Mind Wellbeing

A Manual for Achieving Mental Wellness and Healthy Relationships

Sahba Saberi

In preparing this publication, every effort has been made to provide accurate and evidence based information in regard to the subject matter covered. This publication is not intended as an alternative to medical and dietary advice or psychological care tailored to your specific needs. Individuals should always consult appropriate healthcare professionals about their specific conditions.

All examples, conversations or stories shared in this book reflect typical and generic experiences common to many individuals and are not a reflection of specific stories shared with the author by clients or others.

The author and publisher make no guarantees about the results of this program for individual readers. The ultimate results you will experience rest on innumerable factors, including your efforts in applying the strategies and recommendations covered in this book as well as various aspects of your unique circumstances.

This edition published in 2023

Illustrations by Sahba Saberi & Yasaman Rezvani
Edited by Evelyn Bach & Kiran Wilson
Proofreading by Dorsan Imani

PO Box 15, Thornlie
Western Australia 6108

61-8-94941327
info@fount.com.au
www.fount.com.au

ISBN: 978-1-7647124-9-1 (A5 paperback)

Also available as: 978-0-646-70943-7 (A4 paperback), 978-0-646-71269-7 (audiobook), 978-0-646-72358-7 (ebook), and 978-0-646-87241-4 (A5 exclusive to Fount™ Institute).

This book is dedicated to:

Mr Farid

(who showed me a glimpse of the astounding world of mental health, even if it meant patiently answering a million of my questions, one after another),

the Esfahan Centre for Counselling and Mental Hygiene

(the 3 incredible psychologists who started the project that inspired the Fount programs),

my mum

(for all her support and for not leaving me alone until I agreed to meet Mr Farid),

and my husband

(for walking alongside me and supporting me, even though the entire course of our relationship so far has been interlaced with 'Fount this' and 'Fount that'),

without whom this book would not have been possible!

Preface

'I'm not really interested in understanding the mind or learning about mental health. It's not really something I'm into.' I have frequently heard variations of this sentiment over the years. Why do we lose interest in our own inner wellbeing? To me not being interested in the working of one's own mind is like a person who has no interest in their house being nice to live in, or their body being comfortable.

In fact, our minds are even closer to us than our bodies or homes. Anyone who has found a moment of peace, laughter or an enjoyable connection with a friend or family member despite feeling sick with a bug or experiencing other physical hardship can tell you that our wellbeing doesn't completely rest with physical comforts.

However, our wellbeing is inseparable from the wellbeing of our minds. We can relax and enjoy the ordinary aspects of our lives to the degree to which depression, anxiety or other mental anguish allows us to do so. Our happiness and unhappiness are quite literally our mental health.

Often the people who are uninterested in their mental health or the working of their minds are those who have been convinced that the key to their happiness or unhappiness resides purely on their external circumstances. Or they may be those who have, at some point, opted to stay focused on the more surface level expressions of life in order to cope, survive or escape the pain and discomfort of

their minds. Or perhaps life has been so unkind to them that they have given up on the idea of happiness or wellbeing entirely!

I personally fitted all these boxes at one point in my life. I was a teenager who viciously fought back when my mother suggested that I would consider seeing a psychologist for my own mental health problems. I had been suffering from deep depression and anxiety for years but I had no idea that this had been the case. The only version of life that I knew was the version that I was living: a life that was dark, heavy and full of moment to moment struggles. I could not appear in public without my heart pounding and my knees shaking. I felt so tired from trying to survive my harsh inner critic and had, on many levels, given up. What was a psychologist going to do for me? They couldn't change the reality of the world that I was living in.

Oh, how wrong I was about all of this. I was lucky enough to see an amazing psychologist who expertly helped me understand my own mind in a new way and showed me a glimpse of what mental health was all about. Instantly, I was like a thirsty person with an unquenchable thirst for learning about psychology, mental health, meditation, mindfulness and self-image. For months and years this quest consumed me and followed me everywhere.

As I peeled off the layers of my unhelpful past learning and emotional pain, I frequently marvelled at thoughts like 'I did not know such peace was possible! Is this what it's like to be free of anxiety? Everyone in the world needs to know about this. Why aren't we taught about this at school, or through some other system of education? If everyone was educated about this, life on the planet as we know it would be so different.'

I believed that surely someone had a plan for educating the masses and it was just a matter of time. Later on in my career I realised that there was, in fact, a gap in the field of mental health for programs of prevention and mental health promotion, with a clear strategic plan for large scale implementation. This is, at least partly, due to the fact that up until now, the field of psychology has been so busy with trying to understand and treat already existing mental health issues.

One thing was for sure, I did not want to enjoy this alone. I wanted to help others experience it. I had my mind set on becoming a psychologist and understanding how to fill the gap that I saw in the global mental health arena.

Of course, my own path towards mental health was not free of obstacles by any means. At times, I found that the programs or self help books that I came across explained well what needed to be achieved, but when it came to the 'how' department, I was unable to execute what was being explained. It felt like what had worked for many others before me wasn't working for me.

As a result, I spent over two decades of my life navigating the complex world of psychotherapy, psychoanalysis, self-help, mindfulness meditation, and mental health promotion. In addition, I have become well-acquainted with the latest advances in the exciting areas of transdiagnostic psychology, emotion regulation, schema therapy, acceptance and compassion based therapies and a myriad of other therapeutic schools and modalities.

My aim with all of this has been to develop cutting edge methods for bringing mental health to a greater subset of the population. I am excited to make this recipe or formula available to everyone. In principle, it is no different to what the science of psychology, as well as many teachers of mindfulness and self discovery have written about or taught before me. What is new and different here is the 'how'. The language used, as well as the method of teaching, instructions, analogies and formulas are designed to make this knowledge more accessible, and more easily appliable, for a larger subset of the population.

Below are some of the features of Fount™ programs which comprise its framework:

Innovation - Fount™ programs are developed with innovation in mind. Programs have been carefully formulated and extensively trialled to provide an effective solution for the growing concerns around global mental health issues. It takes advantage of the latest in the field of transdiagnostic psychology to prevent mental disorders, assist in the treatment of already existing mental health conditions and improve overall mental wellbeing for participants.

Transdiagnostic research in psychology seeks to find common underlying patterns across various mental health issues, and to offer treatment that targets multiple mental health concerns simultaneously. Fount™ programs offer tools based on evidence based psychological interventions, such as mindfulness, emotion regulation, CBT, ACT and compassion based therapies. Fount™ places special focus on promoting healthy relationships and community building through training the participants to adopt healthier communication strategies.

Flexibility - Since their original development in 2012, Fount™ programs have been pilot tested with various consumer groups, while consumer feedback and outcomes were used to enhance the evolution of programs and publications. In developing Fount™ programs, every attempt has been made to attend to the needs of various social groups such as adults, children, adolescents, parents, corporate groups and workplaces, as well as linguistically, culturally and ability diverse people.

Scalability and Sustainable Development - A unique feature of Fount™ is that it is designed for scalability. The *Mind Wellbeing* book is designed to lend itself to being readily studied by communities and groups without a need for heavy training or resources. In addition, workshop facilitators, from various cultural and linguistic backgrounds, can be trained to deliver a range of programs to their own communities and workplaces. Trainers are not required to hold previous training in the mental health sector.

Hence program delivery will not be dependent on the availability of experts in local communities. This will allow us to reach remote or socially and economically disadvantaged populations based on a sustainable development model. Considering the epidemic scale of mental illnesses worldwide, and the ongoing dilemma of providing quality mental health treatment and prevention to areas lacking in expert services, this is a highly promising development.

In studying this book, whether by yourself or together with your friends, family or community members, consider the fact that achieving the goal of global mental health advancement can only be possible as a collective effort.

With this book and program becoming available to the public, the next step rests with each of us to consider the role we have to play in improving our own mental health and educating those around us to do the same.

I hope you enjoy this book and find it beneficial to your life and to the pleasantness of your journey! And remember, achieving mental health is a task for all of us!

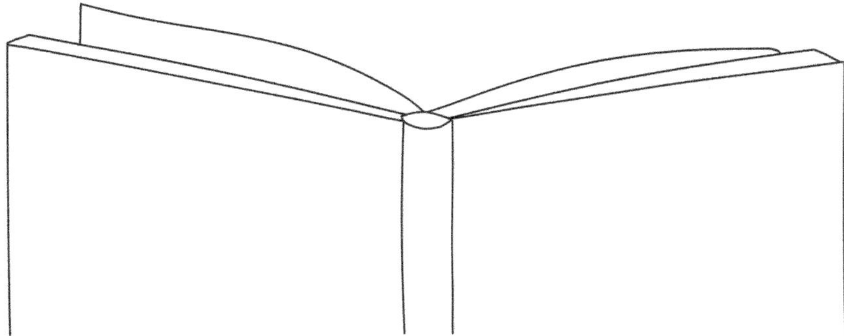

Introduction

What does it mean to be healthy? What is wellbeing? A healthy body is comfortable. A healthy body works well, feels well and is free of pain and discomfort. An unhealthy body, on the other hand, doesn't work as well as it could - so there might be pain, discomfort or some other dysfunction. So, can our minds be healthy or unhealthy? How do we measure the health of our minds?

Just like the feelings in our bodies can tell us if we are healthy or unhealthy, our emotions and thoughts can tell us about the health of our minds. How we feel and what we think can give us pleasant or unpleasant experiences.

Both pleasant and unpleasant emotions are completely normal and healthy. At times you may feel sad, angry, worried or scared. At other times you may feel happy, excited, and positive. These up and down emotions are a perfectly healthy part of life.

But what if our emotions become too intense? What if we experience negative emotions too often or for very long periods of time? What if our thoughts and emotions constantly agitate us and don't let us rest or relax? What if they begin to disrupt our normal life, work or social relationships? What if we lose our ability to enjoy things because negative emotions begin to dominate our moments? These may be signs that we are experiencing mental illness.

Mental illnesses come in so many shapes and forms, and impact people far more often than most of us realise. Just like people can catch a cold or flu, or other physical illnesses from time to time, they can also go through periods of being affected by mental illnesses.

So given how common mental illnesses are, why are we so afraid to talk about them? For a lot of people, the concepts of 'mental health' and 'mental illness' are intimidating ones. Because, for years, society has created a negative stigma1 around these concepts. But today we would like to paint you a different picture. Mental health and mental illnesses are a normal part of our daily lives and it's okay to talk about them.

First, let's explore the idea of mental health a bit more. Does mental health only mean being free of mental illnesses? Not exactly. Mental health is a lot more than that. Mental health means wellbeing and comfort for your mind - and your mind can infinitely grow towards more contentment, more happiness, more comfort, and more peace. Sure, it's good to be free of mental illnesses. But it doesn't have to stop there. There is always room to improve your mental health more, which can affect the following areas of your life:

- Helping you become happier, less anxious, more relaxed and more content

- Helping you sleep better and feel more rested
- Helping you cope better with the problems and stresses of daily living
- Improving your relationships with your friends, family members and coworkers
- Helping you feel more confident and less self-conscious
- Helping you work more productively and efficiently
- Improving your learning, memory and concentration

As you can see optimising your mental health can affect so many areas of your life! You don't have to be suffering from mental illness to have an interest in improving your mental health.

Here's another reason why everyone should have an interest in working on their mental health: prevention is better than cure! Consider this: If you had a car, when would be the right time to look after it? Before it's broken down, or after?

Most people would agree that the right answer is: both. If you completely neglect your car and keep on driving it without looking after it, you will end up with a much higher chance of a broken-down car and an expensive trip to the mechanic. You need to regularly do things like change the oil, check the engine fluids and so on.

Our minds are no different to that car. They also need looking after every day. The difference is that no one tells us how to look after our minds! As a society we have wrongly learned that only people with already broken-down mental health need to look after their minds. Everyone else just keeps driving their minds every day without ever servicing them! And that's why we have such a huge problem on our hands when it comes to mental health. More than 1 in 4 people worldwide experience a mental illness at some stage of their lives. And this doesn't even take into account milder issues that aren't severe enough to be classed as 'mental illness', but are still a cause of problems to our daily lives, relationships and work. They still take away from our satisfaction and the enjoyment of life.

It's also worth noting that mental illness doesn't just affect certain groups of people. We can experience it no matter where in the world we live, regardless of our ethnicity, regardless of whether we are young or old (and that includes young children), male or female, rich or poor, educated or uneducated, strong or fragile and so on.

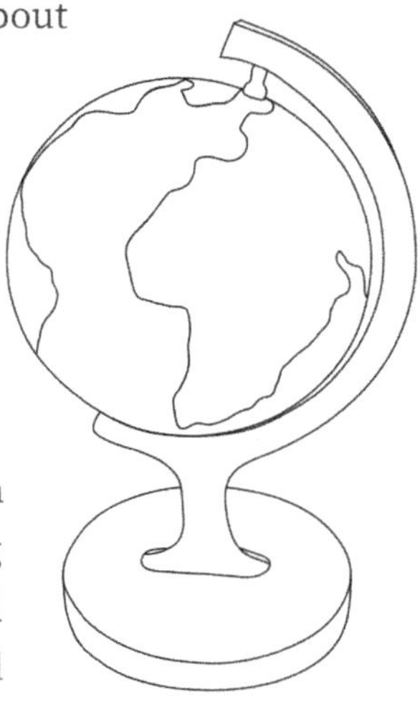

It's clear that we need to do something about this. Wouldn't it be nice to have a happier, less anxious and more content world? We know that prevention is better than cure. It's easier to prevent a problem, than to fix things after they're broken. Just as general hygiene and awareness can prevent many things that could go wrong with our bodies, we need to learn ways to prevent things that could go wrong with our minds. People all over the world need to know how to look after their mental health, using scientific techniques that have been shown to make the mind fit and enhance its functioning.

Fount Programs have been created to do just that! This book has been designed to help people from all walks of life improve their own mental health and the mental health of their families. It can benefit people who are already suffering from mental health problems, as well as those who aren't suffering from mental health issues but simply want to learn how to service their minds regularly to:

- Keep improving and optimising their mental health
- Prevent mental health problems for themselves and their families

Think of this book as a 'how to look after the vehicle of your mind' manual to teach you to become your own mind’s mechanic.

As you can see, improving mental health is a task for all of us. At the end of the day, mental health is about you. It is about your quality of life. It is about how you travel through your life: with ease and satisfaction? Or with stress and discomfort?

And, what's more, your mental wellbeing so often impacts the mental wellbeing of those around you. So this is also about the wellbeing of your loved ones: your family, friends and community. Mental health matters! Let's take it seriously and make a real effort to improve it.

Mental Health and Mental Illnesses

Let's learn a little bit about mental illnesses. There are different types and degrees of mental illness. They can be mild, moderate or severe; short term or long term. Depressive and anxiety disorders are the most common types of mental disorder. Every year millions of people are impacted by these conditions. You may have personally experienced them or know someone who has. Let's take a look at what they are.

Depression: the most common signs of depression are feeling down and having less interest in activities that you used to enjoy. You may feel sad and hopeless. You may have negative thoughts or feelings about yourself. You may also notice changes in your appetite (decreased or increased) and sleep (too little or too much sleep) and may have lower energy and motivation than normal. Depression can feel like an emotional exhaustion: tiredness from over thinking. It may feel like your ability to cope with normal life stressors is all of a sudden less than it used to be.

Remember, people can experience depression at different degrees of intensity and for varying lengths of time.

Anxiety: anxiety comes in different shapes and forms:

- At times it is in the form of fears and phobias.
- Some may experience anxiety around people, especially crowds, and fear of being negatively judged.
- At times people feel anxiety that forces them to obsessively perform certain tasks, such as cleaning excessively or checking the lock over and over again.
- At times a person who has experienced terrible events in their past might continue to be disturbed by the memories of these events.
- At times the mere fear of having anxiety episodes creates anxiety.

- Some people may feel anxious if they leave the house.
- For some, performance, exams, interviews or other types of assessment are a cause of anxiety.
- Some people may worry about bad things happening in the future or becoming sick.
- Other types of anxiety or panic may seem to be there all the time or just appear out of the blue.

For those of us suffering from a mental illness at a given point, we should remember that change is possible. With the right kind of help, most people recover from mental disorders and enjoy increased life satisfaction and health. Mental illnesses should not be considered a life sentence.

The Causes of Mental Disorders

By now you may be wondering: so, what causes these mental disorders? The answer is not so simple. There are a range of things that can increase the risk of us developing a mental illness, and also a range of things that can protect us from it. Some of the things that can increase our risk of developing a mental illness are:

1. **Stress** - such as financial hardship, social pressures, physical illnesses and so on.
2. **Genetic Predisposition** - which means that some of us are just a little more genetically prone to developing certain mental disorders.
3. **Childhood Environments and Experiences** - so much of our opinions, fears, and ways of viewing the world around us are

shaped by our childhood experiences. You could say that what we experience in childhood forms a foundation for our experiences as an adult. Harsh, critical or uncaring childhood environments are detrimental to our mental health.

4. **Unhealthy Relationships** - humans are social creatures. The health of our relationships plays a big part in our emotional wellbeing.

5. **Drugs and Alcohol** - people are attracted to them as a way of feeling better, but in the long run they can create more emotional suffering and anguish.

6. **Significant Traumatic Events** - trauma can be an important risk factor, increasing our chances of developing a mental disorder.

On the other hand, there are positive factors that can protect us from developing mental illnesses and improve our mental health. Let's see what they are:

1. Using healthier ways to cope with stress

2. Using healthier ways to think, manage emotions and process memories of past trauma

3. Increasing the health of the body through better diet and exercise

4. The existence of kind, understanding and supportive people in our lives, in our childhood, adolescence or adulthood.

5. Enjoying healthier relationships through good communication

This book takes advantage of psychology's latest advances and methods to present you with a package to help your mental health by improving your life in all of the 5 areas listed above. We may not be able to change factors like our genes or external stressors, but we can all develop healthier ways of thinking, dealing with emotions and managing relationships. By doing so, we can live happier, healthier and more enjoyable lives!

Myths

Most people do not fully understand mental health. And when people don't understand something, they often try to explain it with myths or hearsay. Unfortunately, there are many myths attached to mental disorders across different cultures around the world and they are often unhelpful. It is important for us to know these myths and challenge them in the community around us. You may have heard some of these before:

Myth: Mental illnesses are a sign of weakness.

The truth is, you cannot use strength or willpower to break free from mental illnesses. It just doesn't work like that. The more risk factors from the list that we looked at earlier, and the less protective factors, the more likely it is for a person to develop mental illnesses. It's as simple as 2 + 2 = 4! And remember, you can never look at a person's life from far away and think that you fully understand their risk and protective factors. Even when it comes to people closest to you, you may not fully understand all their intricate life experiences, and their private thoughts and emotions. If you see a person grappling with mental illness, don't see them as weak. See them as a person who has had to deal with larger hurdles in life.

Myth: The person with the mental illness is just not trying hard enough to control their thoughts or emotions.

No one chooses to experience a mental illness. Those who are experiencing it have often tried, in every way that they know of, to break free and recover from the suffering caused by it. If they haven't managed to do so, it's safe to assume that the task has been too difficult.

Myth: Having a mental illness means that you are unusual or different

As we have already discussed, mental illnesses are extremely common and can impact many of us at some stage of our lives. There is nothing unusual about them. The people who might be suffering from mental illnesses are the very normal every day people around you.

Myth: People don't recover from mental disorders.

With the right kind of help, people can and do recover from mental illnesses, or at the very least, learn to manage their symptoms.

Myth: Being depressed or anxious is just part of life and it can't be any different.

Depression and anxiety are common, but are not a necessary part of life. Even if most people around you are suffering, it doesn't mean that you have to as well.

Myth: Children do not experience mental illness.

Mental illnesses can impact people of all ages. Sadly, children also often suffer from mental illnesses.

Myth: If you enjoy good mental health, you should be proud, as you have done better in life.

There is no shame in mental illness, just as there is no pride in being mentally healthy. We simply seek mental health because it brings us comfort and life satisfaction.

As a society it is important that we begin having a different attitude towards mental health and mental illnesses. We need to accept mental illness as a normal part of life, that can impact many of us. But not as a necessary part of life, meaning that we can recover from it and should not consider it a life sentence. We should learn to become okay with its existence and get rid of the shame attached to it. It is okay to speak of our mental illnesses with those around us who understand and are supportive.

Activity Ⓕ

Create an artwork that shows one or several of the ideas that have made an impact on you in this chapter. You can create a song, a dance, a painting, build a sculpture, create a skit or use any other creative methods to express yourself. If you are studying this book with a group, you can turn this into a group activity.

---

1 Acknowledgment: 'Stigma' is already considered to be a negative term, as it means a trait that people believe to be shameful. Although the addition of the adjective 'negative' before 'stigma' may appear redundant, the author has done so to aid the general public's understanding of the concepts being discussed.

How to Use This Book

Mind Wellbeing is designed to lend itself to group study. Although you can simply grab a copy and enjoy reading it by yourself, it's even more enriching to study it in a group setting. Alternatively, you can read by yourself first and later recap or re-read it as part of a study group or book club. As we will discuss later, it so happens that re-reading this book is encouraged.

Studying with others allows you to discuss the topics, support and motivate each other, learn from shared experiences, and much more. In doing so, you're also joining Fount's broader initiative to transform how mental health is addressed on a global scale.

Symbols

Below are 2 symbols which you will notice throughout the book, along with a description of what they each mean.

Go within: This symbol means: it is now quiet reflection time! It is suggesting that you sit in a comfortable position and begin paying attention to your own thoughts, emotions or the world around you. We suggest that when you see this symbol, you close your eyes. This might help you with focusing. But at times you may find that keeping your eyes open is more helpful to you.

Homework: This is the 'Homework' symbol. Homework practices emphasise specific activities that you could focus on to build on what you have learned in the book. You are your own homework police, so see if you can come up with ways to remind yourself to practice what is suggested.

A gift to yourself

Imagine someone you really love and care for. Now imagine finding out that this person has a wish. A wish for something that would make them really happy. Something that would change their life in a really good way. Would you try to give them what they wish for? What if giving them what they wish for meant that you had to put in a bit of effort? Would you put in the effort and work hard to make your friend happy? Now what if that friend was you? Would you work hard and put in a bit of effort to grant yourself more happiness and peace? If your answer is 'yes', let us tell you a little secret. Your commitment and hard work can help you get so much more out of this book. Achieving mental wellbeing is a comprehensive journey, and every part of the Mind Wellbeing Manual is designed to contribute to this goal. To truly benefit from this program, it's essential to complete 100% of the manual. This ensures you gain the full spectrum of insights and practices designed to enhance your mental wellbeing. Consider the following points:

1. Each section of the manual builds on the previous ones, building towards holistic mental health outcomes. Skipping sections can leave gaps in your understanding and healing.

2. The exercises and reflections are carefully crafted to provide

maximum benefits when completed in sequence. Skipping sections may mean you won't fully grasp or benefit from any subsequent sections that build on the ones you've missed.

Tips for Staying on Track

We are surrounded by so many programs, books, and so much self-help advice. While this is great and we can pick up many beneficial insights this way, getting sidetracked and pulled in different directions in our mental health learning journey can prevent us from fully benefiting from a comprehensive program like Mind Wellbeing. Constant distractions can make it challenging to follow through with a single program. Here are a few tips for staying focused and completing the program:

Take Advantage of Group Support: If you're studying with a group, make a pact to support each other in staying on track. You could even set up a buddy system where if a member misses a session, another member can support them to catch up with the reading and exercises. Discuss with your group how this system could work and who might pair up with whom.

Celebrate Milestones: Set yourself goals and reward yourself once you achieve them. For example, decide on a reward for yourself when you reach certain percentage points in the book, when you complete the book, or if you manage to organise a Mind Wellbeing group and bring everyone together (see pages 225-229 for more insight about how to organise and lead a group of your own).

Get Excited about Highlights: You could also get motivated by looking through the table of contents and marking any sections that excite you or would be particularly helpful to your circumstances. This can motivate you to keep reading so that you can get to the chapters you're looking forward to. Here are three topics within the book that we consider to be key highlights and particularly impactful:

1. Learning the technique of emotion exposure in Chapter 5 can be considered a game-changer for mental health. Let's face it, most of us don't know what to do with our emotions and how best to handle them!

2. Learning about our self-image — how we view and treat ourselves — is another game-changer. You'll learn about these topics in Chapters 6 and 7.

3. Our final highlight is Chapters 10 and 11, which are packed full of essential skills you're going to need in your communication toolbox if you wish for happy and long-lasting relationships.

Set a Schedule: Set a regular schedule that fits your routine for your study sessions. Whether you are studying alone or with a group, having consistent times dedicated to reading and practicing can help you stay committed and avoid falling behind. For example, you might say to yourself, 'every Saturday morning with breakfast, I will dedicate one hour to studying Mind Wellbeing.' Set reminders on your phone or calendar to help you stay consistent. What would be a good time or day for your Mind Wellbeing study sessions?

Catch-Up Plan: If you're studying with a group and miss a session, make a plan to catch up on the reading in your own time. Of particular importance is Chapter 5, as it is a foundational chapter that all future chapters depend on. If you miss it, be sure to catch up on it quickly, so that you don’t fall behind and can participate fully in the next session. Only tick the 'completion' checkbox at the end of each chapter once you've completed all the content in that chapter.

Certificate of Completion: Finally, motivate yourself by looking forward to your Certificate of Completion. To be eligible for a Certificate of Completion (which is located after the final chapter), you must complete 100% of the book. This means that if you are studying the book with a group and happen to miss a session, you need to catch up on the reading in your own time to be eligible for the certificate. This certificate is different from others because, when it comes to Mind Wellbeing, you are your own police. Based on an honour system, you can monitor your own progress and have the option of signing your own certificate of completion.

Now take a moment to make your own plans for staying on track and completing all the sections of the book. You can write down your plans below:

Getting the Most Out of Mind Wellbeing

Below are a few other tips that may help you get the most out of this book:

Keep an Open Mind and Open Heart - you will learn a lot of new ideas. We recommend you keep an open mind, try what you learn and be open to allowing positive change into your life.

Be Patient - this book is structured to achieve long lasting change and improvement in your life. The first few chapters are about building a solid foundation. Then the following chapters use that foundation to empower you and help in improving your wellbeing. So be patient. Early on you may start wondering 'When will I start feeling better?' And if that happens, remember that a foundation is being built. For some, change will take longer and for some it will be quicker. Both are okay, as everyone's journey is different. So be kind and patient with yourself as you journey towards improved mental wellbeing.

Be Curious - a good attitude to have when reading this book is curiosity, a wish to understand yourself and others. It is important that you do not blindly accept any ideas that are shared with you. Instead, aim to really understand these ideas for yourself and put them to the test.

Don't Skip Ahead - Most of us have done it - picked up a book, were so excited to get to the section that was relevant to us that we flicked through the book and only read those specific sections, or only read sections that seemed interesting. This style of reading lends itself more readily to some books than others. And this book is certainly not one of them. For starters, the first few chapters of the book provide you with a foundation that you will need in order to understand or practice effectively what comes later in the book. By not having the proper foundation, you will simply not benefit from the later chapters as much as you would otherwise.

The second reason for this is that this book has been written based on a foundation of transdiagnostic psychology. Transdiagnostic psychology looks beyond our traditional complaints and diagnosis and instead looks at the common features that connects most mental health issues. In other words, regardless of what issues you are trying to tackle in order to improve your life, you will most likely benefit from learning what is in most other parts of this book. So if you do get tempted, flick through the book and read ahead, at least make sure you come back and read what you missed in a chronological order.

Only Apply What You Learn to Yourself - everyone learns at a different pace. Regardless of whether your friends and family members have read this book or not, they may be at different stages of learning to you. Make sure you accept where they are, as we all learn at a different pace. So don't expect them to understand and apply all the new ideas that you have been learning and applying. It is okay to hold dialogues with others about what you learn. But allow them to learn at their own pace and to take away from this book whatever they are ready to take away.

Revisit This Book from Time to Time - as you practice what you learn in the months and years to come, you might find that it helps to come back to this book and read parts of it again. This is in part because, with time and

practice, you may be able to put into place more and more of the strategies and tips offered in this book. Another reason is that at times when a lot of new ideas are presented to you, you may not retain everything all at once. So re-reading what you have learned can refresh your memory.

Readers with Disabilities - Some disabilities may impact your practice of specific exercises in this book. If you find that your disability stops you from being able to practice an exercise, consider using creative strategies to help you practice the exercise in another way. For example, if you have significant hearing loss or deafness, you could replace any mindfulness of sound activities with mindfulness of your own breath, heartbeat or taste (e.g. the taste of a sultana or other food in your mouth).

When to Seek Further Help - There are times when it's a good idea to seek extra help. This includes the following scenarios:

- If you're overwhelmed with depression, anxiety or struggling emotionally in other ways. Basically, if you feel that you're not coping on your own. Particularly if you feel that you may put your own safety or the safety of others at risk.
- If you find that strong emotional challenges, lack of motivation, agitation or restlessness are disrupting your ability to read this book or practise the exercises and strategies covered. A bit of extra help might help you get more out of this book at a later stage.

Expert help could include seeing a mental health trained medical doctor, a psychologist, or other mental health professional. An expert could help you in a variety of ways, such as one on one therapy sessions or, at times, with medications like antidepressants.

Managing Challenging Emotions

Given the introspective nature of this book and its subject matter, it's natural that some of the exercises or content might bring up difficult emotions or trigger memories for some readers. Although difficult emotions are a completely normal part of the healing process, it's important to navigate them in a way that feels manageable for you. So, it might be worth exploring some ideas to help you navigate any challenging emotions that arise as you read this book.

Firstly, as you read on and work through the exercises, allow yourself to take things at a pace that's right for you. If you encounter a memory or topic that feels overwhelming, it's okay to shift your focus and give yourself permission to concentrate on other areas that feel less triggering for now. Practise the exercises with milder memories until you feel more confident, and explore the more challenging areas once you feel ready or more experienced. You can move at a pace that's right for you.

If you find it difficult to shift your focus away from overwhelming emotions or memories once they've been triggered, it may be a good idea to have a self care plan in place. Your self care plan could include:

Taking a Break: If you're reading the book by yourself, give yourself permission to take a break and return when you're ready or have the right support in place. If you're studying with a group, make an agreement that it's okay to walk out and take a break if anyone needs it. Explore practical strategies, like having a quiet corner for those who need to process emotions alone. If your group is held online, normalise logging out and returning at a later point if any members need a break.

Using Grounding and Soothing Techniques: Grounding and soothing activities can help bring you back to the present moment and restore a sense of calm. Consider the following techniques:

- Imagery Anchors: Create a mental 'good place' that you can visualise when you start feeling distressed. Imagine a place where you feel completely safe and relaxed—it could be a real location or a fictional setting that brings you peace.

- Practise Soothing Activities: Engage in activities like deep breathing, listening to calming music, gentle walking, or journalling to help centre yourself and process your emotions.

- Physical Grounding Techniques: Focus on physical sensations, such as feeling the ground beneath your feet or holding a comforting object, to help anchor yourself in the present moment.

Reaching Out for Support: If you feel comfortable, consider discussing your feelings with someone you trust. This could be a member of your study group, a friend, or a family member. You may also consider reaching out to a mental health professional, such as a therapist or counsellor, who can assist you in processing these feelings in a safe and supportive environment.

Now, take some time to reflect individually or with your study group on strategies that can support you if strong emotions arise while reading this book:

....Ⓕ

....

....

....

....

With all that groundwork out of the way, you're almost set to start your journey into Mind Wellbeing! But before we begin, have you considered studying Mind Wellbeing with a group? If you're interested in learning more, keep reading.

Studying This Book With a Group

As previously mentioned, this book is best to be studied within a group setting. This means you can read it with a friend or a group of friends, as part of a book club, or as part of a workshop. Can you think of one or several people that you would like to study the book with? Other readers have studied the book with one or several of their friends, family members, university or work peers, or other community members. Many have found it particularly valuable to study Mind Wellbeing with their partner or spouse, finding this beneficial to their relationship and bond with one another.

Below are a few questions which you may wish to consider when planning your group:

- How to introduce the book to your potential group members and inspire them to want to read it?
- Which days and times are suitable for you to come together and study?
- Where will you meet with everyone? If meeting in person is not possible, meeting online is also a great option.
- Do you each prefer paperback books, audiobooks, or ebooks?
- What's a good start date?

Tip: We have made a free downloadable exercise book available, which you can print for each member who doesn't own their own copy of Mind Wellbeing, or if you're using an audio or ebook. You can download this from: www.fount.com.au/resources

Take a moment to have a think and make any notes to organise your next steps:

.... Ⓕ

....

Note: When inviting others to study the book, make sure they don't feel pressured. They may not be interested in the book at this time or in studying it as part of a group. If so, honor their wishes and preferences. Provide them with all the information and then leave them to decide if and how they would like to study it.

What Your Sessions Could Look Like

Running a *Mind Wellbeing* group is easy. You just need to let the book guide the sessions! Simply get the group together and let the book do the rest!

If the group members don't all know each other well, you may like to start with some ice-breakers and get-to-know-each-other activities to help everyone feel relaxed and comfortable. For example, each member could share a bit about themselves, like their interests or a fun fact. You could also play a small game or try other activities that encourage laughter and help break the ice.

Then, begin by reading the 'Preface' (optional), 'How to Use This Book', and 'Introduction' sections. You can take turns reading from the book (or have a designated reader), or simply listen to the audio provided at: www.fount.com.au/group

After this, you could meet weekly and read a chapter together each time you meet. For longer chapters, allow more time as needed. Other ways to get through the book are:

Intensive Sessions: You can also plan intensive sessions where you cover more of the book in a shorter time frame. For example, you could create a 'weekend retreat' where you read several chapters, or have longer or more frequent sessions.

Designated Reading at Home: Another option is to do some reading at home and then recap, re-read or practice exercises when you meet. If you choose this method, it's important that everyone is committed to keeping up with the reading to ensure no one falls behind.

Feel free to try other arrangements that suit your group. The key is to ensure that as a group, you get through the reading and practice the exercises. The way you do it is up to you!

Group Dynamics

It might also be worth spending some time discussing the types of group dynamics that could make this experience more pleasant for you and the rest of the group. Here are a few suggestions to consider:

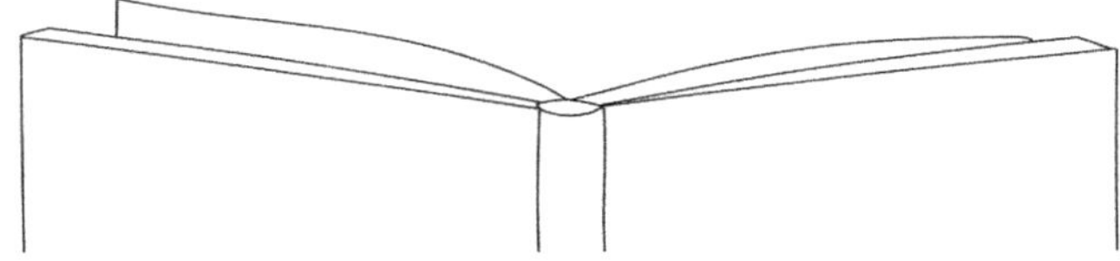

Respect and Kindness: This includes all the obvious things - respecting each other's opinions, maintaining a non-judgmental attitude, showing kindness, and giving mutual respect.

Comfort with Silence: It's okay to be quiet and not talk much during your time with the group. You never have to share your personal experiences at any stage if you don't wish to.

Emotional Safety: Some people may find that studying this book can be emotional at times. Make sure your group is a safe space for emotions. Discuss with your group what this may look like. For example, you may agree to be supportive and non-judgmental, and normalise tears and other expressions of emotions.

Fostering Genuine Growth Conversations: When reading a self-help book like Mind Wellbeing, some readers might find themselves more inclined to focus on the sections that highlight their strengths or areas where they're already doing well. While it can be encouraging to recognise what you're doing well, placing too much emphasis on these areas can sometimes lead to missed opportunities for deeper growth.

First, by concentrating primarily on what's already working for you, you may overlook the broader value of the book. Mind Wellbeing offers a variety of strategies and insights tailored to diverse needs, and not everything will be relevant to everyone. The goal is to identify the areas where you can grow and improve, rather than focusing solely on sections that affirm what you already know or do well.

Second, in a group setting, this emphasis on strengths can unintentionally make it harder for others to discuss their own challenges. When conversations are centered around successes, it might create an environment where some participants feel less comfortable sharing their struggles. To foster genuine growth, it's helpful to balance becoming aware of your strengths with exploring and addressing your challenges. This approach not only benefits you but also contributes to a more supportive and open group environment, where everyone can engage in meaningful discussions about their personal growth.

Managing Exercise Timings: As your designated readers read out the 'Go Within' exercises, the question may come up about how much time to allow for each exercise. Since people need very different lengths of time for these types of exercises, a good practice is to watch for signs like people opening their eyes and their body language suggesting that they're done with the exercise. You could even come up with an agreement as a group about a signal to suggest when you're done. After the first few exercises, reflect with the group about whether or not you allowed enough time and if it needs to be adjusted next time.

Quiet Activities: If you finish a 'Go Within' exercise before the other group members, do your best to stay quiet and not distract them from their practice. Be particularly mindful of any fidgeting or restlessness in your body if your mind is a bit busy. Use this time to relax with some artwork or mindfulness exercises. You could even enjoy colouring in some of the illustrations from the book!

Exercise Formats: Throughout the book, exercises are marked with the following symbols to guide their use in group settings:

Ⓟ **Private:** This symbol indicates activities meant for individual reflection. Group members are not asked to share their answers with the group, but they can do so if they wish.

Ⓖ **Group:** This symbol marks activities recommended for group discussion. While most benefit from private reflection before sharing, facilitators should use their discretion to decide if some can be done entirely as a group. Participation in sharing should always be voluntary.

Ⓕ **Flexible:** This symbol indicates activities that can be done privately or discussed as a group, based on facilitator discretion and member preferences. Members can be invited to share their responses if they wish.

Confidentiality: Your group may also come to an agreement not to discuss personal matters brought up by any group members with people outside of the group.

Support for Struggling Members: If a member of your group is struggling, refer them to a doctor or other appropriate mental health services in your local area.

Any other ideas for making the group a safe and comfortable atmosphere for everyone? Have a chat with your group.

Table of Contents

Chapter 1: The Building Blocks

You are a universe.

Your mind, your psychological existence is an amazingly vast world that is unique to you. Only you know how it feels to live in this world of yours. Only you know how your emotions feel, what you think about, what things you believe in, deep down. Only you can decide to exercise your will power. Only you know how it feels to live within your body.

Most people never take the time to ask themselves some very important questions: 'What makes up my internal world? What are my thoughts? What are my emotions?'

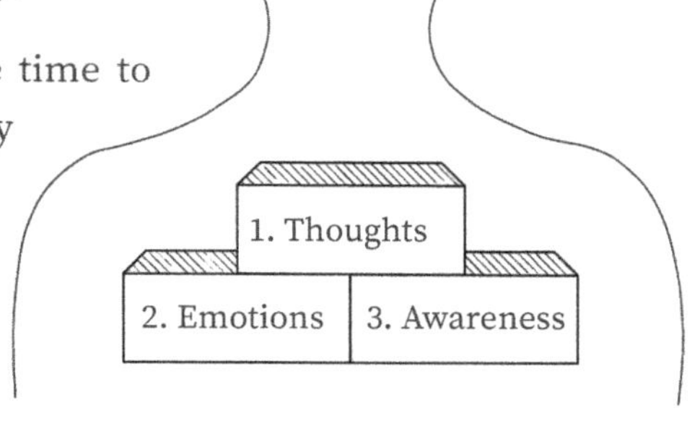

This chapter is all about trying to answer these questions. Before we can learn how to have a healthy mind, we need to learn about the mind itself. There are three building blocks that make up our psychological existence: thoughts, emotions and awareness.

It is important that we learn the differences between these 3 building blocks. Can you tell the difference between them? Take a moment, go within and pay attention. See if you can tell the difference between your thoughts, emotions and awareness.

What did you find to be the differences between these 3 blocks?

.... (G)

....

....

Thoughts - so, here is the most important thing you need to know about thoughts: they are made up of words, images or ideas. Thinking can be like an internal conversation, or a cinema screen in your mind. It can be like a dialogue with yourself which is often happening in the background, as you go about your day. Just like a sports commentator, commenting on everything, forming judgements, planning, organising etc. It may look a little like this:

And the dialogue keeps on going, and going. Logic, rationality and imagination are properties of thought. We use our thoughts to judge things, analyse things, to plan, come up with new ideas and logically explore things.

Take a moment to pay attention to your internal dialogue. Notice any thoughts that come into your mind. Notice how they are made up of words or images.

Emotions - unlike thoughts, emotions are not made up of words. They are not based on language. An emotion is an experience, just as the taste of an apple is an experience. You can never quite explain what an apple tastes like using words and language, can you? You normally feel your emotions somewhere in your body. For example, if you are scared, you may feel your heart beating faster or your knees shaking. The feeling of your heart beating fast feels like fear. If you are angry, you may feel a pressure in your throat, or you may feel your face getting hot, or a sensation in your hands. These feelings in your body are the emotion that you are feeling in that moment. You then use your thoughts to give these feelings a name, so you call it anger, fear and so on.

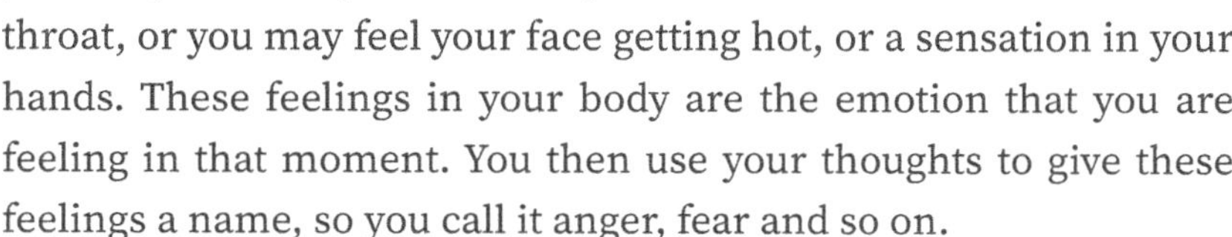

Once we think a thought, we might have an emotional reaction to that thought. For example, if a person thinks 'I don't think my friends are enjoying my company', they may then feel a sensation in their body, like a sinking feeling in their chest, or a pressure in their throat or a turning in their stomach. If someone asks them 'what are you feeling?' they then use their thinking to give their emotion a name. They may call it sad, or nervous, or embarrassed.

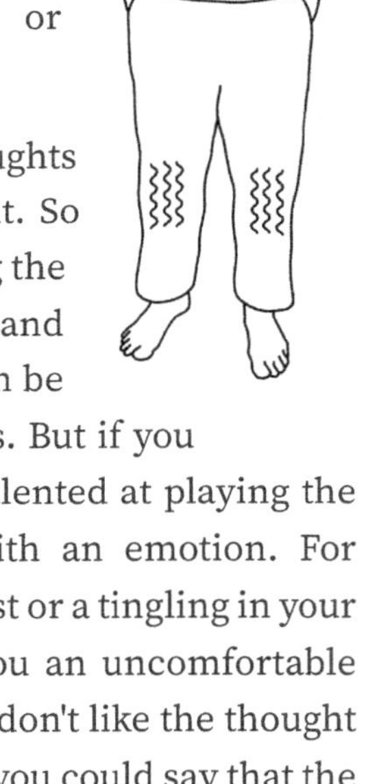

Emotions can be pleasant or unpleasant. Thoughts by themselves are not pleasant or unpleasant. So you may think 'I'm not very talented at playing the piano'. That thought by itself is just a thought and may not have any feelings attached to it. It can be just a neutral observation about your abilities. But if you are unhappy with the fact that you are not talented at playing the piano, you may have the same thought with an emotion. For example you might feel a pressure in your chest or a tingling in your belly. These physical sensations then give you an uncomfortable experience and that's how you know that you don't like the thought 'I'm not very talented at playing the piano'. So you could say that the experience attached to the thought, that makes it either pleasant or unpleasant, is what we call emotion.

Take a moment to pay attention to your emotions. If you don't feel any emotions right now, think of a time when you felt excited, or sad, or happy or nervous. Can you remember how your body felt when you were experiencing these emotions?

And finally, the third building block is...

Awareness - we often mix up awareness with thinking, or emotions. Yet awareness is a completely different thing. Just like emotions, awareness is not made up of words and sentences. Awareness is the simple act of noticing things. Looking, listening, tasting, smelling, feeling. The simple act of being attentive. There are no words when you notice something. You just see it, feel it or hear it.

We humans are so used to thinking about everything that often as soon as we notice something, we quickly start thinking about it. So you may notice a pink flower. The noticing is just seeing the flower, its shape, colour and smell. But very soon you start thinking about it 'I like this flower, but I like red flowers better. I wish my partner sometimes bought me flowers'. And then because of that thought, you might experience an emotion in your body. Maybe it is a pleasant emotion because you remembered you like flowers. Or it could be an unpleasant emotion because your partner doesn't buy you flowers. But although you started thinking and feeling emotions soon after noticing the flower, thinking, feeling emotions and noticing are not the same things. They have a different quality to them and being able to tell them apart is important. Here is a practical exercise to help you see the difference between thinking and awareness:

Pick up an object and hold it in your hand. It can be a pen, a book, a spoon, a flower etc. First spend some time thinking about this object. Notice that your thoughts are made up of words. They may look like this:

'This is a nice looking pen. I like the shape. But it doesn't write so well. My other pen writes better. I wonder where it was made. Is it cheap or expensive? I should write with the other one though, it's nicer to write with.' And so on.

Notice your thoughts as they take place.

Now spend a bit of time just looking at the object. No thoughts. No commentary. Just look at it. And feel how it feels in your hand. Maybe smell it. Notice the object, with all its little details, with all of your attention.

This is called awareness, or the act of mindfulness. We will practise mindful awareness and discuss it thoroughly in chapters to come.

Mindfulness of Sound

Mindfulness is the practice of increasing our awareness. Many of us have forgotten to pay attention and be aware, because our minds are so busy with thoughts and emotions. When we practise mindfulness, we practise being aware more often and for longer periods of time.

Let's try a little mindfulness exercise: mindfulness of sound. It's simple. Just close your eyes and listen. Listen to all the sounds around you. As you listen longer, you might hear sounds that are far away, sounds that are repetitive or not very loud. We normally miss a lot of these sounds. But when paying careful attention, we can start to notice them. Go ahead and try it for a few minutes...

How did you go? Did you find that exercise calming? Do you know why people usually find that exercise oddly relaxing? It's because while they're listening to the sounds, they're not thinking. They give their thinking a break. Just as your body needs rest, so does your mind. You could say that thinking is like work, and mindfulness is like rest. Can you see the difference between them a bit more clearly now?

A good way to tell thinking and awareness apart is that thinking is often about creating ideas or interpreting what has happened in the past or is going to happen in the future. But awareness is just about taking in everything that is happening now, without interpreting or creating new ideas. Unlike thinking, awareness is never about the future or the past. It is about this moment. Thinking about the past or the future often brings up painful memories or worries and concerns. So thinking can be a stressful process. But the present moment is free of what has happened in the past, or what may happen in the future.

In fact, you need to do nothing when you are practising awareness. We mean that. You need to do nothing. You don't need to try to change anything or fix anything or understand anything. You just notice and receive what is already here. Thinking, on the other hand, is about doing things or understanding things, or creating things. It is an activity.

In your normal day to day life, you need work and you need rest. Both working and resting have their places. Similarly, both thinking and mindfulness have their places and they complement each other. But if you were to work every single moment of your life, and never give yourself time to rest, you would soon become exhausted and begin to struggle. Similarly, if you give yourself thinking time, you should also give yourself plenty of time for mindfulness. Or else, you will start feeling exhausted, mentally and emotionally.

> **“Just as your body needs rest, so does your mind. You could say that thinking is like work, and mindfulness is like rest.**

Healing

Mental illness can impact us on the level of each of these building blocks:

- Our **thoughts** can become overly negative, or we may think too much or have trouble slowing down. We may have so many thoughts that it becomes hard to focus on work or studies.
- Our **emotions** can become very intense or uncomfortable for long periods of time.
- Our **awareness** becomes reduced, because we are too distracted by our thoughts and emotions. When awareness is reduced, we find it hard to pay attention to what is happening around us. We may become forgetful, distracted or restless. Our thoughts and

emotions can disturb our ability to fall asleep, enjoy a peaceful moment or concentrate on work or studies.

Improving our mental health can also happen on the level of each of these 3 building blocks. We can improve our thinking, improve our way of dealing with emotions and increase our awareness. Healing these 3 building blocks will make up most of what we will learn about in the chapters to come. So, stay tuned!

Conditioning

Learning is important. It shapes our thoughts and emotions. And we are not just talking about deliberate learning, like the type that we go to school for. The kind of learning that we are talking about can happen without our awareness or control.

Let us start with a story about a Russian scientist called Ivan Pavlov who lived during the 1890s. Pavlov accidentally discovered something interesting one day. He discovered that if, each time he was about to feed his lab dogs, he rang a bell, soon the dogs made a connection between food and the sound of the bell ringing. Which meant that as soon as the dogs heard the bell, their saliva and stomach acid increased, as if the bell and the food were the same thing! Even if the bell was rung and no food was anywhere to be found, the dogs' digestive system still treated it like food!

This phenomenon was named classical conditioning and it became the basis for a large school of psychological research and treatment.

Classical conditioning doesn't just impact dogs and their digestive systems. It's relevant to humans and animals alike and impacts so many areas of our lives. For example, picture the following scenarios:

- A person who once felt sick after eating a kiwi fruit, now gets a sick feeling every time she sees a kiwi fruit.
- A person who smelled a perfume on a person he cared about, now gets the same pleasant emotions every time he smells that perfume. Even if he smells the perfume on a perfect stranger.
- An unhappy employee who did not get along with her boss and decided to leave the job, now gets the same uncomfortable emotions every time she drives past her old workplace.
- An advertising company created a commercial that showed a product being used by an attractive, successful and happy looking person. So now the audience experience a positive emotion when they see that product.

Classical conditioning is also relevant to our eating habits, as well as dependence on drugs or alcohol. For example, imagine a person driving along a street, deciding to stop at a local shop to buy some lollies. The next time he drove down that street, he again stopped to buy some lollies. Soon, his brain associated driving along that street with eating lollies. Years later, he again passed by that street and immediately thought to himself 'I don't know why I am craving lollies all of a sudden?' See, he may not even have any memory of the time when he bought lollies driving down that street. But his brain automatically made the association anyway!

The same applies to our habits around drugs and alcohol. For example, a person who often uses drugs or alcohol in the living room of her house, or when with certain friends, or at a specific time of the day, would automatically experience a craving next time they are in those situations or with those people. Even certain emotions or feeling stressed or relaxed can become conditioned and trigger an urge for using drugs or alcohol.

Take a moment to think about some of your habits. Can you pinpoint any time, place, people or emotions that trigger the urge to go back to your habit?

....Ⓟ

....

....

Here is some good news. Conditioning may be powerful, but we can get rid of it. Let us go back to Pavlov's story. He learned another interesting thing from the experiments with his dogs. He realised that after the dogs were conditioned to associate the bell with their food, if he began ringing the bell without presenting the food, and continued doing this for some time, the dogs' bodies gradually learned something new: that the bell was no longer associated with food. At that point, saliva was no longer secreted when the bell was rung.

This phenomenon leads us to a very effective technique for changing unhelpful conditioned behaviour: we need to allow our body to gradually become aware that the two things are no longer associated with one another. So if the person in our earlier example drove along that street and resisted the urge to buy lollies, after some time he would stop craving them. His body would stop associating the street with lollies. Or if he decided to eat a fruit when driving along that street, he would soon begin craving that fruit instead of lollies. This technique is called exposure therapy.

This rule can also assist with giving up alcohol or drugs. Let's say that, coming home from work and the need to de-stress has been linked to drinking or smoking a cigarette in your mind. You may choose to replace this with other ways of relaxing, such as taking a bath, watching a comedy or cooking a nice meal. Persevering and resisting your habit may be difficult at first. But soon the cravings will reduce.

Exposure therapy can help with a lot of our fears as well. For example, Phil has been afraid of heights for as long as he can remember. He can't remember how his fear started but his mother tells him that he almost fell from a high place when he was little. We don't always have a clear memory of how we became conditioned in the first place and knowing how it started is not really necessary. What's important is that Phil knew that he

needed to face his fear of heights. It's important to start small and easy and gradually make the task harder as you feel more comfortable. So Phil began with a place that was just high enough to be a little scary, but not too scary. He just stood there and looked down. Initially he felt his heart pounding and his palms getting sweaty with fear. But he didn't quit. Instead he stayed there for 10 to 20 minutes. Gradually his heart stopped pounding fast and he began feeling normal again. His body had just learned to let go of this fear a little. In a few days' time, Phil found a place that was just a bit higher and repeated the exercise. Gradually he became less and less scared of heights.

Take a few minutes to make a plan to gradually face one of your fears, the way Phil did with his. Make sure your plan is gradual enough to be achievable. If your fear is very strong, you can even start to face it using a picture, a video or by imagining it. You would also have to rely on pictures or imagination if your fear is around something that can actually harm you (e.g. wild animals, drowning etc).

.... Ⓟ

....

....

Just a little reminder: what you learn in this book is to be used for yourself only. Pushing others to face their fears is never helpful. If you want to help a friend or family member with this, the best thing that you can do is to encourage them to study this book for themselves. They may face their fears only when they are ready to do so, and at their own pace.

Homework

1. Carry out the exposure plan that you've made today.
2. Practise mindfulness every day, even for a few seconds. Make a plan right now by writing down a time of the day that would be best for practising mindfulness:

.... Ⓕ

Now make an internal commitment to give your mind a break from thinking by practising mindfulness every day at the time you just decided on. If it helps, think of some ways to remind yourself to practise it at the allocated time. Some good ideas for reminding yourself are to leave a note to yourself where you will see it, an alarm or notification on your phone or to wear a piece of jewellery as a reminder.

Relaxation Exercise

Let's finish this chapter with an exercise that can help with relaxing your body. Long periods of stress can teach our bodies to hold onto tension. So, one way to teach the body to return to a more relaxed state is using relaxation exercises. Sit in a comfortable position and close your eyes.

Please note: this exercise involves tensing and relaxing different muscles in your body. If you have injuries in any part of your body, please skip that part and don't put extra tension on those muscles.

First, try and tense the muscles in your feet and lower legs. Once the muscles are nice and tense, let them go and relax them. Now let's do the same with the muscles in your upper legs. Again, tense and then relax those muscles. Now repeat the same process for the muscles in your abdomen and lower back: tense, and then relax. Now your chest and upper back. Now move on to your shoulders, arms and hands. Let's repeat the shoulders again. This time tense and relax the muscles in your shoulders and neck. Now tense up the muscles in your face. Don't be shy, go ahead and make a face! And relax. Finally, tense the muscles in your jaws, around your ears and all over your head. And relax.

Take a few moments. Enjoy the relaxation in your body. If any part of your body is refusing to relax, tense and relax those muscles one more time and keep your attention on that part for a little while.

Interesting to know:

Since we learned about thoughts in this chapter, it might be worth mentioning what beliefs are. Beliefs are also a form of thought, but they are more deep-seated and general. When we believe in something at a very deep level, that belief forms a lot of our thoughts. So a belief can be seen as a tree, and each related thought is a branch of that tree. For example, if a person believes, deep down, that they are unlikable, then they may think many thoughts in line with that belief, such as 'I can tell my neighbour doesn't like me', 'I bet I am going to end up lonely' etc. And to the contrary, if a person believes, deep down, that they are loved, their thoughts would look more like: 'How lovely of my friends to go out of their way just to do something nice for me!', 'I am surrounded by kind people'. If you notice you are having a lot of similar thoughts, ask yourself: 'What is the belief underneath these thoughts?'

I've just completed 12% of the book! □

Chapter 2: Emotion Regulation

Noticing the Body

Before we begin, notice how your body feels right now. Is it comfortable? Relaxed? Tense? Restless? Does it feel warm or cool? Do you feel any pain or pressure anywhere? What is your heart doing? Can you feel it beat? What about your breathing?

Close your eyes and pay attention to your body for a moment.

Paying attention to the feelings in your body is something that we will get you to do from time to time in the chapters to come. We have a purpose in doing so, which we will explain a bit later in this book.

Let's Recap! ☺

Please take a minute to remember the differences between thoughts, emotions and awareness. Close your eyes and notice your thoughts, then any emotions you may have in your body and then your awareness of everything around you.

Now, see if you can remember which of these statements are true and which are false:

Thinking is an internal conversation.

True ☐

False ☐

Emotions and awareness are made up of words.

True ☐

False ☐

Thinking is made up of words.

True ☐

False ☐

An emotion is an experience that can be pleasant or unpleasant.

True ☐

False ☐

Awareness is about being attentive to and noticing what is here right now.

True ☐

False ☐

To be aware of something is the same thing as thinking about it.

True ☐

False ☐

Emotion Regulation

Emotions are powerful! They can create pleasant and enjoyable life experiences, motivate us, and inspire us. Or they can drive us deep into unhappiness, suffering and unease. So it's not surprising that emotions can influence a lot of our actions, decisions and social interactions.

And since emotions are so powerful, we often try to control them. We try to shape them, avoid uncomfortable ones, or bring about pleasant ones. These attempts to control or shape emotions are called emotion regulation.

Unfortunately, regulating emotions doesn't always go according to plan. Sometimes the techniques that we use just don't work. They don't help us feel better. Or, at times, they may seem to help us feel better in the short term, but in the long run they do us more harm than good. In order for us to experience improved mental health, we need to learn about helpful and unhelpful ways of dealing with emotions.

In the next few chapters, we will look at many different emotion regulation strategies. We will learn ways to combat those strategies that are not helpful, and we will also learn helpful alternatives that can increase our happiness and life satisfaction.

But first, let us introduce to you a notorious emotion regulation style that is known to pose particular harm to our mental health and wellbeing....

Behold!

The King of All Unhelpful Emotion Regulation Strategies!

Before we tell you what this king is, let's see if you can guess it. Research shows that overusing this style of coping is linked with a large variety of mental disorders, including depression and anxiety.

It gets in the way of our ability to cope with stress. It reduces our general life satisfaction and happiness. And that is why we've named it the King of All Unhelpful Emotion Regulation Strategies!

Take a guess...what do you think this harmful way of dealing with unwanted emotions is?

Hint: This strategy might help with uncomfortable emotions at first, but it can cause us harm if we overuse it.

Ready to guess? Pick one of the following options: Ⓕ

A. Thinking too much about our problems and becoming overly emotional about them .... ☐

B. Thinking negatively .... ☐

C. Trying to avoid experiencing unwanted thoughts, emotions and memories .... ☐

D. Facing uncomfortable situations and attempting to brave through them .... ☐

Ready for the answer?

If you guessed option 'C', you are right! This toxic strategy we use in trying to deal with uncomfortable emotions is called experiential avoidance.

Experiential Avoidance

Imagine the following scenarios:

A man believes that having jealous or selfish thoughts makes him a bad person. So, every time a jealous or selfish thought enters his mind, he scolds himself and tries to push the thought away. Unfortunately, this method doesn't quite seem to work, as the thoughts come back again and again.

A woman hates remembering something that happened in the past. That memory brings up painful emotions, so she tries very hard to never think about it. Unfortunately, this doesn't quite work either. The memory comes back to her when she least expects it, time and time again.

A man often feels worried and anxious. He tries to get rid of these feelings by keeping busy and not thinking. So he tries to fill up every waking moment with work or entertainment so as to avoid thinking. The distraction helps a bit, but it doesn't get rid of the anxiety that's always in the background.

These are all examples of experiential avoidance. Any internal effort that we make to avoid, escape or control internal psychological experiences is called experiential avoidance. And by psychological experiences we mean anything ranging from thoughts, emotions, beliefs, sensations, wishes, impulses, memories and so on. We might try to distract ourselves, try not to think, pretend that certain realities don't exist and so on.

Here is the problem with experiential avoidance: emotions, thoughts and beliefs don't just disappear because we want them to. Imagine a person who just received some upsetting news. Her heart is filled with sadness. But she decides to deal with this news using experiential avoidance: by pretending that she was never given this news, forgetting about the whole thing and ignoring the sadness in her heart. Instead she decides to go out partying and laugh as much as she can.

But unfortunately, no matter how hard she tries to forget, a part of her deep down knows the news that she has just received. No amount of pretending to be happy will completely rub off the sadness in her heart. Her laughter is not coming from a place of pure joy. Not only does she not feel better, the effort that she is putting into avoiding the painful thoughts or emotions soon becomes exhausting. She might feel numb, but this numbness is as uncomfortable as the emotions that she started out with.

It is clear that experiential avoidance is never really effective in getting rid of unwanted emotions, thoughts or beliefs. Surely there has to be a better, more effective way, right?

There is. And ironically, it starts with facing our painful emotions and thoughts, as opposed to avoiding them. But if you notice that you tend to avoid your thoughts and emotions a lot, please don't be in a rush to fully change that yet. In the next few chapters you will learn about new, healthier ways of dealing with your thoughts and emotions, and you will gradually be able to let go of avoidance in various areas of your life, as you feel ready to do so. There is no rush. You can determine a comfortable pace for yourself! For now the task is to simply learn about experiential avoidance, and to consider whether it's a good idea to change your relationship with pain and discomfort in life.

A Harmful Strategy

Okay, so we understand now why experiential avoidance is not helpful or effective. But why is it so harmful? There are many reasons for this. But the bottom line is that experiential avoidance stops us from dealing with the causes of our emotions. Let's look at a few examples.

The first example is conditioning. You have already learned about exposure and the way that it helps get rid of your conditioned reaction to things. For example, remember the person with the fear of heights that we learned about in the previous chapter? It wasn't through avoiding high places that this person managed to get rid of their fear. It was through facing them. As we will learn in future chapters, a big part of overcoming unhelpful internal patterns is through facing them. But those who have a habit of constantly avoiding discomfort, don't give themselves that chance to overcome their internal issues.

Another harmful result of avoidance is that it stops us from acting on thoughts or emotions that have helpful messages for us. If an emotion is there, there is a reason for it. If you get a splinter in your finger, is it smarter to remove the splinter, or to close your eyes and wish for the pain to be gone?

The pain may be unpleasant. But it is there for a reason. It's telling you that you need to remove the splinter. Emotions are similar. They are not enemies to be feared or killed off. They are often trying to raise our awareness that areas of our internal and external world need attention. By ignoring, avoiding or fighting them, we are missing their message. Here's an example:

Sonia has an exam next week and hasn't even started studying. She has a thick book to get through and it's very daunting. Every time she opens the book to start studying, she thinks of the impossible task in front of her, panics and turns on the TV! It is easier to pretend that the exam doesn't exist. But the more she avoids studying, the louder her anxiety gets. Sure, she might be watching her favourite TV show. But she is not enjoying it because, deep down, she is feeling more and more anxious! That is because Sonia's anxiety is telling her some useful information: that she needs to do something about her situation. She needs to focus on her studies. Ignoring the anxiety isn't the answer. Listening to it and finding a way to tackle her studies is a much more useful strategy.

There is another very important aspect of experiential avoidance that causes us harm. Experiential avoidance stops us from reaching acceptance around the realities that we cannot change. What is acceptance and why is it helpful? Let's explore that now...

The Bird

Imagine a bird in a cage. A human captured him, took away his freedom and placed him in that cage. It is a sad reality. But how does our bird deal with this reality? He has 3 choices before him:

1. He could spend the rest of his days having an **internal**, mind based, battle with this reality. His thoughts may look like this:

   - 'This should not have happened!'
   - 'Why did this have to happen?'
   - 'Why me, when all those other birds are flying freely?'
   - 'That human shouldn't have been selfish enough to put me in this cage. My life should have been different. Things should have turned out differently!'

   Unfortunately, no matter how hard our bird mentally resists the current reality, the reality won't change for him. Do you see that his internal battle will never result in a different reality? It will only make him more tired, more stressed and more unhappy. That's why thoughts that are based on 'shoulds' or 'what ifs' always make us very unhappy. It's because they are always about fighting and resisting a reality that just won't change right this minute.

2. He could get up and act. Make a plan to break free from the cage. This is an **external** effort, rather than an internal

resistance. When this option is available to us, it is a good idea to take it. This means that when, in life, we have the option of working towards improving our life condition, we should make an effort and act.

But as great as this option is, it is not always available to us. The bird can try his best, but he may never be able to break free from the cage. This is where the third option can come to his aid.

3. He could **accept**. Acceptance is not giving up. To accept doesn't mean that we stop working towards improving our lives. Acceptance is an internal quality. It is about having inner peace, even while we continue to make efforts to improve our circumstances.

   Acceptance is about making peace with our current reality, as it is. Not because we like it. But because reality does not change simply because we want it to. Acceptance means facing the hard truth that even if this reality were to change in the future, it could not be any different right this minute. So internally fighting it and expecting it to be different will only result in emotional suffering.

   In the case of our bird, acceptance may result in thoughts like:

   - 'It is the way that it is. Whether I like it or not.'

   - 'The future might change, but this moment is as it is.'

   - 'Instead of fighting this reality, what can I do to make this cage more bearable? I could enjoy this moment: the view around me, singing a song or having a nice meal.'

- 'What is the point of thinking that things should be different, when they are the way they are? If I don't accept, reality won't change, but I will suffer more.'
- 'What is the point of comparing my life to those birds that are free, when comparing or wondering won't change the reality?'
- 'Whether I accept it or not, the reality is that this human acted unjustly, and placed me in this cage. I don't have to be okay with his actions. But if I don't accept the reality, I will suffer more.'

As a result of these thoughts, our bird could find a way to make the most of his life. Sure, his life is not ideal, nor is it fair. And sure, through his efforts it may change in the future. But right now, this is the only way that it can be. So why waste energy with 'should have's'? Instead, our bird could enjoy the meal provided for him, or the scenery in front of him. Or might have fun singing a song. Enjoying these little things would not be possible if the bird was constantly engaged in an internal battle with his current circumstances, and thinking non-stop about how it should be. Would you agree?

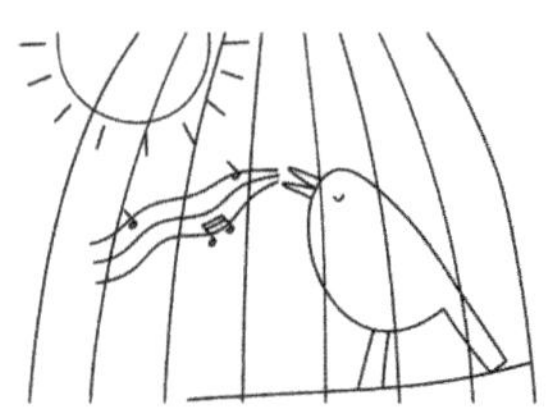

Our bird could even develop an escape plan and work towards it. But acceptance means that our bird's happiness would not depend on the success of his escape plan. His happiness is real now. It is not a hypothetical possibility somewhere in an unknown future.

Acceptance in Practice

Let us challenge a few common misconceptions about acceptance:

- Acceptance doesn't mean being defeated, giving up, becoming complacent or not trying.

- Acceptance doesn't mean forcing yourself to like the present reality - you can still dislike your circumstance, but also accept that it is what it is.

- Acceptance doesn't mean pretending that injustice doesn't exist in the world, nor does it mean becoming okay with it. It is simply facing the reality that things are the way that they are right now.

- Lastly, to accept doesn't mean that you push away your painful emotions around the reality that you are experiencing, be it grief, hurt, anger or resentment. In fact, your emotions are part of the package of the present reality. So it's important to accept them as well! Your emotions may be uncomfortable, but they are as they are right this minute. Fighting them or wishing them to be gone will not result in feeling better. Accepting them will be far more helpful.

A constant comparison between your current reality and the way things should, or could, have been, results in non-acceptance. Giving up this comparison can result in your current reality being much more tolerable and perhaps even sweet and pleasant. To achieve this, you need to be disciplined and completely focused on what is here, right now. Not on comparing what is here right now to something else. Your focus cannot be divided. It needs to be simply here: on your current life in this moment. Let's try it...

Exercise 1

Notice that this moment is as it is, regardless of how you feel about it. Sit with the reality of this moment without thinking or judging. Just sit with an awareness of everything outside and inside of you, without fighting, challenging, judging or wishing things to be different. Try this for the next few minutes...

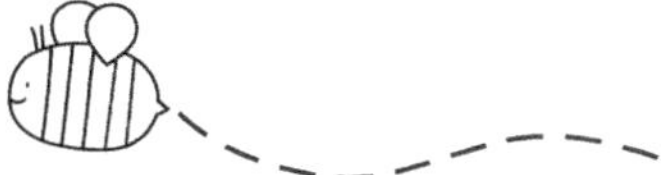

Exercise 2

Now take a moment to privately explore some of the current unwanted circumstances in your life. Make a list of these below:

....Ⓟ

....

....

....

Can you practice acceptance around these circumstances, even while making plans to improve them?

Acceptance and Change

Sometimes acceptance means accepting that change can take time.

We may want the things we want to happen 'right now'! But just because we want it, it doesn't mean that it will happen that way. So acceptance means making our peace with the length of time or the amount of effort needed to see a change. If you are finishing an assignment, quitting a habit, improving your fitness, or working towards any other goals, work hard, and if you realise that it will take longer than you thought to reach your desired outcome, keep going! Don't give up. If you truly accept the amount of time or effort necessary, you will feel more patient. The key to remember here is that those who are patient and keep going, even if it takes a long time to achieve their goals, are the ones who finally get there! Remember the famous story of the rabbit and the turtle? The thought of a turtle racing a rabbit seems funny at first. But it was actually the turtle that won the race. Why was that? Because even though the rabbit ran fast, he only ran for short distances and then kept stopping. But the turtle was patient and consistent. He might have walked more slowly, but he kept going and going. The reality is that slow and steady does often win the race! Those who accept that it takes time and patience to achieve goals are more likely to get there.

This also goes for the changes that you hope to see in the people around you. You may be a parent wanting to see a positive change in your child, a teacher trying to train your students, a spouse working on improving your relationship with your husband or wife, or a friend watching your friend give up an unhelpful habit. Accept that change for them may also take time. Your acceptance, while you await the desired outcome, will reduce the stress on yourself and on them. For example, this may help you notice smaller changes and reward them, instead of expressing your disappointment that the change wasn't bigger or faster.

And now you are reading a book that will start a process of positive change that will take time to gradually unfold. Every new skill that you learn in this book is only a beginning. The more you practise that skill, the more gradual change will unfold in your life. What better place to start practising acceptance and patience than here? As you learn various skills in this course, take care not to pressure yourself to fix everything at once. Take care not to pressure yourself to master all the skills in one go. A piano player may have to play a piece many, many, times before they can play it well. Hours of patient practice is needed. What you learn in this book is meant to make life easier and reduce the pressure on your mind. Patience and acceptance mean that you take the skills away and practise them at a pace that feels comfortable and comes naturally. Feel excited about the changes to your life, but not stressed because you expect the change to happen sooner and faster. That excitement should be enough to motivate you to keep practising what you learn here.

What we learned in this chapter brings us to the powerful words of the American poet Robert Frost: 'The best way out is always through.' Experiential avoidance means running away from reality. It is about clashing with reality, wanting it to be different and making a constant effort to resist or ignore it. It comes from a place of fear. Acceptance is embracing or facing reality, looking it in the eye and working with it to create positive change. It comes from a place of strength.

Yay,
I've now completed
17% of the
book! □

Chapter 3: Thoughts

Noticing the Body

Let's do that little exercise again. Notice how your body feels. Is it comfortable? Relaxed? Tense? Restless? Does it feel warm or cool? Do you feel any pain or pressure anywhere? What is your heart doing? Can you feel it beat? What about your breathing?

Close your eyes and pay attention to your body for a moment.

Revision ©

1. Emotions are powerful, so we try to control, shape and .... them.

2. .... is an unhealthy way of regulating emotions. It means avoiding our internal experiences, such as thoughts and emotions.

3. Acceptance means:

   Letting go of our internal resistance and war against the reality of this moment ☐

   Letting go of our external resistance and war against the reality of this moment ☐

4. Repeat the following exercise from the previous chapter:

Notice that this moment is as it is, regardless of how you feel about it. Sit with the reality of this moment without thinking or judging. Just sit with an awareness of everything outside and inside of you, without fighting, challenging, judging or wishing things to be different.

Recognising Your Thoughts

Today we will start learning about our thoughts. What are they? How do they impact us? And how can we have healthier thinking?

In the previous chapter we learned that thoughts are made up of words and mental images. They are like internal conversations. We also learned about awareness. We learned that awareness is not the same thing as thinking. Awareness is not made up of words or mental creations. It is just about paying attention to what is here right now, in the world around us or within us. When we practise mindfulness, we give our full attention to what is happening right now. We might pay attention to the sounds around us. To the feelings in our body. To the smell of a flower. To the taste of a spoonful of food in our mouth.

But here's an interesting little twist! What happens if, while we are thinking, we pay attention to those thoughts? Paying attention to our thoughts is another aspect of mindfulness. That's right! In those moments, it could be said that we are thinking and are aware, all at the same time! Or rather, thoughts are happening and we are watching them. Mindfulness of thought is about allowing your thoughts to go through your mind, as they do, but being aware of them at the same time. Noticing your thoughts as they happen. As people practise mindfulness of thought, they often find that they fall into one of three different categories. Let's take a look at what they are. As we describe these categories, we ask that you close your eyes and take your attention inside. See if you can notice which description is closest to your experience.

Listeners

These are people who find it easier and more natural to listen to the internal dialogue, or their thoughts. See if you experience your thoughts like an internal conversation, just like you would hear the conversation between two people sitting next to you. See if you can listen to the conversation without needing to change, modify or control anything. Just listen.

If you belong to this category you might find it helpful to close your eyes while practising mindfulness. This will help you to focus more and not get distracted.

Go ahead, see if this is how you experience your thoughts.

Observers

People in this group find it easier and more natural to watch or observe their thoughts. If you belong to this group, watch your thoughts as if you are watching a movie on a cinema screen. Your thoughts might look like various pictures and images related to ideas, memories, opinions and so on.

See if you can watch the pictures without needing to change, modify or control anything. Just watch.

If you are watching your thoughts, you might find it more natural to keep your eyes slightly open. If it helps, look to a quiet corner to avoid distraction.

Go ahead and practise this approach. See if this is how you tend to experience your thoughts.

Feelers

People in this group find it easier and more natural to feel their thoughts, as if they were energy charges within the body. If you belong to this group, it is likely that your thoughts have a high emotional charge, and at times it is difficult to distinguish between thoughts and emotions. Simply feel your thoughts as they move about in your body or around your head.

Become aware of what your thoughts are saying and all the experiences that they are creating. Stay aware of the thoughts as they appear and disappear. Be aware of how they feel and where in your body you feel them.

It may help you to consider the following analogy: imagine you are standing in a river with waves of water washing against your legs. Imagine your thoughts and emotions to be like the water. Your job is to stay aware of the water current (i.e. thoughts and emotions) as they come and go. You do not need to control, analyse, or understand the current. Just let it flow and stay aware.

If you belong to this category you may also find it helpful to close your eyes while practising mindfulness, to help prevent distraction.

Go ahead, see if this is close to how you tend to experience your thoughts.

A Few Points to Remember

Most people are a combination of listeners, observers and feelers and experience their thoughts in a variety of ways. The point is to start becoming aware of your thoughts, in whatever form they appear.

It is also important that you do not interfere with your thoughts. This means that you should only notice them and pay attention to them. You do not try to control them, censor them, create them or get rid of them.

Often people ask 'But what if I am not thinking any thoughts? Should I be making myself think about something?' The answer is, mindfulness is never about changing, creating or controlling. Mindfulness is about observing what is there already. So if there are no thoughts, just sit with the silence. Just pay attention to the silence. And if a thought appears, pay attention to it. Just notice whatever is here right now.

On a side note, the moment you ask yourself 'Well, there are no thoughts here. What am I supposed to be paying attention to?' or 'Am I even doing this right?' you are thinking. Those questions are the very thoughts that are going through your mind. Notice them.

Now let's practise a bit more. If you can, this time go for a bit longer.

We want to give you a small challenge. See if while you read the rest of this chapter, you can stay aware of your thoughts. Realistically, there will be moments when you forget to pay attention to them. That is okay. Practice makes perfect. But whenever you remember, pay attention to your thoughts again. We will try to help by reminding you from time to time.

So, what do you think happens to our thoughts when we don't pay attention to them? Do you think our thoughts change when they are just happening in the background and we are not looking at them? Do you think they might behave any differently?

....Ⓖ

....

Healthy Thinking

Let's do a little activity. Use any material or objects that you see around you, in your stationary drawer or in the kitchen, to build a structure that can support a pen... or several pens. You can build a bridge, a tower, a table or any other structure that you like. Your aim is to use your raw material to build the most robust structure you can think of to support your pens. What ideas can you come up with?

Now have a think of the following question:

Which one of your inner building blocks did you use to come up with your structure?

....Ⓖ

You would probably agree that it was your thinking. Problem solving and coming up with ideas are mostly properties of thought. Another property of thought is logic. What is logic? Let's do another activity to help us answer that question. Grab yourself three equal sized glasses. Fill two of them with water. Keep the third one empty.

Now, have a think and see if you can figure out a way to fit all the water from the two full glasses into the one empty one.

...Right now, you may be feeling a bit confused. How can you fit the contents of two glasses into one? You might be thinking that what we are asking of you is not possible. What part of you is able to tell you that it's not possible? It is your logic that is telling you this. Your logic has an understanding that water, in its normal form, cannot be shrunk into a smaller space. Your logic just automatically knows that. Isn't that clever? Our thinking is like a very smart computer. But we don't always make the best use of this computer. Thinking can be a blessing or a curse. It can help you solve complicated problems to improve your life and the lives of others around you. Or it can cause you to become restless, unhappy or unable to relax. So what makes some thinking so helpful and some so unhelpful? How can we be more in charge of our thinking and use it in positive, helpful ways, rather than in destructive and unhelpful ways?

Reminder: don't forget to notice your thoughts!

Passive Thinking

Passive thinking is when you are going about your daily business, but in the background your thoughts are churning at the speed of a hundred miles an hour while you're not paying attention. You may be semi-aware of these thoughts, or not aware of them at all. Before you know it, all kinds of emotions could be running through your system. You may be feeling sad, angry, worried, self-blaming, and so on. But if someone asked you 'what were the thoughts that made you feel this way?', you would scratch your head and answer 'no idea!'. Or you would have to trace back your thoughts in order to try to remember. So in simple words, passive thinking is when you are thinking, but you are not paying attention to your thoughts. It's as if you are on autopilot mode and your thoughts are automatically running, without your involvement.

Often the same automatic thoughts are repeated over and over again. So, for example, the same negative thoughts about your worries or concerns might repeat every day or every week, without ever reaching a resolution. It's as if their only purpose is to ruin your mood and make you feel negative emotions! They rarely help you find solutions or break free from your problems. Because you're not actively assessing these thoughts and, as a result, blindly accept everything that they say as if they were absolute truth.

On the other hand, when we are aware of our thoughts, when we pay attention to what we are thinking, we can become active participants in them and assess them. This is called active thinking. The more we are aware of our thoughts, the better we can manage them.

Don't Believe Everything You Think[1]

So, here's the problem with passive thinking: when we don't pay attention to our thoughts, we're not able to use our logic in the best of ways. Thoughts do not always tell us the truth! No matter how real or convincing they seem to be, there are often subtle mistakes mixed in with our thoughts. And when we don't pay attention to these thoughts, we are not there to see these mistakes and correct them. Instead we blindly believe everything they say. Here's an example to show you what we mean by this. Sarah always felt a subtle, nervous feeling in her gut if she left the water tap running a bit too long. She never took much notice of it. She would just get rid of the anxious feeling by quickly rushing to turn off the tap. She had lived for many years with this experience, without ever questioning why it happened. The thoughts were automatic, and she didn't really pay attention to them.

But one day, when she was 25 years old, she finally became curious. 'Why do I feel this way?' She began paying attention. Thinking back to her childhood, she remembered where it all started. She must have been really young, maybe 4 or 5 years old, when her mother said to her 'Sarah, turn that tap off. You're going to flood the house!' Her mother may not have put much thought into what she said. She just wanted Sarah to close the tap and not waste water. She would have definitely not meant it literally when she said

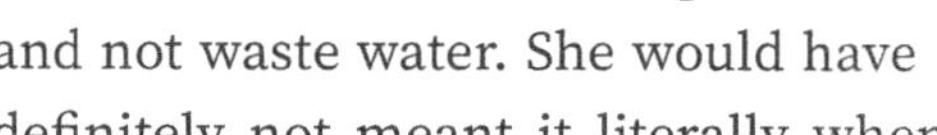

that the house would get flooded. But Sarah was too young to understand all of that. She took it literally and developed a fear.

The interesting part is that Sarah lived many years after that and grew up to be a rational adult who could obviously understand that it takes a lot more than a tap running for a few seconds to flood a house! So why did she still feel afraid when running the tap?

You guessed it: passive thinking!

And that day when she finally began to pay attention to her thoughts and reassessed them, she was practising active thinking.

As you can see, Sarah's beliefs were formed at a young age, before her logic and ability to reason were very advanced. But she continued to treat that belief as true and accurate because she never noticed or questioned it. She just accepted it as a fact and never looked at it again. Instead she absentmindedly acted on it each time by turning the tap off quickly in order to avoid the 'flooding'. Until the day when she finally questioned her thought, every time the thought had gone through her head, the logical adult Sarah had been absent. The thought had controlled her emotions and behaviour without Sarah having a say in it.

The problem with passive thinking is that you, the driver, the logical thinker, the brain that should rationally assess these thoughts, are not fully present. So in your absence, the thoughts can run amok.

It is like a factory that has been running for years without a manager overseeing the workers, or a car that is left running without a driver. You, the driver, have an extremely important job in ensuring that the power machine of your thinking will benefit you rather than harm you. Active thinking simply means that you, the manager, the driver, become present, begin paying attention and become actively involved with the thoughts that are taking place.

Reminder: don't forget to notice your thoughts!

Thought Errors

Thought errors or thinking mistakes happen when our thoughts tell us things that sound logical or rational, but really aren't logical when we dig deeper. Let's take a look at a few ways in which our thoughts commonly make mistakes. As you hear the descriptions for each of these thinking mistakes, consider whether or not you have experienced them in your own life:

Mental Filter

This is when we focus on a specific area of a problem and leave out the rest. Often the negative aspects of a situation are focused on and the positive aspects are ignored. So we paint the whole picture with a single negative detail. Picture an employee who has had many great achievements at work and often gets praised by her boss and colleagues for her good work. But one day her boss criticised a small aspect of her work. She felt very down and worried, thinking 'I'm a bad employee. I never get things right. I can't believe I made such a silly mistake. Others managed to get it right! I think my boss is really disappointed in me. Maybe he'll fire me. I am just not good at this job!' She decided she was not good at her job by focusing on her one small mistake and forgetting all her achievements.

Jumping to Conclusions

At times we may be quick to jump to conclusions, even though we have insufficient information about a situation. For example, we might try to make predictions about the future on the basis of very little evidence (e.g. 'I just know that I'm going to fail the exam tomorrow'). Or we may assume that we know what someone else is thinking. Remember, the check-out lady at the supermarket could have been unfriendly towards you because she had a migraine, because she had just had an argument with her husband, because she felt as though she didn't fit in with her colleagues, because she has social anxiety and so on. To assume that 'she must not like me' is an example of jumping to conclusions. Perhaps, next time, if you were to smile and ask her how she is, you could help her feel a bit better and see a completely different side to her.

Personalisation

At times we take things personally when they are not personal at all. For example, we may think it is completely our fault when things go wrong, even if we are only slightly responsible or not responsible at all. And even if the events were completely outside of our control. For example, a woman who lost her husband might blame herself completely for not being a better mother to her children while she was experiencing grief and depression. What she was forgetting was that if, while she was grieving, her mental health was so poor that she was not able to do any better, she was just as much a victim of the situation as her children were. It was not helpful to blame herself for something that was not within her control.

It's all about me!

Catastrophising

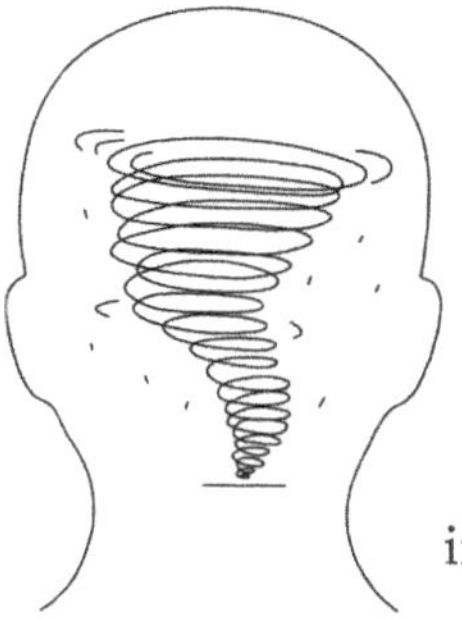

We may believe that a problem is much bigger that it actually is. We may see the problem as horrible, dreadful and highly alarming, when in reality it may not be very significant at all. Or we may underestimate our own coping ability and skills in being able to deal with the problem. For example, you may find out that you have some important guests arriving, an important exam coming up or a large bill to pay, and you are swamped by thoughts like: 'I can't do this. How am I going to cope? This is so huge!' You miss the fact that you would have passed many similar challenges in the past. It may be hard work but, based on history, you have the ability to cope and find solutions. You just need to take it one step at a time and, before you know it, it will be over!

Overgeneralisation

Human beings show a need for finding consistency and patterns in life. What happened in the past, is expected to happen in the future. This results in a common thought error called overgeneralisation. So, for example, if the first couple of people who saw your artwork didn't like it, you might expect that no one else is going to like it. If your past has been difficult, you expect that your future would be difficult also. If you didn't achieve your goals in the past, you would not expect to achieve them in the future either. We just assume that there is a consistent pattern written for our lives. However, there is no reasonable evidence for this. No matter how long your difficulties have been going on, there is no logical reason to believe that things will stay the same in your future. People's lives do change. Ups and downs do happen. People do experience significant life changes across the different stages of their lives. And there is no reason to believe that you are an exception to this rule.

Magnification and Minimisation

At times we simply misjudge the proportions of things. This means that we minimise or magnify certain aspects of a situation. Like magnifying other people's positive characteristics while minimising or explaining away any positive characteristics of your own. This may even impact what we see when we look into the mirror, or when we judge the outcome of a project we have been working on. We may magnify the things that we don't like about ourselves or our work, while minimising what we do like. For some, the reverse is true: they may magnify what they like about themselves or minimise any personal areas needing improvement.

Reminder: don't forget to notice your thoughts!

Activity

Read the following story and explore what thought errors the character might be showing. What would be an alternative, more helpful way of thinking?

Rose was not invited to the wedding of a friend. She and her friend hadn't seen each other for a long time, for no reason other than having grown apart and finding different friend groups. But Rose couldn't help wondering if not being invited to the wedding meant that she was an unlikable friend or her friend hadn't considered her worthy of friendship. So she felt quite hurt.

.... Ⓖ

....

....

....

....

Helpful Thoughts

Our thoughts aren't always inaccurate or unhelpful. Often they have helpful messages for us. Passive thinking means that we may also not notice these helpful thoughts. So we don't act on the messages that they have for us. For example, James felt anxious, stressed and exhausted. He just assumed that he felt stressed because his life was difficult and he had a lot of responsibilities. But one day, he decided to practise active thinking. He paid attention to the thoughts that made him feel stressed and wrote them down. He realised that he had a lot of tasks that needed doing. Thoughts about what needed to be done kept churning through his mind, but because they were passive thoughts, he never organised himself to actually do these tasks! Instead he just felt overwhelmed. As a result of paying attention to these thoughts, James made a to do list, prioritised the things that needed doing first, and made practical plans to do them. He immediately felt better. By paying attention to his thoughts, James practised active thinking and became the manager of his internal world, rather than being passively pushed around by his thoughts.

Reminder: don't forget to notice your thoughts!

Active Thinking

You could say that there are 4 steps to active thinking:

1. **Paying attention to what your thoughts are saying** - this step is the simple act of mindfulness of thoughts. We have discussed the fact that mindfulness is not about changing thoughts, but simply about noticing them, watching and becoming more and more aware of them.

2. **Becoming curious about how accurate your thoughts are** - as you become aware of your thoughts, at times you may become aware of inaccuracies within them or realise the need to assess certain thoughts. So every now and then you may ask yourself, 'Is this thought in line with reality?', 'Is it true?', 'Is it based on facts?'

3. **Letting go of inaccurate thoughts** - if you realise that a thought is inaccurate or not in proportion with what is actually happening, you no longer need to believe that thought. You don't need to get rid of that thought. You just need to realise that it's not true. A lie is only effective if we believe it to be true, right? The moment you realise that it is a lie, you automatically stop believing it. The same applies to thought errors.
   If you realise that your thought is not in line with reality, there is no longer a need to believe it. You don't need to force your thoughts to change or fight the thoughts. You just need to stop believing them. At times this results in immediately feeling better. But at other times, even though your thoughts have changed, your emotions remain unchanged. For example, you may logically

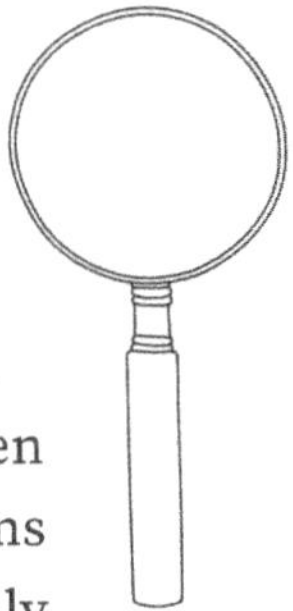

believe that you are safe, but still feel the emotions of fear and anxiety. Do not worry about these emotions for now. We will learn how to manage emotions in future chapters. At this point, all you need to do is to stop believing the thoughts that are inaccurate.

4. **Noticing helpful information and acting on them when necessary** - bring your focus to the tasks at hand, carefully assess all angles, plan and organise yourself.

Homework Ⓕ

See if you can come up with a way to help yourself remember to notice your thoughts and practise active thinking every day. Create an art-work or a note to yourself that you can leave near your work-station, on the dashboard of your car, on the fridge or anywhere else that you regularly look. You could even make yourself a piece of jewellery as a reminder.

Making progress!

I've now completed 23% of the book ☐

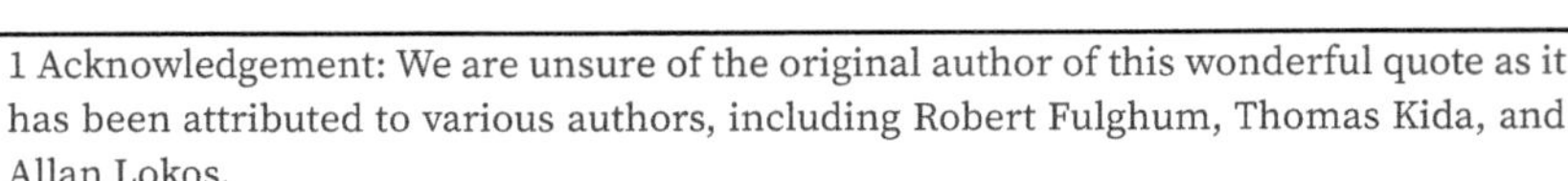

1 Acknowledgement: We are unsure of the original author of this wonderful quote as it has been attributed to various authors, including Robert Fulghum, Thomas Kida, and Allan Lokos.

Chapter 4: Fine-tuning the Art of Thinking

Noticing the Body

Let's do that little exercise again. Once again, notice how your body feels. Is it comfortable? Relaxed? Tense? Restless? Does it feel warm or cool? Do you feel any pain or pressure anywhere? What is your heart doing? Can you feel it beat? What about your breathing?

Close your eyes and pay attention to your body for a moment.

As you read through the rest of this chapter, you'll be reminded to bring your attention back to the body from time to time.

Now, let's do a quick mindfulness of thoughts exercise. Remember, if you are an observer, you will see your thoughts as if they were pictures in your mind. If you are a listener, you will hear them like an internal mind based conversation. And if you are a feeler, you will notice them in your body. So, sit back and pay attention to your thoughts for a while. Allow your mind to do whatever it wants to do. If your thoughts are very active and fast paced, you may notice that after watching them for a while, they become quieter and more still. So take your time and don't rush this process.

Revision ©

1. Which of the following statements are correct?

   We should believe all of our thoughts. If we think them, they must be true.

   True ☐

   False ☐

   We need to be like a scientist when dealing with our thoughts: examining and testing them before believing them.

   True ☐

   False ☐

2. Active thinking means:

   A) Paying attention to ....

   B) Checking the ....
   of the thoughts.

   C) Letting go of..

   D) Acting on ....

3. What is experiential avoidance?

....

....

A Helpful Tool

When children begin to learn to ride bicycles, they use training wheels to help them with the learning process. And once they have finally learned to cycle with some confidence, the training wheels have done their job and can be ditched! We have a tool that can act like training wheels in helping you master the art of active thinking. That tool is writing. When you write your thoughts down, you are forced to slow down and pay attention to them.

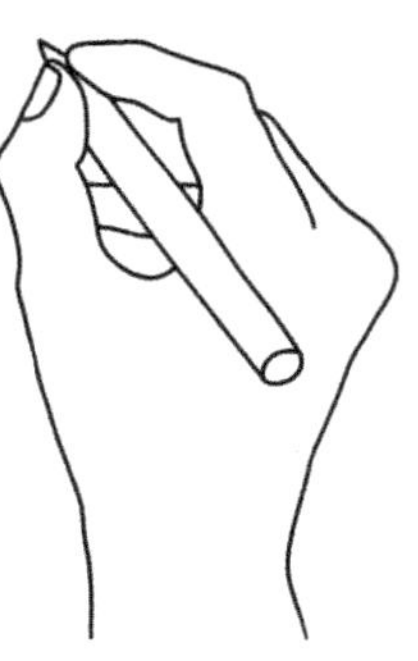

As you practise active thinking with the help of writing, you begin to develop the habit of paying attention to your thoughts. And at some point, you will notice that you are noticing the thoughts automatically. At that point, you are ready to ditch the training wheels, meaning that you can practice active thinking without the help of writing.

Please note: although writing is a helpful tool for achieving active thinking, it is not a necessity. If you don't find it helpful, or you're not able to practise it for any reason, feel free to replace it with the regular practice of paying attention to your thoughts.

Another tool that can help you with active thinking is talking. Whether you choose to talk to a trusted friend or family member, a professional like a psychologist, or counsellor, the process of saying your thought out loud helps with active thinking. Some of you may have noticed that at times, the moment you speak to someone about a problem or a challenge, you suddenly start finding clever solutions, or see the issue from a totally different angle. At times you don't even need to hear the other person's point of view. Just by saying your thoughts out loud, active thinking has helped you figure it out. At other times, it's the process of exchanging ideas while speaking to another person that helps you reassess your thoughts and understand things better. That is all part of active thinking.

Points To Remember When Active Thinking

What you write is for your eyes only - you may even wish to dispose of your writing once you are done with it. So be honest with yourself and don't hold back. Even write about those thoughts and emotions that you feel you shouldn't have, or you dislike. This is a good way to reduce experiential avoidance. If a thought enters your mind, it is okay to be honest with yourself and acknowledge it.

Write about your thoughts, not just the external situation - we often think that our emotions are a direct result of our external, real life situations. It is easy to assume that something happens in the world around us, and as a result, we feel a certain way!

What if we told you that often it is not the external situation that causes your emotions? It is your thoughts about the situation that lead to the emotions. This is because we use our thinking to interpret and understand the external events. Imagine a teacher who is not managing her classroom. She feels disappointed and frustrated after class. She attributes her emotions to the behaviour of the students: 'I feel frustrated because the kids are so difficult to manage! They don't listen to me.'

One day, she decides to use active thinking to understand her thoughts and emotions better. She begins writing her thoughts down:

> 'What is it that causes me to feel frustrated and disappointed after class? What are the thoughts that go through my mind?' She pays attention and notices these thoughts: 'I'm not having an effect on these kids. I should be doing better. I'm not good enough. I am a failure. If I had been more capable, the kids would have listened to me.'

She then checks whether her thoughts are accurate: 'Am I really having no effect on these kids? Actually, the kids are changing and improving, only it's at a slower pace than I expected.' She lists all the progress that individual students are making. For students who had not made much of a progress, she makes a plan:

> 'Johnny is writing a bit better. Sarah is still not writing better, but she manages to sit through the class and listen more. She is definitely learning more. Mike is not showing much improvement. He seems quite uninterested in what we are learning in the class. Can I find a way to make the topic more interesting to him? Maybe I can have a chat with him to see why he is so bored in the class. Maybe he is so far behind in his studies that I need to teach him more basic things first. Or maybe he's far too clever and he already knows everything we are learning and so he gets bored. Or maybe I can give him activities that are more practical, visual or physically active to keep him engaged.'

She then reassesses her own performance as a teacher. After listing her strengths and weaknesses, she realises: 'Maybe any other teacher in my shoes would be struggling too. This is a tough class. I'm not doing as badly as I thought. From today on, I will start practising acceptance. If I accept the challenges facing me, it will be easier to cope.'

As you can see, it wasn't the external events (in this case, the students' behaviour) that caused this teacher to feel frustrated and disappointed. It was her thoughts and the way she had interpreted the events. By reassessing and changing those thoughts, she began feeling calmer and more at peace with the situation. But without active thinking she wouldn't have been able to do any of that.

Don't overgeneralise - as you write your thoughts down, be specific. Don't stop at overly generalised statements like 'people are not to be trusted'. Get to the more specific thoughts going through your mind. For example, a person might write 'I feel like I can't trust anyone because many people have mistreated me in the past. This includes Donna, Michelle, Uncle Steve, and Rob. I trusted them but they all did hurtful things to me.'

Once this person has written down these specific thoughts and beliefs, they can start to reassess them:

> 'Okay, so let's see if everything that I'm thinking is true. My relationship with Donna, Michelle, Uncle Steve, and Rob was initially good. But when they hurt me, I never spoke to them to understand why they did what they did. I don't truly understand what went through their minds. Could it be a misunderstanding? Could it have been momentary selfishness resulting from their own stress and anxieties? Could it be that somewhere along the line they were hurt at something that I did, but instead of telling me they acted in vengeful ways?

Could there be more to the story that I don't know? If they truly didn't care about me and wanted to take advantage of me, why did they put effort into our relationship in the past?

Is there a way for me to better understand their motives? And if it turns out that some of them did truly set out to take advantage of me, does that mean that this rule applies to all of them and everyone else in my life? Can people really all be the same? Or are they all very different from one another in their motives?'

And of course, beliefs like that may take a long time to be tested and shifted. This person may need to gradually assess and reassess their belief over time, while communicating with and learning about the people around them.

Don't fight with your thoughts - there is a common misconception that in order for us to feel good, we need to make sure that all of our thoughts are positive. This results in people having constant internal struggles where they try to fight off negative thoughts and force positive ones in to replace them.

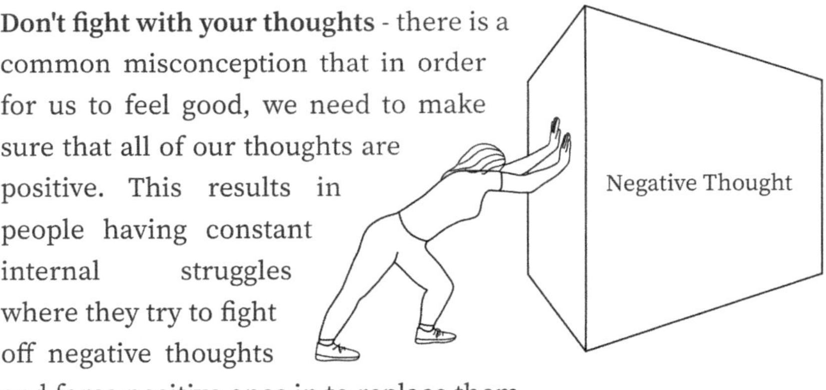

Here's a question for you: by avoiding and censoring thoughts that have negative content, what are these individuals actually doing?

If you guessed 'experiential avoidance', you are right! The practice of 'only thinking positive thoughts' results in an internal struggle, a constant fight against your thoughts. In the long run, it can cause emotional exhaustion. This is while deep down, a part of you still believes in the negative thoughts that you started off with.

The purpose of active thinking isn't to simply be positive. The purpose is to put your thoughts to the test, just as a scientist would put their theories to the test. The purpose of active thinking is to stop blindly accepting any idea as true, whether positive or negative. Finding what is real and true is your aim.

Your beliefs and emotions don't have to match your thoughts yet - as you practice active thinking, there may be times when you think of a more rational idea than your old ideas, but find it hard to believe this new idea on a deep level. For instance, the teacher in our earlier example might logically realise that she is capable, but on a deep level still struggle to believe it, or her emotions may still cause her to feel incapable. If this is the case for you, don't concern yourself with having to believe the new rational views, or fixing up your emotions right now. Your job at this stage is only to consider the alternative views, even if they are hard to believe. So, simply look at the facts and write down any alternative possibilities. The believing part may naturally fall into place gradually and some of the skills that you will develop in future chapters will help with that process. You may find the following structure helpful when writing your

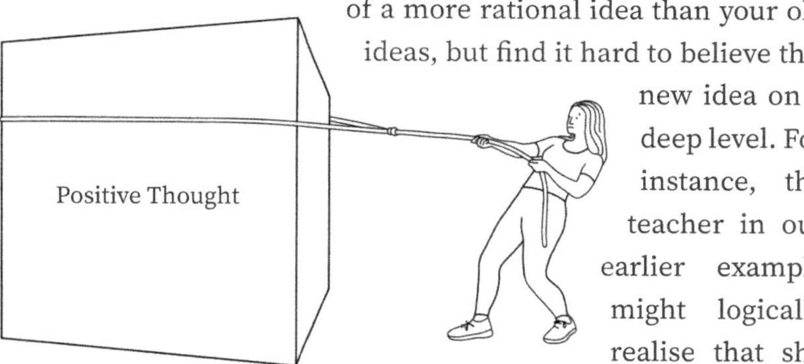

thoughts. If you are using a notebook, you can copy this table into your notebook, or just use similar headings to guide your writing process. Ⓟ

External Situation/ Circumstances	My Thoughts	Thought Errors	Alternative Thoughts

The Scientist

Remember the story of Sarah and her fear of flooding the house if she left the tap running a bit too long? Sometimes the decisions that we have made about our lives are based on thought errors in our past thinking. If we never question these ideas, we may carry on living the rest of our lives with the assumption that they are true. This section is about rethinking our past decisions about the world, which may have turned into deep seated beliefs. Consider this as a space to reflect and to renew.

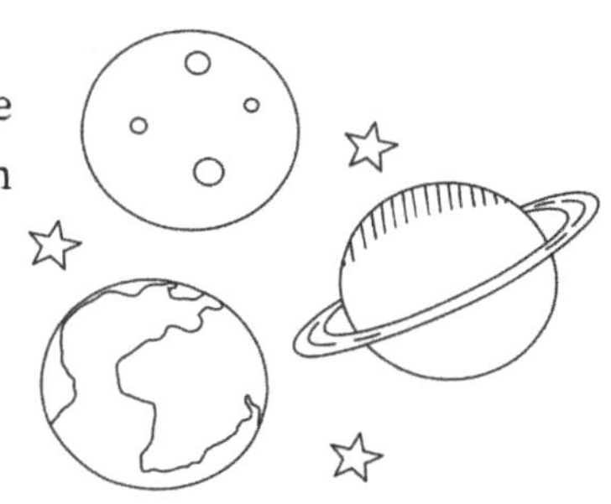

Meet Mark. Mark is a scientist. He knows that the most important rule in science is to not believe something as true before it is tested and proven. While researching, Mark often has theories about how things might work. But no matter how convinced he is by a theory, he always puts it to test before believing it. Why? Because Mark knows that human opinions are not always correct. No matter how convincing they may seem.

But Mark often forgets to use the same rule when it comes to his personal life. For example, when he was a kid at primary school, he struggled with spelling. Other kids in the class seemed to get it without much effort. But somehow for Mark learning to spell was very difficult. On one occasion, his classmates laughed at him for struggling to spell. At that time, he decided 'I must not be very clever. Maybe I'm not as good as the other kids.'

Since then, many years have gone by. Mark has had many achievements. He realised that although spelling was not his strong point, he did pretty well when it came to studying science. He fixed many complicated problems in his personal life and career. But deep down, he still believed 'I am not very clever, so I'm not as good as other people.' He even felt like a fraud when he received praise for his good work as a scientist. It was almost as though nothing could change the decision that Mark had made about himself when he was a kid. He continued to believe his theory about himself, despite so much evidence to the contrary.

One day Mark decided to begin active thinking about this subject. He decided to take a fresh look at this matter using the scientific principles that he knew best. 'I decided that I wasn't clever as a primary school child struggling with spelling. Let's see if I was right!', he wrote. 'What would I do if I came across another child struggling with spelling today? Or a child who was being laughed at by their classmates? Would I decide that this child is not clever and generally a failure in life? Or would I feel empathy towards them, reassure them and remind them that different people have different strengths and weaknesses? Of course, I would be kind and reassure them. If I came across little Mark being laughed at by his friends, I would want him to know that this is just a phase in life and that he's not the failure that he thinks he is. He's just as good as anyone else. Just like everyone else, he has strengths and weaknesses. So perhaps I need to reconsider what little Mark decided about himself. I need to realise that when little Mark decided "I'm a failure in life", he was actually believing a thought error, and not the truth.'

Notice how your body feels now. Does it feel any different to before?

Self-Fulfilling Prophecies

Here's an important piece of information about beliefs. Beliefs have a way of proving themselves right. When you expect something to happen, you make it more likely to happen. What do we mean by that? Well, if you convince someone that they can't do something, they are a lot more likely to fail at doing it. But if you convince them that they can do it, they are far more likely to succeed. If you believe that you're unlikable, you are a lot more likely to push people away. But if you feel secure that there is no reason for people to dislike you, then you will tend to behave in ways that are more likely to attract people. Let's have a look at how this works:

Example 1 - A student who believes 'I'm not going to do well in my studies' may find that whenever he doesn't understand something in class, he either quits early or persists in studying but becomes so anxious with these thoughts that he can't concentrate well and ends up with

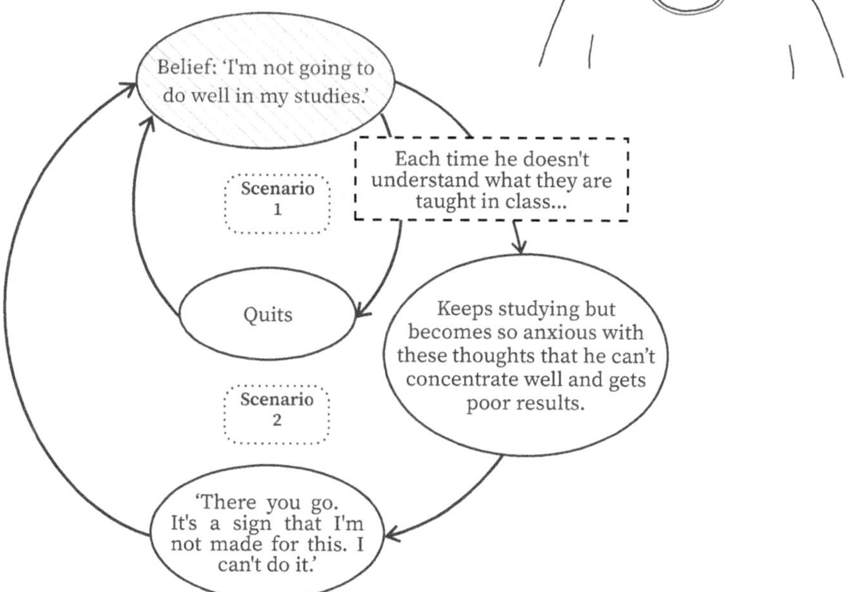

poor results. Both of these scenarios provide him with evidence for his original belief: 'I'm not going to do well in my studies.' In both cases, his belief proved itself right.

Let's take a look at what would happen if this student were to believe that he could do well in his studies. In this scenario, every time the student finds something difficult or doesn't understand an aspect of what they're taught in class, he thinks: 'This is normal. If I don't understand it, it must be hard. Maybe other students are struggling with it too. How can I understand it better? Who can I ask for help? Let me read that section again. Let me research.' So he keeps trying until he eventually succeeds. This proves his original belief: 'I can do well in my studies.'

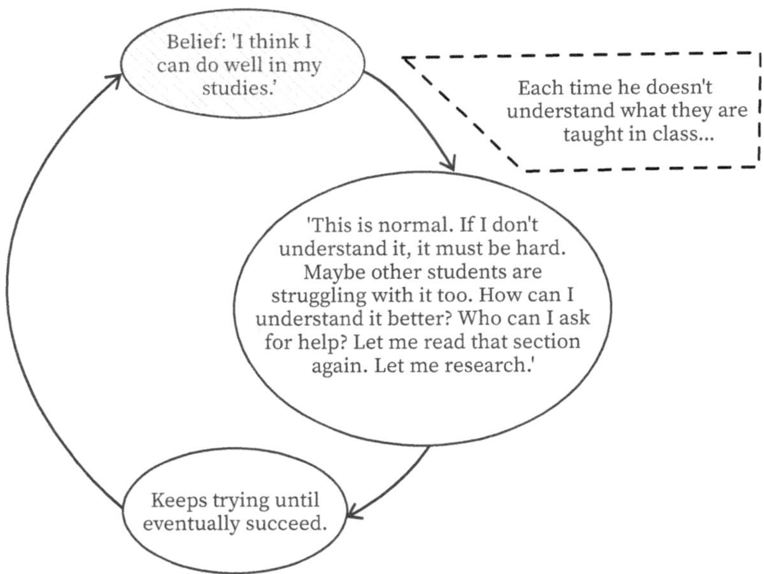

Example 2 - Now imagine a person who believes that she is unlikable, or that people generally don't like her.

This belief can lead to 3 possible scenarios. In scenario 1, she pulls away from people. Won't make eye contact. Won't enter conversations with people. This behavior causes people to assume that she wants to keep to herself. They feel she's not interested in mixing in. So, they leave her alone. As a result, this person would get plenty of 'evidence' to support her belief: 'I'm unlikable' or 'people don't like me.'

In scenario 2, she may try a different, yet equally unhelpful tactic. She may try extra hard and show clingy, attention-seeking behaviour. She may make excessive efforts to not disappoint others. She may be overly apologetic. This behaviour could lead to emotions like irritation in those around her, so they may snap at her or push her away. This, again, would confirm the belief: 'I'm unlikable' or 'people don't like me.'

Finally, in scenario 3, this person could show a heightened tendency to feel insulted or rejected in relationships. She could interpret innocent behavior as a sign that people dislike her. This can result in more conflict and tension being stirred up in her relationships with others. She would be more likely to push people away as a way of self-protection. Once again, these outcomes would confirm the belief: 'I'm unlikable' or 'people don't like me.'

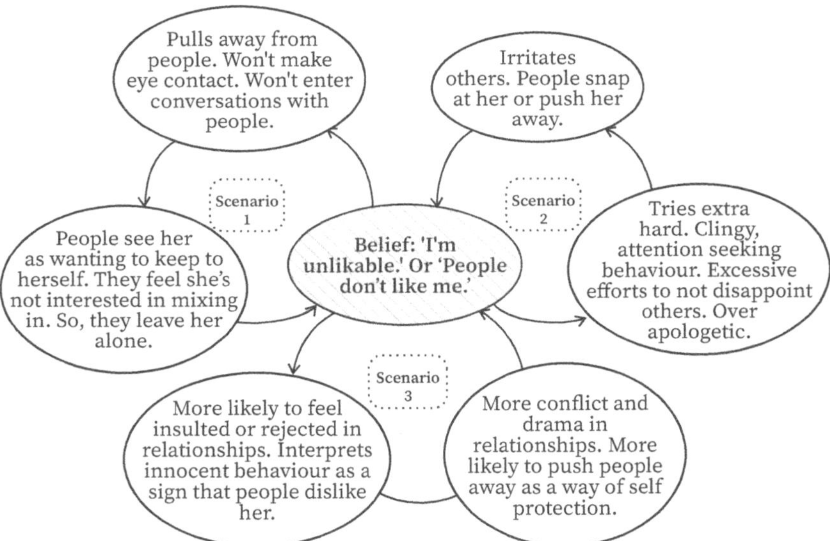

Now compare this to how things could pan out if she believed that people generally did like her, or that she is acceptable as she is. In this scenario, she would have a calm, relaxed, and positive demeanor. She wouldn't feel the need to over-exert in order to receive other people's approval or affection. She would gain the ability to effortlessly be true to her authentic self. People around her would enjoy the pleasant and happy energy that she exudes.

They would likely choose to be around her as her company would make them feel calm and safe. This would then confirm her original security in the belief: 'People generally like me' or 'I am acceptable.'

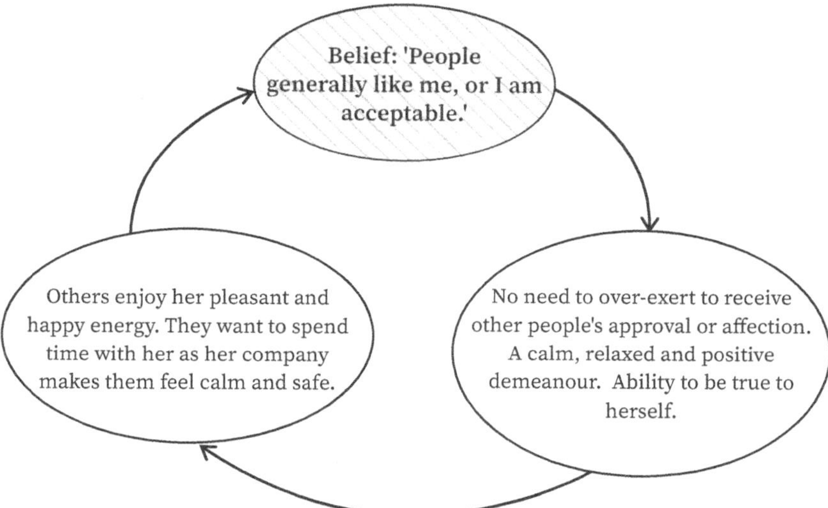

And we could give you so many more examples of this. The point to remember is that just because you have gathered lots of evidence that supports your negative views of yourself and the world, it doesn't necessarily mean that they are true. Consider the possibility that your negative views are actually largely responsible for those negative outcomes. A careful examination of your beliefs and their impact on those around you may be necessary.

Activity Ⓕ

Take a moment to draw a chart, similar to the ones we just looked at, that explores one of your key beliefs and any ways in which this belief may be proving itself right.

Decisions About the World

Sometimes our thought errors are about the world around us. These may be thoughts about how the world works or life in general. For example, Julia spent years being intensely sad about the fact that her father, who was very sick before he died, suffered in his final days. One day, when reassessing her thoughts, Julia realised that although her dad's suffering was very tragic, the reality is that it is over. Her dad was not suffering right now, and so there was no point to her holding on to a suffering that was no longer real. The past is nothing but a memory, if we are able to see it for what it really is. This realisation helped Julia come back to the present moment, where her dad was not suffering any longer. Of course, we are not suggesting here that, by correcting these thought errors, Julia's pain and grief would have necessarily disappeared immediately. As we will learn later, she may still have needed to give herself plenty of time to grieve, and that's completely normal.

Another example is Antonio. He was afraid of death. He wondered what would happen to him after dying. Reassessing his thoughts made him realise that there are only two possibilities:

1. There is no life after death, in which case he would not exist to be sad or upset about it.

2. There is a life after death, in which case the adventure of life continues! It would be just like migrating to another place, with lots to see and discover. And if there were moments of struggle, just like in this life, he would find the strength to handle them.

This helped Antonio let go of the fear of death and focus on living his life well.

Notice how your body feels now. Does it feel any different to before?

Rethink Your Past Decisions

Is there a decision that you have made about yourself or the world around you that needs revisiting? Can you use Mark's scientific approach to reassess your beliefs about yourself or the world?

Please note: if there are significantly painful, emotional areas of your life that need revisiting, you may like to leave those for a later point. Today is about practising and mastering this valuable skill, so please take it easy on yourself and try it on an area that is less emotional or painful. But gradually you'll become more experienced, so we recommend that you visit those more painful areas of your life and reassess your unhelpful thoughts around them at a later point.

First, on the left side of the box below write a description or draw a picture that represents the current view that you have towards yourself or the world around you. Take your time and write down whatever is on your mind. Even if you feel like filling the whole column with just a sentence or word. Let your emotions pour onto the page. Once you are finished with filling out the left side of the box, pause and notice how your body feels. Does it feel any different to before?

Ⓟ

My current life view	A more rational alternative life view

Now, on the other side of the page write an alternative view or draw an alternative picture. Assess your thoughts using the skills that you have learned in this chapter and the previous one. Can you find any thought errors? You don't need to worry about believing the alternative picture yet. You just need to explore the alternatives.

Now once again, notice how your body feels. Does it feel any different to before?

The Emotion

What you did in the previous section was to change a thought. Or maybe several thoughts. How did you do that? You looked for any facts, information or logical reasons that would suggest that your thought wasn't accurate. If you found that, then you simply stopped believing in your thought and VOILA! Your belief was automatically changed!

But did changing your thoughts automatically change the emotions in your body as well? Or do you still have a left-over emotion from that exercise? The emotion may feel like a heavy chest, a pressure in the head, restlessness in your hands or feet, a tickle in your belly, or some other sensation in your body. You may be wondering: 'if my thoughts have changed, then why hasn't my emotion changed with it?'

The reason why your emotions may remain unchanged is that thoughts and emotions don't always match! They don't always tell us the same thing. And you can't use the same tools to change them both. In the same way that you can't hammer in a nail using a screw-driver. Even though the screw-driver is a very useful tool if you are screwing in a screw, when you want to put a nail into the wall, you would rather take out the hammer. Similarly, your logic and reasoning are not always good tools for changing the feelings in your body.

So, what is the right tool for changing emotions? The simple answer is, emotions change when we experience them. With our full attention. Imagine you have a child and you buy him an ice cream. But then he accidentally drops the ice cream on the ground and starts crying. Can you snap him out of his sadness with logic, telling him things like 'Stop being sad! It's fine. Look, other kids don't have ice creams either. It's not a big deal.'? I think you would agree that saying these things will not stop him from feeling upset.

What if, instead, you said to him: 'Come sit on my lap, it's okay, you can cry', and you let him have a good cry? What would happen after a few minutes? That's right, your child would probably forget about the ice cream and go off to play! What that crying did was to help his emotions be felt, experienced, digested and then relieved! We are about to show you a technique that uses the same principle to help you manage your emotions effectively.

It's simple. First, close your eyes and see where the emotion is in your body. Do you feel a pressure, a heaviness, a tickle or another sensation somewhere in your body? Or maybe a feeling of restlessness or agitation? Maybe your heart is beating faster. Maybe your breath is shallower? Whatever it is, focus all of your attention on that sensation. That's it. You don't need to try to relax that feeling or make it go away. You don't even need to understand it or figure it out. No, all you need to do is to focus on it. As if nothing else in the world exists right now, other than that sensation in your body. If you can do that, after a few minutes, that feeling in your body is likely to go away by itself. Try it.

How did you find it?

What you just tried is called emotion exposure. You might find that mastering the skill of emotion exposure is particularly helpful to your mental health and wellbeing. If you are going to focus on perfecting one skill out of everything that you learn in this book, let it be this technique. You may not be feeling very confident in it yet, but don't worry at all. We'll be learning a lot more about it in the next chapter.

A Good Place

Let's finish this section on a happy note! Do you have a happy place that you like to go to? It could be a happy place out in the real world, or one from your imagination and dreams.

Thinking of your happy place might appear like a childish activity. But it can be a helpful exercise for several reasons. For most people, this happy place can represent a break from normal daily stressors and uncomfortable thoughts or emotions. This activity can also assist you in getting to know yourself a bit better. If you don't have a happy place, this is your chance to create one!

If you had a magic wand that could suddenly take you to a place where there would be no pain, suffering, anguish, stress or anxiety, what would this place look like? What would be its characteristics? Now let your imagination run free. Enjoy this place, explore it. Get to know it. This place can be realistic or abstract. Create it however you like it!

Notice how your body feels now. Does it feel any different to before?

Homework Ⓕ

Now take a moment to make practical plans around writing your thoughts down. Have a think: do you have a notebook or diary that you could use for this purpose? Will it be a notebook that can fit into your pocket or handbag? This way you can carry it around with you and use any free time during your day to write down your thoughts.

Or you could allocate a time at home to writing down your thoughts (e.g. every night before bed).

In the coming week, work towards getting into a habit of regularly writing your thoughts down. You might choose to do it at a set time of the day (e.g. just before going to bed at night) or whenever you are struggling with emotions or stress.

....

....

....

....

Chapter 5: Emotions

Noticing the Body

Once again, notice how your body feels. Is it comfortable? Relaxed? Tense? Restless? Does it feel warm or cool? Do you feel any pain or pressure anywhere? What is your heart doing? Can you feel it beat? What about your breathing?

Close your eyes and pay attention to all of that for a moment.

Revision ©

Classical conditioning is...

....

....

(Can't remember the answer? For a recap, refer to Chapter 2: Conditioning.)

Exposure therapy means that we face those things that we have been conditioned to fear or dislike, instead of avoiding them. What happens when we perform exposure therapy?

....

....

Acceptance can help relieve mental anguish and discomfort and it brings us a greater level of inner peace. Choose which one of the following two statements is true about acceptance:

Acceptance is letting go of our internal resistance and war against the reality of this moment.

True ☐

False ☐

Acceptance is letting go of our external resistance and war against the reality of this moment.

True ☐

False ☐

(Can't remember the answer? For a recap, refer to Chapter 2: The Bird.)

Artwork Ⓕ

Using any art form that you like, express a thought or emotion that has been on the surface a lot for you lately. You can use symbols. You can use colours and shapes or any other ways of expressing yourself.

The Body Matters

Most people would agree that our thoughts are very important. Our thoughts seem to make up so much of who we are. When we want to make sense of the world around us, we think. When we want to solve complicated life problems, we think. When we are feeling down or anxious, we also use our thoughts to understand and process what is concerning us.

But what about our emotions? You know, those physical sensations in our bodies, like the pounding heart, the heavy chest, the butterflies in the belly and so on? Are they really that important? Aren't they just some mildly significant sensations that we often find reasonably easy to ignore and move on with our lives? Not really. Emotions are so much more important than many of us realise.

Those sensations in the body are not insignificant. It's as if your thoughts are food and your emotions are the flavouring! Emotions make our thoughts pleasant or unpleasant. Enjoyable or uncomfortable. In fact, we would like to suggest that those sensations are often what fuel and drive our thoughts, and not the other way around! Let's explore this.

What comes first? The thought or the emotion? Is it the thought that creates the emotion? Or the emotion that creates the thought? This question is somewhat like asking if the chicken came first or the egg. The answer is not very simple. Let's just say that a thought can be the start of an emotion. But once the emotion is there, it can become the fuel that starts creating new thoughts with a similar flavour.

So, for example, if you are feeling sad and gloomy, it is much more likely that you will keep thinking sad thoughts. Your thoughts are more likely to focus on the negative side of everything. If someone was to suggest a happy idea or activity to you, you would probably not be drawn to it. You become attracted to all kinds of things that are in line with the emotion that you are already feeling.

So the emotion is like the fuel that keeps the fire of your thoughts burning! If you want to stop the fire, you first need to remove the fuel. In other words, you could say that thoughts lead to emotions, and emotions lead to thoughts.

And then, when an emotion is in place, we see the world through its lens and it's hard to believe that what the emotion tells us is not reality. But when the emotion clears, we suddenly see things in a different light. We realise that what we saw as the only possible reality was actually just an emotion.

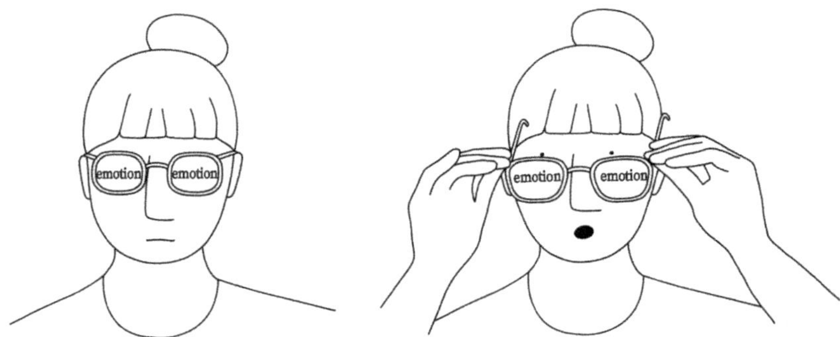

Let's say you have had a bad day at work, and you are feeling angry about something your boss did. You arrive home, everything is as usual. But you are more likely than usual to feel stressed or agitated over things such as your child knocking over a glass of water or your partner laughing loudly at a joke.

Take a moment to close your eyes and picture yourself in this situation. Would the emotions that you brought home from work cause you to react differently to things today?

Now, say, your child does something trivial and because of your already existing anger, you begin snapping at them. Your partner asks you why you overreacted. Would you be likely to realise that you overreacted? Or are you more likely to think that your reaction was perfectly reasonable?

And what if your partner had never brought to your attention that you had overreacted? Would you have realised it? Would you have noticed the original source of your anger, which was your bad day at work, as the cause of your overreaction? Or would you be more likely not to be aware of it?

Not everyone would notice that their reaction to what their child did was an overreaction and simply a result of leftover emotions related to what their boss did. This is a rather important piece of information. Each day, every day, we carry many emotions around with us, without realising what started them off, where they came from or why they are there. We simply carry them with us from one situation to the next, and the next. New emotions are added to the pile and at times we feel like we have no choice but to run to things such as alcohol, a shopping spree or junk food to help us numb those emotions.

To be perfectly clear, what we are saying is that those bodily sensations that we have come to know as emotions influence our thoughts, just as much as our thoughts influence the emotions. And to feel better, we need to learn ways to manage those bodily sensations, just as much as we need to change our unhelpful thoughts.

Imagine if a snake suddenly appeared in front of you. What would your reaction be? Fear? Panic? Heart racing? Palms getting sweaty? Knees shaking? An urge to run away?

Okay. But let's imagine that a person you trust then assures you that this snake is not dangerous: 'Don't worry, it's a non-venomous and harmless snake. Quite friendly too!' How do you feel now?

People react in two different ways in situations like this. The first group would go 'Phew! That's awesome! Can I pet him??' The new information given to this group is enough to calm the emotions of fear and panic.

The second group would continue to feel fear: 'No way, I still won't go anywhere near it!' This group can logically understand that the snake is not dangerous. But on an emotional level they are still experiencing fear: their heart is still racing. Their palms are sweaty. Their knees are shaky. Their thoughts changed, but the emotions did not go away. No amount of logical reassurance quite gets rid of the fear that they feel in their body.

Sometimes we can change our emotions through changing our thoughts. But at other times that's not enough. The body needs to change as well. And that is why we need to master the art of emotion exposure.

Experiencing Experiences

Emotion exposure is an intricate skill. Mastering it takes time and practice. But it is a skill well worth mastering. To learn it, we first need to improve our ability to become aware of experiences that are non-verbal and not language based. Let's do a small experiment. First, grab a piece of fruit, say an apple.

If you don't have access to any fruit, another food item or just a glass of water would do. Close your eyes.

Take a bite from your fruit, or a sip of the water. Place all of your attention on the taste, texture, smell and temperature. The feelings as you chew on and swallow your fruit. Take your time and notice all the little intricate details.

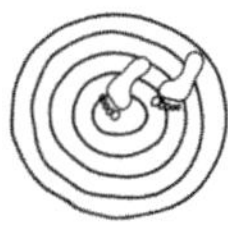

Now, take a look at a few hypothetical situations: 

- Imagine you just met a person who has always lived inside a big bubble with a constant warm temperature. This person has never experienced the feeling of being cold. Can you use words to explain to this person how it feels to be cold? Please note: your explanation needs to show this person exactly how 'cold' feels.
- Imagine you just met a person who has never tasted anything salty. Can you use words to explain to them how salt tastes? Please note: through your explanation, this person needs to understand exactly how 'salty' tastes.
- Imagine you just met a person who has never seen the colour blue. Can you use words to explain to them what blue looks like? Please note: your explanation has to show this person exactly what 'blue' looks like.

How was this exercise? It is not an easy task trying to communicate an experience to someone who has never experienced it before, right? You can use words to describe the experience, but the other person won't actually know what it's like to feel cold, or to taste salt, or what blue looks like, unless they experience these for themselves. They won't know exactly what an apple tastes or smells like. Words alone are not able to communicate experiences, because experiences are not language based.

Emotions are similar. Most of us are familiar with the experiences of our emotions, which we normally feel in the body. Let's take a look at a few common emotions and consider how they feel to you. First up, anger. How does anger feel to you?

.... Ⓕ

....

....

If your answer was along the lines of 'anger feels like everything is unfair', 'it feels like no one respects you' and so on, you are actually using your thoughts to describe the feeling of anger. The kind of answer that we are looking for is a lot simpler than that. Just pay attention to your body. We are looking for answers like 'it feels like my face is getting hot', or 'I feel a pressure in my throat and chest' and so on. Try one more time. How does anger make your body feel?

.... Ⓕ

....

And what about the following emotions? Don't forget, you are not describing your thoughts here. You are only paying attention to your body and trying to describe how the emotion makes your body feel:

Fear .... Ⓕ

Sadness ....

Shame ....

Worry ....

Excitement ....

Nervousness ....

Boredom ....

Disgust ....

As you can imagine, these emotions could feel different for different people. For example, a person may feel sadness, anger, and anxiety all as sensations in their chest. Another person may call a sensation in their chest 'sadness', but also name another sensation in their head, and a third one in their belly, different shades of sadness. They may be felt in different parts of the body, but this person recognises them all as the same emotion.

You may have also experienced those times when you feel an emotion, but don't quite know what to call it. What is important to notice here is what the body is feeling, and not so much what we may decide to call that emotion or how we use our thoughts to describe it. To understand our emotions better, it's important to develop a closer connection with the sensations in our bodies, just like the way you became familiar with the taste of an apple in that earlier exercise.

It's also worth mentioning that not all emotions behave the same way. Some emotions are still and stay in one part of the body. Others may feel like a sensation that moves around or pulsates in the body. Some may feel identical to a physical experience. Others are experienced as partly physical, but not entirely!

Some of you may be wondering: what about the advice that you often get, that it's best to not pay too much attention to your emotions? Wouldn't giving them too much attention make us more emotional? Well, if you are sitting in a corner and passively thinking about emotional matters, then yes, you are right. Passively obsessing over issues will not be helpful. Awareness is a different matter. And awareness of the body will help improve your coping with the issues you are facing, not reduce it.

A Little Note

Before we go on with the rest of the chapter, it's worth having a quick chat about a challenge that some readers may face with the upcoming exercises. As we invite you to notice your emotions, some of you may respond with 'Well, I'm not feeling any emotions right now'. What to do if this applies to you?

Firstly, forget about the term 'emotion' and just focus on your body. How is your body feeling right now?

At times, you may feel sensations like a pressure in your head, tension in your muscles, heat in your body, a restlessness in your legs and so on. You may not associate these sensations with emotions. It is not always easy to tell the difference between emotional reactions and purely physical ones. But for the purpose of practising the exercises in this chapter, don't worry so much about telling them apart. Just treat your physical experiences as if they are emotions and practise the exercises on them anyway. If they have emotional roots, you may find some relief from them.

But some of you may find that your body is calm and free from any tension. Your mind is also calm and at peace. That is great! This is how it feels to be in an emotionally neutral state and in fact we hope that the practice of emotion exposure will help more people experience that calm state. But like everyone else, you will experience emotions from time to time. So, to help you get some practise in performing emotion exposure, for those times when you will be needing it in the future, try the following exercise:

Use your thoughts to navigate through some scenarios in your daily living that would normally bring about emotions for you. Think of the various events that happened today, this week or at any point in your past. Or think about the future, your worries, plans or hopes. Or remember a song, a scent or a place that holds emotional value for you. As you journey through your thoughts, notice how the sensations in your body shift and change. There you have it: you are noticing your emotions now. These may be memories of your past emotions, but by remembering them, your body still reacts, and you will experience the emotion now.

Once you feel an emotion, start practising emotion exposure as instructed. Please don't overwhelm yourself by bringing too many emotions to the surface. Once an emotion is there, stop thinking and begin practising emotion exposure.

Now with all the above points in mind, let's have a go at practising emotion exposure. Close your eyes again. Notice any emotions that you are feeling right now. Ask yourself: do I experience my emotions somewhere in my body? Do they move around or are they still? Don't concern yourself with trying to find a name for your emotions or figuring out why you are feeling them. Just become familiar with how they behave.

Quality Attention

Some of you may be wondering 'What does it mean to pay attention to an emotion? How do I know if I'm doing it right?' We will try to answer these questions in this section. It is helpful to improve the quality of our attention. So we'll dedicate a bit of time to mastering this seemingly simple skill. First, let's place a little dot on the page...

•

What we will get you to do now is very simple. Just stare at the dot for a while and keep your attention on it. That's it. You don't need to do anything else. Just fix your gaze on the dot for a little while.

How did you go? Were you able to keep your attention there?

Let's try that exercise one more time. If thoughts distract you, gently bring your attention back to the dot and keep staring at it. The longer you can maintain your attention there, the better. And if you can't go very long, that's okay! Practice makes perfect. Let's try again.

•

This is what we mean when we say, 'keep your attention on the emotion in the body'. It's just like keeping your attention on the dot, except you would be keeping your attention on the part of the body where you feel the emotion. Of course, when it comes to emotions, you won't be using your physical eyes, just your internal awareness.

So, notice what emotion you are feeling in the body, then fix your attention on that part of the body and keep it there as if you are staring right at it and cannot take your eyes off it. Do this even if the emotion is uncomfortable. The discomfort is likely to pass soon. Keep your attention there until the emotion eases. Don't fight the emotion or try to make it go away. You just need to keep your attention on it.

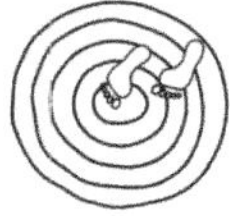

But what about emotions that move around in the body, pulsate, or appear and disappear? How do you keep your attention on moving sensations within the body?

To help you develop the skill of keeping your attention on moving emotions, please visit www.fount.com.au/dot for a video resource. If you do not have access to the internet, you can still practice this exercise by watching any moving object in your environment. A good choice might be to go outside and watch the movements of a leaf on a tree as it dances in the wind. The rule is the same: your attention needs to remain on the leaf wherever it goes. But see if you can keep your eyes still while maintaining your attention on the moving leaf. Even though your eyes aren't moving, you should be able to see it from the corner of your eyes. In other words, your eyes don't need to move around fast to follow the the leaf everywhere. It's better to stay as still as you can while letting your attention follow the leaf as it moves within the sphere of your vision. Take a few minutes and give it a go.

What you practised here is similar to what you would do if you are keeping your attention on a moving emotion within your body. Keep your mind's eye, or your internal awareness, on the moving sensations within your body. It's best to try and keep your eyes still even if the emotion is moving around in your body.

Perhaps the biggest challenge for your attention is emotions that appear and disappear. This type of emotion is often hard to pay attention to, because as soon as it disappears, we tend to lose focus and get distracted. But then it comes back and surprises us again. But with a little bit of practice we can learn to keep our attention on these types of emotions just as we did with the other emotions. It takes time and patience, but the general rule is, first, give your attention to the emotion. When it disappears, you don't need to do anything special. Just stay focused and ready to look at it again once it returns.

> **"See if you can keep your eyes still even if the emotion is moving around in your body.**

Essentially, what we are saying is that at times it would be helpful to shift your attention away from your chattering and analysing thoughts, and place it on the body instead. Resist the temptation to stay focused on your thoughts. Keep your attention on your body until it reaches a calmer state. Then you can go back to thinking and see if you still see the problems in front of you in the same way, or whether the new calm body has changed your view of the issues in front of you. Give it a go and see for yourself!

The Science

By now some of you may be thinking, 'Well, it seems to work. But why does it work?' or more precisely 'How does it work?' In this section we will journey into the science of emotion exposure. Although research shows that emotion exposure is effective, there are still a lot of unknowns around exactly how it works. But there are a few theories that try to explain the reasons behind its effectiveness. The first theory relates to a concept called habituation. Habituation is what happens when something is repeated over and over again, and with repetition it gradually loses its impact on you. For example, say you just moved to a new house next to a noisy street. At first the noise feels loud and overwhelming. You can't hear yourself think! But as the hours and days go by, you start noticing it less and less. At some point you barely notice it, unless you pay attention.

Another example is when you wear a new watch for the first time. For some time, you can feel it clearly on your wrist. You notice its temperature, its weight and every other sensation about it. But gradually you stop noticing it altogether. Once in a while, when you think of your watch, you may feel it on your wrist again. But then it goes on to join the many other 'normal' things that you rarely pay attention to.

Most people have heard the story of the boy who cried wolf. It can be said that by repeatedly crying 'wolf', the boy in the story would have habituated the people in the village so that they were no longer alarmed by it.

Usually when we talk about 'getting used to' something, what is really happening is that our brain has developed habituation towards that thing. When habituation takes place, the brain changes at a cellular and chemical level, causing it to become less sensitive to what it has become habituated to. So every time you are habituated, your brain actually changes a little. That's right, there are actual changes to the structure of your brain or its chemicals, that allow your brain to no longer show sensitivity to that thing. This theory suggests that when we concentrate on our emotions long enough, we get to a point of habituation and that's why we no longer feel that emotion to the same intensity. So, by closing your eyes and keeping your attention on the emotion, what's happening within your brain is very similar to what happened after a few hours or days in that new house in the noisy street.

We often don't let this process happen in our brain because we try to distract ourselves from uncomfortable emotions before the brain has had a chance to reach habituation. When you close your eyes and concentrate on an emotion instead of avoiding it, your brain structures and chemicals may be changing and, in turn, what you experience is reduced sensitivity to that emotional experience.

The second theory is that emotion exposure works in a similar way to normal exposure therapy. Remember, classical conditioning means that our brain makes a connection between two unrelated things. And when we perform exposure therapy, we teach the brain that the two things aren't really connected anymore. We do that by facing the things that we fear or dislike and letting our body do the rest! Exposure is an automatic process. We don't need to deliberately teach our body anything.

Similarly, our bodies can be conditioned to react to certain situations, giving us the experience of an emotion. So a date, like the anniversary of a sad event, or a smell, a place, a person or any other reminders might bring back the memory of an emotion for you. Like a heavy heart, a lump in the throat, a funny feeling in the belly and so on. So that smell, that place, that person or the date of that anniversary are now acting like conditioned triggers that bring back an emotional memory.

> **"Emotion exposure means that we can clear up the fingerprints of an emotion that belongs to the past. The memory can then be just a memory, rather than a trigger for an old emotion.**

Sometimes we don't even know what emotion has been triggered. Here's an example. Imagine that today you are feeling upset because you just had an argument with a friend. You go shopping to get it off your mind. You see a perfume bottle, have a smell and spray a little bit on your wrist. As you smell it for the rest of the day, you are conditioning the smell of that perfume to act as a trigger for the emotion that you're feeling. Months later, you walk past a complete stranger that's wearing the same perfume. You might suddenly feel a heavy emotion and have no idea where it came from. You see how confusing the world of our conditioned emotions can get?

As you can see, not all emotions are new and fresh. Many of our emotions are conditioned responses from things that have happened to us in the past. Our bodies react in similar ways in similar situations, creating similar emotional experiences, over and over again. Emotion exposure means that we can clear up the fingerprints of an emotion that belongs to the past. The memory can then be just a memory, rather than a trigger for an old emotion.

It's also worth noting that some of the conditioned emotional memories that we have, go all the way back to our childhood. Pleasant or unpleasant childhood environments can create all kinds of emotional memories. When parents and other caregivers punish or reward children, for example, some powerful conditioned responses can be created.

So for example, if a parent used to snap at you or tell you off every time you were having playful fun, chances are that as an adult, every time you are having a good time, you also feel a negative emotion deep down. You then use your thinking to make sense of this and say to yourself 'I'm feeling guilty because I'm wasting time'. Or at times, when people are sensitive to criticism, they could very well be reacting to a conditioned response that was created earlier in their life, when they were in trouble with their parents for making mistakes.

The final theory that tries to explain the effectiveness of emotion exposure is that it facilitates acceptance. As you may recall, acceptance is letting go of our internal resistance and war against the reality of this moment. Emotion exposure and acceptance have a few things in common. Emotion exposure relies on the principle of not expecting ourselves to change, control, resist or fight our emotions. In other words, it increases our acceptance of our emotions, just as they are in this moment. And acceptance can help us cope better with unwanted and uncomfortable realities. In turn we may feel a general state of calmness and peace. You may have experienced this during your practice of acceptance in previous chapters.

Thinking vs. Emotion Exposure

Perhaps the real answer to the question of emotion exposure's effectiveness lies in a combination of these 3 principles: habituation, conditioning and acceptance. Considering these principles can help us make sense of those ingredients that seem to make emotion exposure work most effectively! For most of us, emotions are often there, running amok within the body, day after day. And we are often busy thinking about our problems and the emotions attached to them.

So you may say that every day you think about your emotions and wonder why emotion exposure would do anything different or new for you. The answer is that emotion exposure is not the same as thinking about your emotions. There are three main ingredients that distinguish emotion exposure from the way that we normally relate to our emotions.

1. **Awareness, not thinking** - emotion exposure is all about bringing our attention to the body, or to the experience of our emotions. It is a mindfulness practice. The focus is not on analysing the emotions or thinking about them - thoughts like 'What is this emotion?', 'Where does it come from?', 'I'm tired of always feeling down', 'What if something bad happens?', and so on. When practising emotion exposure we take a break from thinking and instead notice what the body is doing. Or what the experience of that emotion feels like.

2. **Sustained attention** - we normally only give quick short-lived attention to our emotions, and our attention is weak and divided as we go about our day or are distracted by a million racing thoughts in our head. Focusing your attention on the emotion and keeping it there a bit longer than usual may be what is needed to allow habituation to be achieved, or to make exposure therapy most effective.

3. **Acceptance** - in other words, giving up the temptation to change the emotion. This is very important. When practising emotion exposure, you are only a passive watcher. You are not trying to change, soothe or escape. The more you give up the temptation to control your emotion, the more quickly it will pass. Imagine getting on a roller coaster. Once you are on the ride, it is not your job to control it or stop it. And you could not do that even if you tried! You just need to sit back and let the ride take you wherever it takes you. Trying to control it is pointless. When practising emotion exposure, we need to treat our emotions in exactly the same way. We cannot control or get rid of emotions using will power. That only results in more internal anguish and distress. So we might as well sit back and experience the ride.

Remember, this is not a process that you can speed up using your will power. So as you have your eyes closed and are feeling the emotion, be mindful of thoughts like: 'When is it going to go away?', 'How can I get rid of it?', 'This is pointless', 'It's not working' and so on. These thoughts are an indication that you are placing your focus on trying to get rid of the emotion, rather than on feeling the emotion and experiencing it fully.

Go ahead and experiment, if you like, in the weeks to come. Put what we are saying to the test. See if you can agree that these three key ingredients are exactly what makes emotion exposure so effective.

You may like to use the emotion as an alarm system to remind you to practise emotion exposure. Up until today, feeling an emotion was your cue to react or avoid. From now on, the emotion is your cue to stop and pay attention!

Handling the Monster

Meet Jasmine. Jasmine had a monster, hidden inside a box. She didn't know how to get rid of it. The monster poked out its scary head every now and then and scared Jasmine. Jasmine spent most of her days trying to keep the monster in the box. She often worked hard to keep the box closed, to make sure the monster didn't get out. Once in a while, though, the monster did get out. Jasmine would feel frightened and overwhelmed, focusing all of her energy on pushing the monster back into the box.

One day, Jasmine got tired of the fight. She decided to let the monster out, and thought to herself, 'Oh well, what's the worst that could happen?!' We are not going to lie, initially seeing the monster was not comfortable for Jasmine. After all, she had spent most of her life avoiding and fearing it. But she was brave and sat with it, looking right into its eyes. Gradually, Jasmine realised that the monster was not doing anything to harm her. It was not attacking, it was not violent. In fact, the monster was not as big and scary as she had initially thought. Perhaps it was even shrinking. And after a while, since the monster had been set free, it decided to go off on its own journey and leave Jasmine alone.

This monster is a lot like our emotions. Some of our emotions may appear like monsters and we may have spent years avoiding them. But when we face them, they will soon become less scary. Unfortunately, most of us deal with our emotions exactly as Jasmine initially dealt with her monster: we put them in a box and try to keep them locked away forever. So the monster remains big and scary.

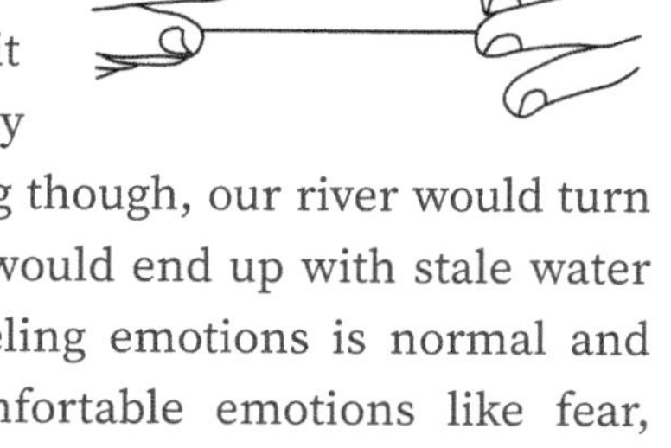

Another way to look at this is to consider healthy emotions as a running river. Water enters the river bed, flows through and then off it goes into the ocean. It does not stay around. If the water stopped flowing though, our river would turn into a swamp. All of a sudden, we would end up with stale water that is not as fresh and clean. Feeling emotions is normal and healthy. And that includes uncomfortable emotions like fear, sadness and anger. Mental health problems are created when our emotions turn into a swamp, meaning that an emotion lingers and becomes a part of us, even when the situation that created it is no longer there. For example, picture a child that felt rejected when his friends didn't play with him at primary school. Many years later, the boy grows into an adult, but he still feels alone and rejected in social settings, even when there is no external reason for it. As you can see, an emotion that was created for him as a child turned into a swamp. It remained a part of him.

Our emotions turn into swamps when we avoid them. When instead of facing them and dealing with them, we treat them like the monster in Jasmine's story: put them in a box and try to keep them locked away. But how do we deal with emotions? What do we do with the monster once it's out of the box? Do we focus on changing the thoughts? Do we focus on improving the emotions in the body? Or do we focus on tackling the external circumstances: the practical life problems. We can summarise the answer in 3 easy steps:

Step 1 - Active thinking - you have already learned about this in chapters 3 and 4. One thing we want to add here is that once you feel that your thoughts are in line with the reality, it's best to move on to step 2. If after you have reassessed your thoughts your emotions are still uncomfortable, don't spend excessive amounts of time trying to use logic to control them. Yes, logic is a helpful tool. But we can't use it to erase emotions.

Take the example of a man called David who was grieving the loss of a close friend who had died recently. He was understandably very upset. He wanted the sadness to be over fast, so he decided to use logic to control the painful emotions. His thoughts went something like this:

'I should stop feeling sad, because it makes no sense. He is not in pain or suffering. He lived a good life. So I should be able to accept his death and put it behind me. What is the point of me sitting here and missing him, when he is not coming back? Life is too short to keep looking back. So I need to move on and stop being sad.'

Although David's thoughts are logical and true, he was forgetting one important thing: he needed to grieve first! He needed to allow his emotions of sadness, loss and love for his friend to come to surface, express themselves and be felt. And only through being felt and experienced, would these emotions finally lift, and only then would he be able to fully accept his friend's death. Logic is the right tool to correct our thoughts. But it is not the right tool to control our emotions. You cannot rush the process of grief, or logic your way out of it. A large part of grieving is the simple act of feeling your emotions, even those emotions that may seem irrational. Those who try to bypass this important step, may end up with emotions that have turned into swamps. They will be forced to keep their monster in a box, because letting it out will once again create fresh emotional pain.

> “ **Remember, this is not a process that you can speed up using your will power.**

Step 2 - Emotion exposure - in this step, you leave the world of mental chatter, logic, rationality, searching, questioning, coming up with ideas and all other aspects of thinking aside, and instead bring your attention to the humble body. Just focus on what the body is doing. Going back to our example, this is the next step for

David to complete his grieving. He may notice a range of physical experiences, perhaps a heavy chest, pounding heart, aching body, or a knot in the throat encouraging him to have a good cry. He should keep his attention on these physiological symptoms, even if they are uncomfortable. He will gradually feel lighter and lighter.

Step 3 - External action - often your thoughts and emotions tell you to act. They may tell you to pick up the phone and give someone a piece of your mind, or to quit your job, or to go off on a huge cleaning spree! When your thoughts and emotions have helpful messages that could improve your life or the lives of other people, it's important to hear these messages and act. But at other times, it's best to act only after you've done steps 1 and 2. You may find that after your emotions are calmer, you change your mind on how you wish to act, or whether you wish to act at all. So, whenever possible, instead of rushing to act on the external situation, act internally first. Work through your thoughts and emotions. If, after the emotion is relieved, there is still a need to do something about the external situation, then go ahead and do it.

For example, imagine that you feel that your friend is neglecting you, and you feel the emotion of being neglected as a sick feeling in your stomach. You then try to get rid of that feeling by fighting extra hard to get your friend's attention. But this causes her to feel irritated and push you away even more. Instead, if you take a minute to practise emotion exposure around that sick feeling in your stomach, you would feel calmer and less in need of getting your friend's attention. You can then interact with her in a way that might encourage her to naturally give you her attention.

An Onion

At times, our emotions are like an onion. If you peel off a layer of the onion, there will be another one underneath it. And another one. And another one. After some time, the layers will stop and you will end up with no more onion. Similarly, at times during emotion exposure you will find that, as an emotion leaves, there is another one underneath it. And another one underneath that one. It may feel like the layers of emotion will never end, and that all you are doing is replacing one layer with the next one. But continuing to practise emotion exposure means that at some point the layers may end, allowing you to experience a calm, peaceful space of no emotion.

It may help you to remember a rule:

- Thinking often brings up emotions (new emotions or old ones)

- Emotion exposure allows the emotions to be alleviated

So you may find that at times when you begin thinking, you begin feeling more emotions. If this happens, practise emotion exposure on the new emotions that are activated. Remember to get into the habit of pausing your thinking and focusing on the body instead, because getting lost in thoughts may result in more and more emotions coming to surface. However, as each emotion lifts up, feel free to allow your thoughts back in again. So allow the thoughts in, and once you feel an emotion, stop thinking and focus on the body. Repeat this process until you feel lighter and more at peace.

Note: don't forget to check for any errors in your thinking as well. If a thought error keeps creating an emotion for you, it's important to first realise the thought error and change your thinking.

Practice

We will now invite you to practise emotion exposure one more time. This time, keep the onion in mind and as each emotion is lifted off, look to see if there is another emotion there. You can also let your thoughts in to see if they bring in another emotion. If so, practise emotion exposure again. If time allows, keep going until you begin to feel calm and relaxed.

The 3 Steps of Emotion Exposure

1. Find the emotion in the body.
2. Place your attention on that part of the body, just like you did with the dot.
3. Keep your attention there long enough for the emotion to subside. Don't try to make the emotion subside. This is an automatic process. Your job is to only sit still and watch.

Homework

In the week ahead, begin developing a habit of being aware of your emotions. Notice them as they arise in your body. Practise emotion exposure daily. Some good times to practise emotion exposure include: just before bed, when you have a quiet moment to yourself, or when you experience particularly strong emotions (e.g. after work or following social interactions).

Frequently Asked Questions

The challenge of practising emotion exposure is not going to be the same for everyone or for every emotion. You might find that certain emotions are more challenging to work through or concentrate on. Others are a lot easier. At times, practising it will result in quick relief to your emotions. At other times it might not work so quickly or smoothly. What is important is to not give up when you face a challenge, but to keep trying. Check that you are correctly applying all the principles that you have learned about in this chapter. Here are 7 common challenges that people report when practising emotion exposure, and tips on how to deal with them:

1. **'I feel an emotion, but I can't find it in my body. What do I do?'** - If this applies to you (and it's one of the things that most people experience from time to time), then don't try so hard to pin the emotion down in your body. Just concentrate on the general experience of the emotion. The overall feel of it. The feeling that the emotion gives you. Sit with that experience and keep your attention still. At some point, you may start noticing it within the body as well. If that happens, start keeping your attention on that part of the body.

2. **'I'm feeling a few different sensations, in different parts of my body all at the same time. What do I do?'** - It's best to focus on one part of the body at a time. Maybe start with the one that you're feeling most strongly, or the one that keeps grabbing your attention. Once that sensation lifts off, move on to the next. The reason that we suggest this is that the more intensely you focus, the quicker you will get results. So, if your attention is jumping between different parts of your body, it might at times reduce the effectiveness of your practice. But, if focusing on only one part proves difficult, then try staying aware of all the different sensations appearing and disappearing within your body, as if you are watching a show. Keep your attention on the show until the feeling calms down.

3. **'I am feeling a sensation in my body, but I'm not sure if it's an emotion or just physical?'** - It is not always easy to tell emotions apart from purely physical sensations. That's one reason why, when our bodies are unhappy, (e.g. when we are hungry, tired, coming down with a cold and so on) we are more likely to feel intense emotions. The key here is to stop getting bogged down with the question 'is it an emotion or just the body?' and instead practise emotion exposure on it anyway. If what you are feeling in the body has an emotional component, you should experience relief after some time.But that said, if you are certain that there is a physical component, attend to that as well. If you are

An Onion

At times, our emotions are like an onion. If you peel off a layer of the onion, there will be another one underneath it. And another one. And another one. After some time, the layers will stop and you will end up with no more onion. Similarly, at times during emotion exposure you will find that, as an emotion leaves, there is another one underneath it. And another one underneath that one. It may feel like the layers of emotion will never end, and that all you are doing is replacing one layer with the next one. But continuing to practise emotion exposure means that at some point the layers may end, allowing you to experience a calm, peaceful space of no emotion.

It may help you to remember a rule:

- Thinking often brings up emotions (new emotions or old ones)

- Emotion exposure allows the emotions to be alleviated

So you may find that at times when you begin thinking, you begin feeling more emotions. If this happens, practise emotion exposure on the new emotions that are activated. Remember to get into the habit of pausing your thinking and focusing on the body instead, because getting lost in thoughts may result in more and more emotions coming to surface. However, as each emotion lifts up, feel free to allow your thoughts back in again. So allow the thoughts in, and once you feel an emotion, stop thinking and focus on the body. Repeat this process until you feel lighter and more at peace.

Note: don't forget to check for any errors in your thinking as well. If a thought error keeps creating an emotion for you, it's important to first realise the thought error and change your thinking.

Practice

We will now invite you to practise emotion exposure one more time. This time, keep the onion in mind and as each emotion is lifted off, look to see if there is another emotion there. You can also let your thoughts in to see if they bring in another emotion. If so, practise emotion exposure again. If time allows, keep going until you begin to feel calm and relaxed.

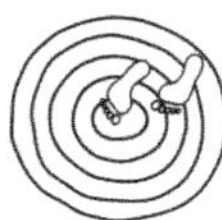

The 3 Steps of Emotion Exposure

1. Find the emotion in the body.
2. Place your attention on that part of the body, just like you did with the dot.
3. Keep your attention there long enough for the emotion to subside. Don't try to make the emotion subside. This is an automatic process. Your job is to only sit still and watch.

Homework

In the week ahead, begin developing a habit of being aware of your emotions. Notice them as they arise in your body. Practise emotion exposure daily. Some good times to practise emotion exposure include: just before bed, when you have a quiet moment to yourself, or when you experience particularly strong emotions (e.g. after work or following social interactions).

Frequently Asked Questions

The challenge of practising emotion exposure is not going to be the same for everyone or for every emotion. You might find that certain emotions are more challenging to work through or concentrate on. Others are a lot easier. At times, practising it will result in quick relief to your emotions. At other times it might not work so quickly or smoothly. What is important is to not give up when you face a challenge, but to keep trying. Check that you are correctly applying all the principles that you have learned about in this chapter. Here are 7 common challenges that people report when practising emotion exposure, and tips on how to deal with them:

1. **'I feel an emotion, but I can't find it in my body. What do I do?'** - If this applies to you (and it's one of the things that most people experience from time to time), then don't try so hard to pin the emotion down in your body. Just concentrate on the general experience of the emotion. The overall feel of it. The feeling that the emotion gives you. Sit with that experience and keep your attention still. At some point, you may start noticing it within the body as well. If that happens, start keeping your attention on that part of the body.

2. **'I'm feeling a few different sensations, in different parts of my body all at the same time. What do I do?'** - It's best to focus on one part of the body at a time. Maybe start with the one that you're feeling most strongly, or the one that keeps grabbing your attention. Once that sensation lifts off, move on to the next. The reason that we suggest this is that the more intensely you focus, the quicker you will get results. So, if your attention is jumping between different parts of your body, it might at times reduce the effectiveness of your practice. But, if focusing on only one part proves difficult, then try staying aware of all the different sensations appearing and disappearing within your body, as if you are watching a show. Keep your attention on the show until the feeling calms down.

3. **'I am feeling a sensation in my body, but I'm not sure if it's an emotion or just physical?'** - It is not always easy to tell emotions apart from purely physical sensations. That's one reason why, when our bodies are unhappy, (e.g. when we are hungry, tired, coming down with a cold and so on) we are more likely to feel intense emotions. The key here is to stop getting bogged down with the question 'is it an emotion or just the body?' and instead practise emotion exposure on it anyway. If what you are feeling in the body has an emotional component, you should experience relief after some time.But that said, if you are certain that there is a physical component, attend to that as well. If you are

hungry, eat something. If you are tired, make sure you get some rest. If you are sick or in pain, speak to a doctor. The bottom line is that the body and emotions are so intertwined, that they regularly impact each other. For example, pain can intensify your emotions, but emotions can also intensify your pain. So it is best to work on both.

4. **'I'm feeling bored, restless or tired. What do I do?'** - Boredom and restlessness are also emotions. Notice how they make your body feel and practise emotion exposure around them. Tiredness can be physical or emotional. If you believe it may be emotional, try practising emotion exposure on the parts of the body where you feel it.

5. **'What happens if emotions come up in situations where I can't close my eyes and focus? How do I deal with that?'** - With continued practice, you can start noticing your emotions even as you go about your day and with your eyes open. Notice how in social situations, as painful emotions arise within your body, you actively try to push them away and ignore them. Instead, stay with the pain in the body and place your attention on it, until it subsides. If, at times, you need to focus more, find a quiet corner (e.g. take a toilet break!)and practise emotion exposure. Alternatively, work on any left-over feelings from the emotion at the

end of the day, when you get home or when you find some alone time. As you work through these emotions, you may notice that they return with less and less intensity over time, or that some emotions never return again.

6. **'The emotion that I'm feeling is too uncomfortable. I find it too painful to pay attention to. What do I do?'** - It is unfortunate that some emotions can be so uncomfortable. It often feels easier to put them in a box and forget about them, like Jasmine did with her monster. But with a bit of determination you may be able to reduce the discomfort of these emotions as well. Here are a few things you can try:

   - Use your imagination to picture yourself yelling, screaming or expressing the emotion however you would like to express it. Or consider expressing yourself while writing or creating art. Now feel the emotion in the body as you express yourself.

   - Imagine a scenario where the emotion is changed. Picture your life situation improved. Or if the emotion is from the past, imagine a scenario with a happier ending. As you imagine these things, keep your attention on the body and feel all the sensations that are happening. Feel the relief as well as any left over emotions.

   - Talk to someone. Seek therapy from a trained

professional, or find a friend who will not rush you to get rid of the emotion using logic, and ask them to allow you to express what you're feeling. It may be helpful to let them know that the purpose of speaking to them is just so you can express your emotions. Now, just talk it out as you feel the body at the same time.

- Focus on one sensation at a time, as we discussed in the 2nd point above. Once you find a painful sensation in your body, don't get distracted by other sensations or thoughts. Just fix all of your attention on it and keep your attention firmly on that part of the body until the sensation is relieved. Now look for other sensations.

- Chip away at it - look at the emotion a few seconds at a time, and then if it's too painful let it go. Do the same again next time. Gradually, by repeating this, the monster will feel less and less scary and you will be able to keep your attention on it for longer.

7. **'My attention is wandering and I am too distracted. How do I concentrate on the emotion?'** - It may be a good idea for you to place your focus on mindfulness of thoughts to begin with. As you practise sitting there and watching your thoughts, remaining aware of their movements, it may help to consider this analogy, which we've touched on before:

   Imagine you're standing in a river with waves of water washing against your legs. Imagine your thoughts and emotions to be like the water. Your job is to stay aware of the water (i.e. thoughts and emotions) as they come and go. Do not think, analyse, try to create the current or stop the current. Just stay aware and let it flow. Practise this as often as you can. You may find that this practice gradually helps your thoughts to slow down and for you to become more mindful of your thoughts and emotions.

Finally, please remember that emotion exposure can be a boring practice! Mindfulness in general may feel boring. That is okay. Being bored is not something to be afraid of. In fact, we suggest that you expose yourself to 'boring' and feel it with your full awareness. So if you are feeling bored focusing on a boring sensation within the body, just tolerate it and keep your attention there anyway. At some point you may find that boredom gives rise to a sense of peace and calm. So this will be worth the effort!

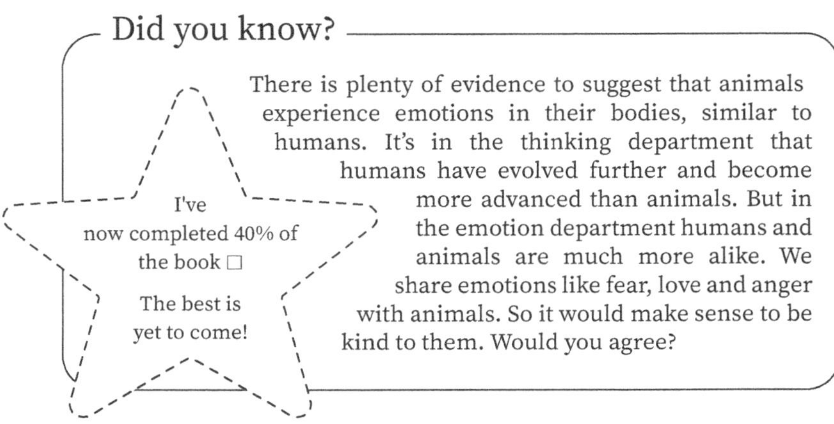

Did you know?

There is plenty of evidence to suggest that animals experience emotions in their bodies, similar to humans. It's in the thinking department that humans have evolved further and become more advanced than animals. But in the emotion department humans and animals are much more alike. We share emotions like fear, love and anger with animals. So it would make sense to be kind to them. Would you agree?

I've now completed 40% of the book ☐

The best is yet to come!

Chapter 6: The Self

Revision ⓖ

What makes emotions uncomfortable is what the body is feeling. So, in order to reduce the discomfort of emotions, what do we need to focus on?

Thoughts ☐

External circumstances ☐

What the body feels ☐

Let us recap the rules of emotion exposure. Decide which of the following statements are true about the practice of emotion exposure, and which ones are false:

When your eyes are closed, you think about your emotions.

True ☐

False ☐

When your eyes are closed, you pay attention to your emotions. You do not think.

True ☐

False ☐

You first check to see if the emotion is somewhere in your body. If it is, you keep your attention on that part of the body.

True ☐

False ☐

If you cannot find the emotion in your body, you sit with the experience of the emotion anyway.

True ☐

False ☐

You try to figure out why you have the emotion, or where it comes from.

True ☐

False ☐

You try to make your body relaxed and make the emotion go away.

True ☐

False ☐

You try to control the emotion.

True ☐

False ☐

You try to make the emotion go away by telling yourself that it's not logical or helpful.

True ☐

False ☐

When you practise emotion exposure, you do not try to control or change the emotion.

True ☐

False ☐

Emotion exposure is not a relaxation practice. Your job is not to try to relax or to make the emotion feel better. Your job is to simply watch the emotion and pay attention to the experience, even if it is uncomfortable.

True ☐

False ☐

Emotion exposure is an automatic process. You don't need to deliberately change your emotions. You just face the emotion and let your body do the rest of the work.

True ☐

False ☐

So now, before we start, take a moment to practice emotion exposure around any emotions that you may be feeling right now.

Self-Image

What do shame, pride, embarrassment, humiliation, self-admiration and self-resentment have in common?

.... Ⓖ

....

Answer: they are all related to your sense of self, which is what this chapter is all about. Your sense of self, or self-image, is about how you view yourself: What mental images you have of yourself. Your opinions and emotions relating to the person that you believe you are.

There are two main components to our sense of self or self-image:

1. **Thoughts:** your thoughts and opinions about who you are, how the world views you, your worth and value as a person and so on. You might also know these thoughts as your 'identity'.
2. **Emotions:** what does it *feel* like to be you. These are emotions that feel like you. Just like any other emotions you would likely feel them in your body, but they feel a bit closer to you than other emotions. They feel like your 'you-ness'.

Research shows that the amount of time we spend focusing on our self-image has a direct correlation with how likely we are to suffer from various mental health issues. In other words, the more time you spend thinking of the things you like about yourself or don't like about yourself, the more likely you are to suffer from different mental health issues. This includes thinking about how other people view you, how you compare to other people, your success or failures in life, whether you are a good person or a bad person, and generally your identity and self worth. Focusing a lot on thoughts about your identity and self-worth is called self-focused attention. In contrast, when we're able to think about our self-image less, and instead bring our attention to the experiences of this minute - which you now know is called mindfulness - we can enjoy better moods, less anxiety, more peace and less restlessness. Let's practise this right now:

First, close your eyes and think about yourself, your successes or failures in life, or how other people view you. Take your time.

How do you feel at the end of that exercise? Do you feel a lot of emotions raging through your system? These can be pleasant or unpleasant emotions. Do you see that the more time you spend focusing on thoughts and ideas about yourself, how others view you or whether or not you're good enough, the more likely you are to struggle with intense emotions? Would you say that you spend a lot of time on a daily basis thinking about your self-image and self-worth? Think about that question for a minute. You don't have to share your answer with anyone. It's for your eyes only.

Now let's switch our attention to something that is happening in this minute - free from thoughts of self. Maybe start by listening to all the sounds around you for a few minutes.

Now turn your attention to your body. Watch as your breath flows in and flows out.

How do you feel after those two mindfulness exercises? Do you feel calmer and more at peace? Do you see that while you were practising these mindfulness exercises, you weren't really giving any thought to ideas about yourself? Your focus was on the reality of this moment, not on any thoughts about who you are, what you're like, or what you do or don't like about yourself. Was that not a more freeing experience?

The World of Comparisons

Take a look at this image of a wooden stick:

Would you say that this stick is short or long? Think about that question for a minute. Is this stick short or long?

Right now, you may be feeling a little bit confused, thinking: 'compared to what?' And you are right to be confused. You are spot on. This stick, on its own, and without being compared to any other objects, is neither short nor long. It is just as it is: a stick. But if we place it next to a longer stick:

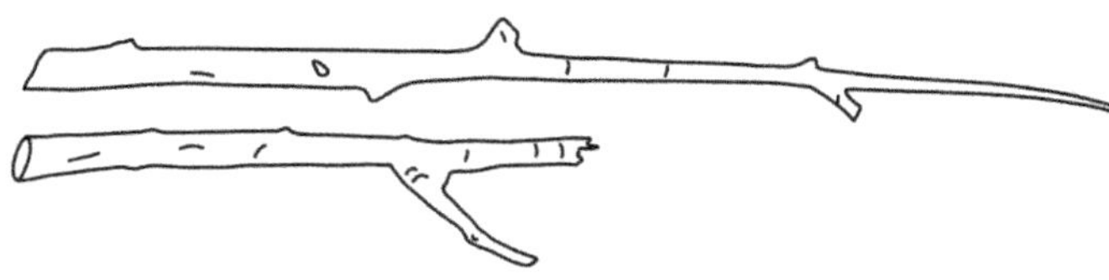

All of a sudden, you may conclude that our stick was short all along.

Your brain would label the stick: 'short'. Now let's remove the longer stick and place our stick next to a shorter one:

This time you may conclude that our original stick is long. Your brain would label it as 'long'.

Our stick hasn't changed one bit. It's *comparison* that has made us see it differently. Our brains are constantly busy comparing things and then using this comparison to place labels on things. We compare children. We compare adults. We compare animals. We compare objects. We compare life events. We might decide that a child is smarter than another child. A shirt is more stylish than another one. A colour is prettier than another colour. One employee is more hardworking than another. One woman is more beautiful than another. We might decide that it's better to be tall than short. Or it is better to have certain facial structures than others. Or it is better to have a particular hair type, or occupation or personal character.

A lot of the opinions that we form about ourselves and others are formed through comparison. One problem with comparison is that when we compare, we expect the person to be the same as someone else, and well, they might not do very well in that test! If we were to set aside the comparison, we might see that the unique qualities are exactly what make that person beautiful! What do we mean by that? Well, imagine if your friend asked you to close your eyes and told you that she was about to feed you a piece of apple. But instead of the sweet crunchy apple that you were promised, your friend fed you a piece of salty spicy olive! What would your reaction be? Surprise? Disgust? Your first thought might be 'There's something seriously wrong with this apple! Why is it soft and salty, instead of crunchy and sweet? Why does it smell strange?' The reason for your negative reaction is nothing but the fact that you had a specific expectation that wasn't met. You may normally love olives, but when the olive was compared to an apple and expected to taste like an apple, it didn't perform well in that test at all. That's right, olives fail as apples, even though as olives they are perfect! This is what comparison does.

Imagine a world where all olives are failures because they are expected to perform like apples. Let's call this the *world of comparisons.*

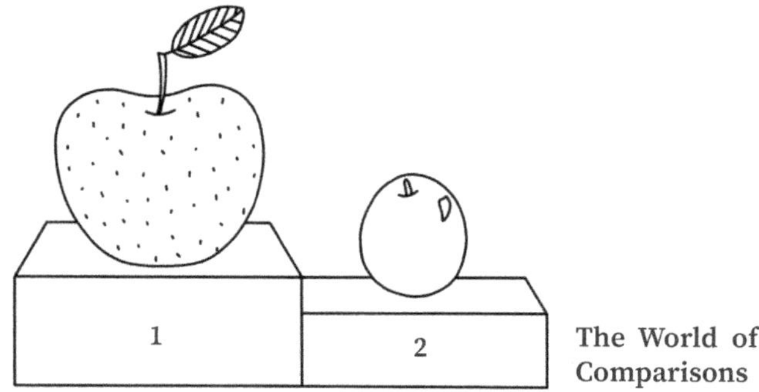

The World of Comparisons

Now, imagine another world where olives and apples are seen as two completely different foods that are both great in their own right. Let's call this the world of absolutes.

If apples and olives had feelings, which world do you think would be a happier one for both? The world of comparisons or the world of absolutes?

The World of Absolutes

Just to be clear, we are not saying that comparison is always harmful. Just like most things in life, comparison also has a purpose, and when used in the right place, it can be helpful to us. For example, when you're at the market you might compare the size of a few watermelons, so that you can buy the largest one possible because you have a lot of guests to feed. While shopping for a vacuum cleaner, you might compare the quality of a few products so that you can buy the best one for your budget, since it would make your life easier. Comparison becomes problematic when it is coated with emotions, instead of being a purely practical tool designed to make our lives easier. This is particularly so when we use it to measure the worthiness of ourselves or others, when it tells us that some people are more worthy than others, or more deserving of love.

It's also worth mentioning that not every opinion that we have about people or things is necessarily the result of comparison. For example, some things, in themselves, are pleasant or unpleasant. No one enjoys a headache or a stomach bug. We don't need to compare being sick with a stomach bug to being healthy in order to know that we don't like it. To know that there is something wrong.

Similarly, conflict, hatred and deprivation in themselves are unpleasant. You can also look at a painting or listen to a piece of music and enjoy it without needing to compare it to anything. You can enjoy that painting or music in an absolute sense.

But a lot of our opinions are born out of comparison. And our minds have a habit of turning our observations into labels which we don't easily let go of. Simply put, when we make our minds up about something, we tend to stick with it and hold on to that opinion for dear life! We don't easily let that opinion go. For example you might label your grumpy neighbour as 'unfriendly' and try to avoid him from that point on - even though, if you got to know him better, you might realise that he's actually quite nice and was just having a bad day when you first met him. So when you combine the two mental habits of comparing and labelling, you end up with an even more unhelpful package.

Make a list of some of the judgements that you have made about yourself or others as a result of comparison:

....Ⓟ

....

....

....

Now go through every item on that list, close your eyes and see if you can create a fresh view of yourself or others by stripping away the comparison and looking at yourself or the other person in an absolute sense.

Imagine that you are that stick from the earlier experiment. Realise that without comparison, you are not long or short. You are just you. Please note, we are not asking you to 'like' everything about yourself or others. We're suggesting that you strip away the comparison factor and see yourself or the other person as if they were the only person on the planet and couldn't be compared to anyone else.

Now, take another look at your list. Return to the world of comparisons - the reality of the world that we live in. What does it feel like to live in this world of comparisons?

Notice the emotions that arise in your body as you think about the world of comparisons. Where in the body do you feel these emotion? Close your eyes and practise emotion exposure. Once you are done, have a think about the world of comparisons again. If any new emotions arise, practise emotion exposure once again. Repeat this several times.

The Coin

In early childhood, children don't think much about their identity, their place in society or whether or not they're good enough. The child concentrates more on experiencing the world than on their worth as a person. But somewhere along the way something changes within us: we learn the concept of self-worth. Somewhere along the way we start thinking of our place within the society, what others think of us and how we compare to other people. We start wondering: 'Am I good enough?' 'Am I worthy as a person?' This is the start of a lot of our emotional struggles. Can you see that the idea of self-worth is only born out of a place of comparison? That it wouldn't exist without comparison?

Imagine a coin. On one side of this coin we have a belief that 'I am of high worth' or 'I am superior'. On the other side, we have the belief that 'I am NOT good enough' or 'I am inferior':

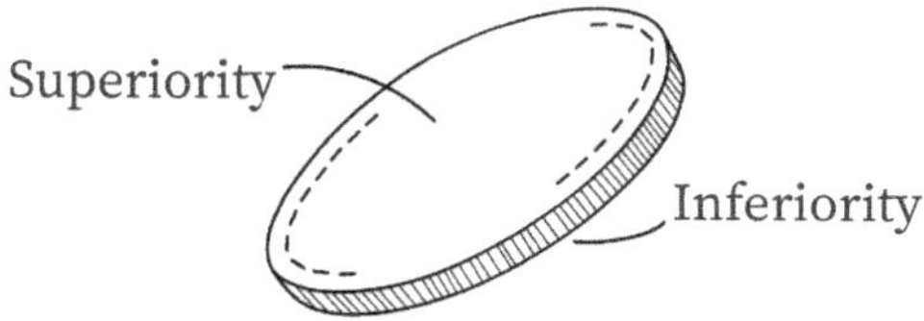

Let's call this the coin of our troubles! Because many of us spend years struggling to stay on the 'good' side of the coin and avoid the 'bad' side. The world around us often tells us to live according to this coin. We feel that there is no choice but to accept it as a reality of life. We feel proud and ecstatic when we experience the 'good' side but depressed or anxious when we experience the 'bad' side. We fear the 'bad' side and so do everything to avoid it.

When children are first introduced to this coin, they may learn that they belong to either side of it to begin with. Some may learn that they are better than other children, others learn that they are not good enough. Both are harmful. For example, a child might start with a period of being bullied at school or struggling with certain tasks and being given the message that they are not as good as the other kids in their class. So, they may decide: 'I am not good enough, I am faulty, I don't belong, I am different to other people', and so on. But another child could start by receiving the opposite message: that they are more special, talented, or worthy than the other kids around them, and that's just as harmful. Because at that point they develop an inner pressure to somehow keep receiving that praise from others. They may even look down on people that they consider inferior, but also on some level fear becoming those people. The more time they spend looking down on others, the bigger their fears of inferiority. They have learned that they live in a world of comparisons, that they live in a world where their worth is constantly being measured and that they may not be loved or valued if at times they don't do so well. They would feel deep emotional pain if one day they feel that they're no longer the image that they had expected of themselves. There is no sense of safety for either of these children, because comparison means that their self worth is on fragile grounds.

If you drop an object from the top of a high cliff...

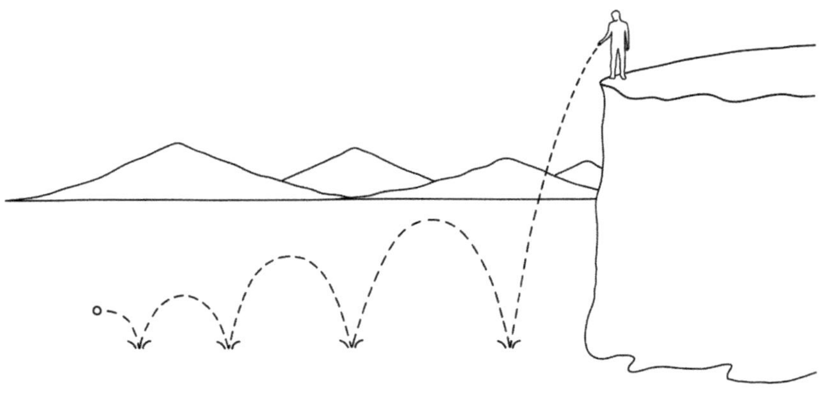

...the impact would be much more than if the same object was dropped from, say, the top of a stool...

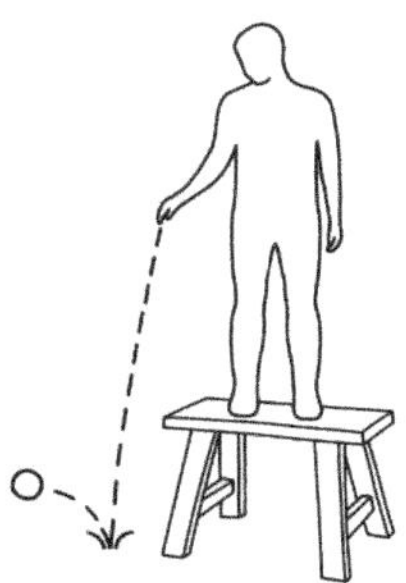

The higher the drop, the bigger the impact, right? It's the same with our self-image. The higher we build our sense of self-worth, the more painful it is if we believe that we have failed. See, as children learn to live in the world of comparisons, they often try to combat their painful feelings of low self-worth by fantasising about a day when they finally become someone who is good enough. Someone who is respected. Someone who is looked up to. Someone who is complimented and praised. They may want to become a superhero. A celebrity. Someone super popular, super successful or super strong. And then these fantasies turn into expectations. They feel a need to achieve the fantasy. And the higher and mightier the fantasy image is, the less impressive their current self appears in comparison. It is like a person who is looking at an object from meters above, and the object looks tiny and insignificant. The bigger the expectation that you have created for yourself, the more significant the drop is, should you fail. The greater the danger of feeling utterly insignificant, should you not meet the expectation.

What are the areas around which we measure self-worth in this world of comparisons? Well, it depends on the person. At some point in your life, you may have decided that the value and worth of people depends on:

- how rich they are
- how attractive they are
- how intelligent they are
- how funny they are
- how successful they are
- how strong they are
- how in control of their emotions they are
- how good a parent they are
- how well dressed they are
- how healthy they are
- how popular or lovable they are

And so on... We're all different in what we consider to be a measure of 'being worthy'. You may consider some of the items on the above list as important measures of worth but consider other ones as not very important at all. The point is that we use certain measuring scales to compare people, and decide who is worthy and who isn't. Who is on the top side of the coin and who is on the bottom.

It's worth mentioning that there is absolutely nothing wrong with enjoying money, a nice car, good education, nice clothes or any of the other things that we mentioned on that list. The problem starts when we measure people's worthiness based on these things. The point is that some people enjoy driving a good car and dressing nicely. Other people have no interest in these at all. Both are perfectly okay. Some like to go to university and have a higher education. Others have no interest in this and have other interests in life. Again, both are fine. Measuring people's worthiness based on these criteria is the problem.

So, as you can see, superiority and inferiority are really two sides of the same coin. In a world where one exists, the other one will naturally exist too. What kind of world is that? The world of comparisons. In the world of comparisons, people are divided into those we consider superior, those we consider inferior, and others who float somewhere in between. It is a cruel and unkind world. A world that creates lots of unnecessary emotional pain. Naturally, comparison also means that 'I'm only worthy if I'm more worthy than other people'. You see, if your worth is measured in comparison to others, you are only more worthy if your competition is less worthy. So this creates a natural competition which is an inseparable part of the world of comparisons. This means that we often don't look at others who are doing well in life and enjoy their success or happiness. Instead when we look at their success, it highlights our own failures.

So, which world would you prefer to live in? If you would like to break free from the world of the coin, you may be wondering: '...but how?'

Well, the first thing to remember is that we each have to start with ourselves and get rid of our own coin. With each of us changing, the world suffers from this coin of troubles a little bit less. Each of us has to make an internal decision to hand in their resignation from the world of worthiness and unworthiness. Let's try a little exercise.

We are about to use an exercise where we use our imagination to paint the past differently. You may be wondering what the point of this is when you can't really change the past. Yes, you can't change the past, but by experiencing the story differently in your mind, you can change the thoughts, beliefs and emotions that are created because of your story. So even if it feels silly, give it a go!

Let your mind go free and take you to whatever point in your past that's relevant to the coin being formed. The earlier the memory, the better. Do you remember a time or circumstances when the coin became a part of your life? Let your mind guide you to its origins.

Keep in mind, at times people are surprised by the specific memory or past event that their mind chooses to go back to. If this happens to you, don't overthink it and just go with the flow.

Maybe it was a teacher, parent or another adult who compared you to another kid? Maybe they shamed you or harshly criticised you? Maybe it was other kids being mean, or picking on you? Maybe it was you comparing yourself to other kids, or deciding that you were inadequate in some way? Or it could have been nothing to do with you. Maybe you observed someone else being harshly criticised or bullied. Or you overheard a coin-related conversation between other people. Or maybe your story was so unique that it doesn't fit into any of the descriptions you just read.

Keep in mind that you may have several significant memories of this nature. If so, pick one to work on for now, preferably the earliest one you can remember. You can return to the other memories at another time.

What would you like to do to support and help your child self? Maybe you'd like to introduce a warm, kind and supportive adult character into your story and get them to help the child (this adult can be you, as the child's 'future self'; or someone else). This adult can show the child what it feels like to be loved without comparison. Loved in an absolute way. Make the child feel 'enough', maybe even have a laugh together and go buy an ice cream. Would the child benefit from making a different decision, acting differently or seeing things in a new light? Provide them with the support or advice they need so that they can do these things. If the child wishes for irrational or unrealistic things, remember that this is your imagination. So no need to limit the child by trying to keep this exercise 'realistic'.

Now speak to the child about adopting a different view of themselves, or the world. We each have the option of starting with ourselves and getting rid of our own coin. With each of us changing, the world suffers from this coin of troubles a little bit less. Each of us has to make an internal decision to hand in their resignation from the world of worthiness and unworthiness. So help the child consider the possibility that even if everyone else around them are operating based on the coin, they don't have to fall for it also. They have the option of being free. It may help to tell the child these things:

You were not wrong. You were not the problem. The problem was that many people have been a victim of their own traumas which has caused them to lack empathy and compassion, or to become stuck in their own cruel world of comparisons. It is a prevalent problem and you became a victim to it. Even adults can be wrong. So have the courage to believe that you are not the problem, even if others tell you otherwise. You don't have to be something else or someone else, in order to be 'good enough'.

In the weeks to come, whenever you remember stories of your past that are related to the coin, go back and try to rewrite them. Also, don't forget to notice the emotions in your body that are related to your self-image and the coin. Emotions relating to your self-image can feel like shame, pride, embarrassment, humiliation, self-admiration, self-resentment and so on. Practice emotion exposure around these whatever chance you get.

Fear of Being Judged

This might be a good time to discuss another separate, but related topic: fear of the opinions of others. Many of you may be finding it hard to imagine letting go of the coin, because, well, what if other people keep judging you based on the coin? We often fear not being considered good enough by others. We fear being negatively labelled by them. We give their opinions so much importance that even when we are certain about something, on some level, we start doubting ourselves simply because someone else disagrees with us.

We particularly value the opinions of those that we consider superior, more worthy or important to us in some way. We may have learned from a young age that the opinions of those around us are more accurate, true or important than our own views and opinions. So it is no surprise that being negatively judged or disliked by others can trigger so many painful emotions for most people. These include feeling lonely, anxious, embarrassed, ashamed, sad, hopeless, angry, and so on.

It is important to realise that even though these emotions might be very strong and painful, they are still nothing but emotions. Begin practising emotion exposure around them whenever they are triggered. Over time, you may find that the opinions of others feel less frightening.

There are two very common thought errors that play a role in our fear of being negatively judged. The first thought error is that, on some level, many of us undervalue our own intellect and overvalue the intellect of others. Take a look at the image below:

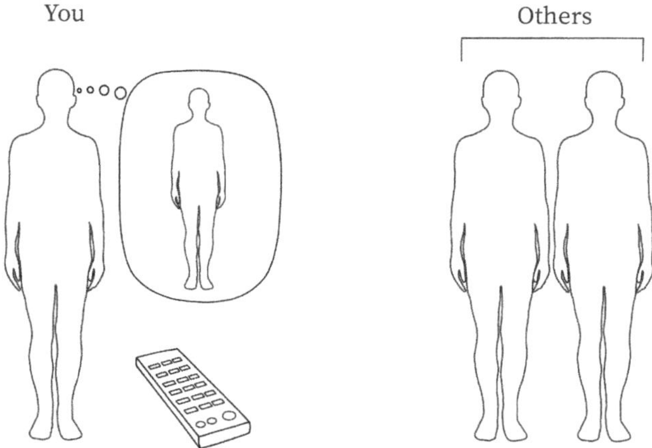

Imagine that the person on the left is you. The image in the thought bubble is what you think of yourself, your identity or self-image.

The remote control down the bottom is what controls the image in the thought bubble. The figures on the right are those around you - other people. Who do you think holds that remote control? Who controls the image that you have of yourself? Do you control it? Or do others control it?

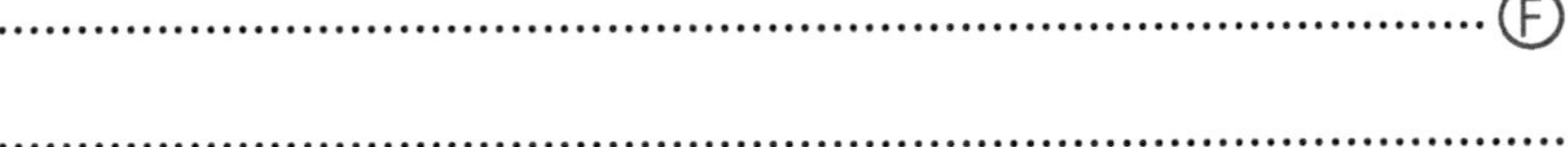

Now, let's try a little exercise. Close your eyes, sit comfortably, and pay attention to the image that you have of yourself, in this minute. Do you like that image or does it make you feel uncomfortable? Does it create positive or negative feelings?

Now imagine that there is a person next to you who has a negative view of you. Does their opinion change how you feel about yourself? Does it become more negative? Then who is holding that remote control? You or the other person? If their opinion changes how you feel towards yourself, then they are at least partially holding your remote control. That is the case for most people.

The truth is, people can be wrong about us. They are not perfect. Their opinions and judgements can contain a lot of errors - just as yours can contain errors. But you can only use your own power of judgement and intellect to navigate the world. You only have access to your own faculties of reasoning and discernment. You cannot think with another person's brain. Even if you were to speak to an expert and choose their ideas over your own, it is still you who is deciding this. You are still using your intellect to choose their ideas. Since, at the end of the day, you have no choice but to rely on your own intellect, you might as well trust it.

> "Since at the end of the day you have no choice but to rely on your own intellect, you might as well trust it.

Yes, we all have thought errors. Your power of judgement may not always be perfect or free from error, but overtime, as you practice active thinking, you can learn to use your vehicle of intellect better. You are good enough to be able to exercise your judgement and trust it. Let us emphasise that one more time: You are good enough to be able to exercise your judgement and trust it. Everyone will make mistakes and you are no exception. But when you make mistakes, you can then use your power of intellect to find your mistakes and learn from them. But if you don't trust your own judgement, you can't use it effectively to learn from your mistakes either.

So, now let's try and imagine taking that remote control back into your own hand. Remind yourself that there is no human being in the world more fit to judge you than you yourself. No one knows you more intimately than yourself. There is no reason why other people's opinions about you are more correct or accurate than your own view of yourself. You are given your own unique intellect with which to judge, so why not trust it? If others have an opinion about you, that is nothing but a thought in their head. It is not the truth of you. Also, remember that their thoughts about you can very soon be replaced by thoughts about someone else. They are all just passing thoughts. So, let them keep their opinion. You don't have to change it. But you don't need to believe it either. You can choose to accept any helpful ideas that they have and dismiss any unhelpful ones.

How did you go with that exercise? How do you feel after it? Remember to practise it next time you worry about other people's opinion of you. Remind yourself that what they think of you is nothing but an opinion.

Personalisation

Logically, most people would agree that we are each just one person amongst many. Most people would agree that none of us are any more or less important than the rest. Still, on a deeper level, people often see themselves as more central and significant than others. For example, if you received a criticism, an insult, or if someone undermined you or questioned your worthiness, you would be more likely to notice it and experience unpleasant emotions as a result, than if a similar thing was to happen to another person around you, say your neighbour or your colleague. Of course you may put yourself in the other person's shoes and feel empathy towards them. But this likely comes no where near the storm of powerful emotions that would hit you if you were the target personally. Personalisation means that there is always a 'me' entity that we are just that much closer to and more vulnerable towards than we are to the rest of the world.

Sometimes you may even personalise other people or things. You may see your child, your family, your community or certain other people in your life as an extension of yourself, and if they are criticised or undermined, it's as if you are criticised or undermined. But the principle still remains the same. Whatever or whoever you associate with yourself may become a much more sensitive subject to you than things or people that you haven't personalised.

Like all other thought errors, the first step towards changing this is to start becoming aware of it. Let's do a little exercise. First, close your eyes and pay attention to the way that you personalise yourself and the things that are related to you. See if you can notice the difference in your emotions when someone criticises you, versus criticising someone unrelated to you.

Now, try the following things:

1. See if you can shift your view and start seeing yourself in a non-personal way. See yourself as others see you: in a non-personal way. Or in the way that you see those people around you that you haven't personalised. Imagine not taking personally how other people see you. After all, to them, you are just one of the many people around. To them, you are not personal. So they don't see you in the way that you see yourself.

2. Notice the emotions that come up as a result of personalisation. Notice them in your body and place your attention on them. After the emotions have lifted, do you see the situation any differently?

How did it feel to see yourself in a non-personal way?

.... Ⓕ

....

....

....

Change Can Start With You

When we are surrounded by a world that is still operating on the basis of comparison, it's easy to be tempted to join in to escape emotions of shame, fear, loneliness or anxiety. Imagine being surrounded by people who express a lot of opinions about who is more amazing and who is generally not good enough. Can you think of some people in your life that tend to do that? Write down some of the comments that you remember them making:

.... Ⓟ

....

....

....

What emotions do you feel as you remember these types of conversations? Now shift your attention to the body and practise emotion exposure around these emotions.

Take another look at your list and repeat emotion exposure a few times.

Can you imagine viewing yourself free from comparison even if you are surrounded by these people? Can you resist believing in their world view? If it is hard to resist it, what emotions are you feeling? What emotions are pushing you to believe in their world view? Practise emotion exposure as needed.

Next time you are spending time with people who make you question your worth or lead you to believe that you need to be a certain way in order to be worthy, notice your emotions, go within and feel them. Practise emotion exposure as soon as you are able to. You don't need to believe this version of the world. Change can start with you.

How to Praise or Criticise

As you can see, our self-image can be easily influenced by those around us, and in turn what we do or say can impact other people's self-image. Our words and actions hold a lot of power when it comes to creating a world of comparison, worthiness, unworthiness, superiority and inferiority. So, a good question to ask is:

'How do I praise or criticise, to make sure I am doing good and not causing harm?'

A rule of thumb is to remind yourself that what people do is not who they are. So, when praising or criticising, choose your words carefully to make sure you are commenting on the person's current behaviour, and not suggesting that this is who they are. Describe the behaviour rather than labelling the person. For example, say 'What you did was so kind', rather than 'You are such a kind person'. You could praise them by saying thank you, showing gratitude or appreciation for their actions. At times a simple, kind, gesture is enough.

The same rule applies to criticism. Instead of saying 'You're lazy', you could ask about their energy levels or motivation. This way, you're acknowledging that there is a reason behind the way that this person acts. When you say that a person is lazy, you're suggesting that there is some sort of intrinsic quality about them. That lazy is who they are. So, the simple rule is, comment on the behaviour. Don't label the person.

Another point to remember is that if you have a habit of comparing people in your mind, you will also be likely to keep your praise mostly to those who seem to be doing better in comparison to the rest. So, for example, if you are spending time with a few friends, you may mentally compare their appearance, success, popularity or some other aspect. Then according to that comparison, you praise the ones that you believe are doing better. Your friends may feel that, and they may measure themselves based on how you have ranked them. They may begin to compare themselves to those that have received the most praise from you or may begin competing or showing jealous behaviour. Instead, you could begin viewing each person free from comparison. This way, you can acknowledge what each is doing well. Or how far each has progressed in their own journey. You can get excited about their strengths or unique qualities. You are more likely to spread your praise more evenly between all of your friends, instead of only giving praise to specific ones.

Homework

Remember, at the start of this chapter, we talked about emotions that are to do with your sense of self? Emotions like shame, pride, embarrassment, humiliation, self-admiration, self-resentment and so on. As you practise your daily emotion exposure in the weeks to come, pay particular attention to your sense of self.

At times, these emotions can become a chronic part of you. Just as we don't always realise that we are surrounded by air, because it is always there, it is easy to forget that we are experiencing an emotion that is there most of the time. So make sure you pay attention to emotions that feel like a normal part of you.

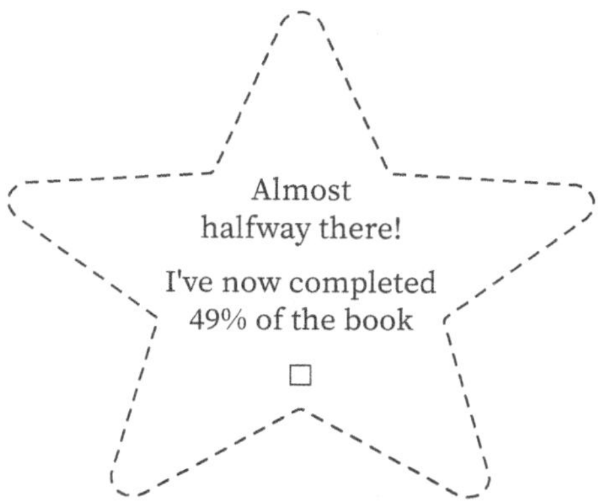

Chapter 7: Self Compassion

Revision

Close your eyes and remember what you learned in the previous chapter, as well as how you've gone with practising it since. Don't pressure yourself to remember everything. Just allow the remembering to naturally happen at its own pace.

At times we are so used to certain emotions that they begin to feel like our identity. Or like the reality itself. It helps to begin noticing these emotions even if they are a bit more difficult to notice, given that we are so close to them. The following exercise might help with this. Close your eyes and sit comfortably. Repeat the words 'I' or 'me' in your mind a few times. As you repeat 'I , I , I' or 'me, me, me' notice how it feels to be you. How does it feel to be you in this minute? Notice any pleasantness or unpleasantness that is attached to the experience of being you or living the life that you live. Once you notice these, place your focus on the experience, just as you would with any emotion. Keep your focus on that part of your body for a while.

Self-Talk

While practising active thinking, you may have noticed that you tend to speak to yourself in your mind, as if you have a relationship with yourself. It could sound like an inner dialogue with yourself. You may be critical of yourself. You may be encouraging towards yourself. Your inner voice may sound like a mean bully, or a person that constantly talks you up or down. You may notice that your self-talk reminds you of the way that an important other person like a parent or ex-partner talked to you. Almost as if you have learned to treat yourself the way that they used to treat you.

For some of you this relationship with yourself may be less thought based and more emotion based. So you may feel a lot of anger towards yourself, feel sorry for yourself, or feel a lot of admiration towards yourself. You may snap at yourself or punish yourself just like your parents or teachers did to you when you were a child. Or you may feel ashamed or proud of who you are, just like your classmates at school made you feel.

Close your eyes and pay attention to your self-talk for a moment. See if you can recognise it. Can you identify where and when you learned to speak to yourself in that way?

Why Do You Deserve Love?

So, you are imperfect. All humans are. You may work hard to improve yourself every day, and that is great. But, in the meantime, can you love yourself despite your imperfections? Or do you believe that in order to deserve love, you need to be a better person, a more organised person, a more successful person, a more likeable person and so on? We would like to suggest that you deserve love right now, just as you are. You fully and completely deserve it. And whose love do you need the most? You need your own love more than anyone else's. Happiness starts with your ability to be compassionate and kind towards yourself. You may be asking, why do I deserve love if I am not the person that I should be? Let us try to answer that by discussing why we withdraw love from ourselves in the first place. Here's a small analogy.

Dylan had a bike. He loved it so much. It had been with him through so many adventures. It was comfortable. It was fun to ride. He would prefer to ride this bike over any others.

But one day a bunch of new kids moved into his neighbourhood and told Dylan that his bike was no good. They told him that only shiny new bikes with a new design and paint job were cool ones. Dylan loved his bike and didn't take the kids seriously at first. But they kept laughing at him for holding on to his bike. They looked down on kids with bikes that were no good. When Dylan wanted to hang out with them, they showed no interest in spending time with him because of his embarrassing bike.

As you can imagine, over time, these kids convinced Dylan that his bike was embarrassing and that he was unworthy because of it. Dylan stopped riding his bike and began envying kids with nice shiny bikes.

You see, there was absolutely nothing wrong with Dylan's bike. It was still fun, comfortable and perfect for him. It was Dylan's view that had been changed. In the past, Dylan was not concerned about whether or not he was worthy or whether his bike was cool enough. He just enjoyed riding. These thoughts were only introduced to him later on by the new kids.

So the question we must ask is not 'Why should Dylan love his bike?' It is rather 'Why did Dylan stop loving his bike?' And the answer is: because he started measuring his worth as a person based on the value of his bike.

Our society teaches us that we need to be a certain way in order to be a worthy person. Just like Dylan, we gradually come to believe what the society around us is telling us. The more we become concerned with being 'good enough' or measuring our worth, the more we forget how it felt when we were simply content with who we were. We forget to be content within ourselves despite any of our imperfections or flaws. Our attention gets shifted from the world around us and enjoying life, to concerns over our self worth.

The reality is that, just as Dylan's bike is still great, if only Dylan could look at it independent of what the society has told him, you too are great, just as you are, if only you could stop believing what the society has told you you should be. Imagine two birds, one small, one big; one skinny, one round. One has a small beak, one has a large beak; one is quiet and shy, one is noisy and playful. Both birds are happy in their own skin, free of thoughts about whether or not they are good enough. They are not concerned with their worth, they just love life! But the human mind comes along and begins trying to measure what is better and what is not as good. We judge our worth based on our size, shape, colour, and personality. And so we forget how to love ourselves and love life.

Close your eyes and see if you can make an internal decision to love yourself, just as you are in this minute. If you are able to love yourself, enjoy that feeling for a few minutes. If not, notice the emotions that are stopping you from being able to love yourself and practise emotion exposure around them.

Self-Compassion

If your self-esteem relies on comparing yourself with other people and coming up better, then your self-esteem is sitting on fragile ground. You may enjoy periods of good self-esteem, followed by periods of excruciating emotional discomfort when life causes you to question if you're in fact good enough. Wouldn't it be better if you could feel good, at times of growth, at times of not doing so well and at times when you are not appreciated by those around you? Of course, if you see a need for it, you can still work towards improving yourself. But what if you could also feel content in the meantime?

Self-compassion means extending kindness and understanding towards ourselves, even at times of weakness, at times of imperfection and at times of struggle. It means accepting ourselves, just as we are, instead of subjecting ourselves to constant self-blame and self-criticism.

“ Happiness starts with your ability to be compassionate and kind towards yourself.

If you see an injured animal, or a crying child, you are likely to feel compassion towards them, meaning that you would like to extend kindness towards them, to rid them off their suffering and make them comfortable again. To feel compassionate towards yourself is the same thing. A person who is compassionate towards themselves doesn't think 'I'm pathetic for being so sad and weak.' They extend love and care towards themselves. They respond to their own imperfections with kindness. And those who can be compassionate and forgiving towards themselves, can be the same towards others.

Research around self-compassion shows that it is correlated with lower levels of anxiety and depression. And it is linked with higher levels of life satisfaction and positive emotions. That means the more compassionate you are towards yourself, the happier you are, and the less likely you are to suffer from depression and anxiety. So you need your own love and compassion to function well. It's not a luxury, it's a requirement. And let's be clear: every part of you needs love and compassion. Even the parts that you don't like, the parts that you are ashamed of and the parts that are not doing so well.

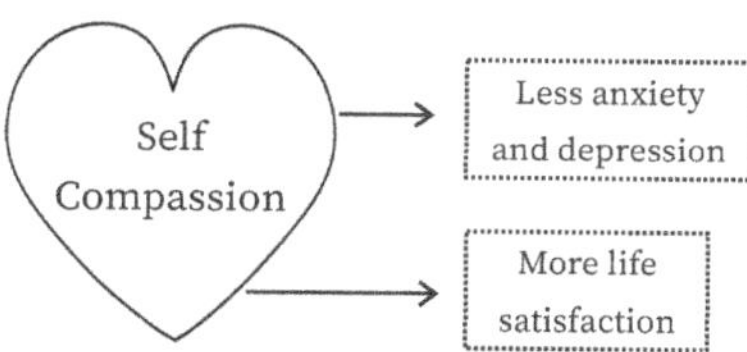

Blame

You could say that the opposite of compassion is blame. Blame seeks to find the person whose fault it is and punish them. Blame doesn't care that they didn't know any better or couldn't help it. When we blame, we just want to express our rage. In that moment we have no regard for the person we are punishing. Our focus is too fixated on the rage to allow us to consider how they might be feeling.

Blame is a form of non-acceptance. Whether we blame ourselves or blame other people, we are fighting the current reality and refusing to accept it. There is very little difference between a person scolding their child for not understanding maths and scolding the sky for being blue. Reality is as it is. Scolding and blaming will not change either of these realities at this moment. The sky is blue whether we like it or not. And if your child struggles to understand maths, that reality is also as it is. There is an explanation for their struggle and scolding will not magically fix that struggle. Trying to understand their struggle and patiently finding ways to meet their needs is a far more effective strategy. No matter what the reason is, scolding and blaming will not magically change the reality. Accepting others as they are and accepting ourselves as we are is a great precursor to creating a better world.

Here is a fact about blame: blame does not seek solutions. It simply seeks to punish. Imagine two drivers. Each knows that their car urgently needs to be serviced. Each driver neglects it for one reason or another. Both are on their way to an important meeting when suddenly the car breaks down on the side of the road!

Driver number 1 stands on the side of the road, thinking: 'How could I let this happen? Why do I do these things? Why do these things always happen to me? Why can't I do anything right? I knew the car needed a service. Why did I neglect it? I'm so useless...' and he goes on and on, blaming and punishing himself over his mistake.

Driver number 2 thinks to himself: 'Oh no, this is pretty bad! I really should have taken the car for a service and I didn't. That was a mistake, but what's done is done. How do I fix it now? How do I prevent it from happening again in the future?' He reflected on his mistake, he owned up to it, and he didn't waste a further minute punishing himself after the lesson was learned.

A few hours later, driver number 2 is focused on fixing the practical issues, while feeling emotionally calm. But driver number 1 is still feeling guilty, full of self-blame, angry, anxious and down. He is struggling to focus on improving the situation or making future plans to prevent similar issues, because his mind is so focused on punishing himself. Which driver would live a happier and more comfortable life? Which driver do you resemble most?

A blaming mind is constantly focused on trying to figure out 'whose fault is it?'

'Is it my fault? Or is it the other person's fault?'

'Is it my mum's fault? Or is it my dad's fault?'

'Is it this TV character's fault? Or the other TV character's fault?'

Not 'how do we understand all parties with their unique challenges and find smart ways to fix the problem?'

Blame ignores the fact that people are imperfect, they make mistakes, they get tired, they have emotional challenges, they forget, they get confused, they get influenced by the society and forget to think independently, and many other factors that explain their behaviour. Blame ignores the fact that people often don't know how to do any better. Blame also ignores the fact that usually people from both sides of an issue contribute to the problems that we see. Neither side is perfect. So usually we can't find one side that is 100% to blame and one side that is 100% free of flaws. When we blame we over-simplify things and ignore all these important details.

> **“Accepting others as they are and accepting ourselves as we are is a great precursor to creating a better world.**

It might be a good idea to explain something here. There is a common misconception that often gets in the way of people feeling compassionate towards themselves and other people. This misconception stems from the fact that many people confuse the following two concepts:

- Excuses

- Explanations

When we understand the challenges faced by someone, we often feel compassionate towards them. But many of us are resistant to hearing people as they try to explain their side of the story, because we feel that they are simply making excuses for their mistakes. We hear their explanation to mean that they don't wish to try harder or shouldn't improve things.

Take a moment to reflect on the following question, or discuss it with your group:

What similarities or differences do you see between explaining a behaviour and making excuses for the behaviour?

.... Ⓖ

....

....

....

Answer: When you make excuses for problematic behaviour, the focus is usually on denying that the behaviour was in fact wrong or unhelpful. You might want to argue that there's no need for change. Or that you have no responsibility in trying to improve things.

On the other hand, when you explain your reasons for a behaviour you may agree that the behaviour was unhelpful or needs to be changed, but at the same time wish for others to understand your challenges. You are simply trying to help them walk in your shoes and see your side of the story. Your purpose is to show them the circumstances, thoughts, or emotions that led to the behaviour, so that they could have more compassion towards you.

Explanations are also helpful because once we better understand the reality of a situation, we are more equipped to help the person struggling with it. It is easier to create positive change from a space of compassion than from a place of blame.

Another difference between these two concepts is that it could be said that excuses come from a place of dishonesty. We expect that a person making excuses would be intentionally manipulating the facts in order to deny that they've done anything wrong. Explanations are, on the other hand, honest and to the point. We are simply explaining how things are and what the real circumstances were that have lead to a behaviour.

So, as you can see, it is helpful to seek and offer explanations for behaviour. It helps everyone involved to understand the behaviour better. If we accuse people of making excuses when they are simply explaining, we are at risk of blocking communication, and making the person feel unheard and alone.

In the example of the two drivers, which we covered earlier, driver number 2 might have spent some time trying to find an explanation for the fact that he didn't service his car sooner. He may have thought to himself: 'Why did I neglect to have the car serviced sooner? That's right, I have been busy and run down. I thought the car would be alright and that I could push it a bit longer, until I was a bit less busy.' Here he is not excusing his lack of attention to servicing his car. On the contrary, he acknowledges the mistake and is seeking to learn from it. By trying to understand his challenges, he gives himself the advantage of recognising his barriers and finding solutions for them. As a result he may decide: 'So I tend to become busy and push back daily tasks like this. How could I avoid that in the future? Perhaps I could write down in my diary future dates when my car needs to be serviced and make a stronger commitment to stick to these dates.'

Now, before we move on, close your eyes and notice how 'blame' feels to you. Whether you are blaming yourself or blaming another person, or if you can remember being in the receiving end of blame, what does the emotion of blame feel like to you?

Feel free to allow yourself to be angry, frustrated, annoyed or experience any other emotions that it brings up for you, while placing your attention on what you feel in the body. Take your time and practise emotion exposure until these emotions subside.

To sum it up, a large part of self-compassion is accepting that all people, including you, are battling their own internal struggles and at the time of their actions, they are often doing the best they can. What if unfortunate things happen in life because of human beings'

internal and external challenges, challenges that are simply reality and need to first be understood and accepted, before any change can happen? What if I am not horrible or useless? What if I am just struggling and need a bit of compassion and understanding? Ponder on these thoughts for a few minutes and see if you can consider offering yourself self-compassion.

Self-Acceptance

Another point to consider is that self-compassion can, in fact, increase our success with difficult tasks in life. Say you are addicted to smoking. Now, no one can disagree that smoking is bad for your health and it is best to quit it as soon as you are able to. But let's look at how your efforts at quitting would look with and without acceptance.

Without acceptance - you might get swamped with thoughts such as:

> 'I should never have picked up a cigarette!'
>
> 'I should not be addicted to smoking.'
>
> 'I should be able to quit with no difficulty.'
>
> 'Why did I even become addicted in the first place?!'
>
> 'I should have known better.'

'It is so hard. I should be finding this easy. I shouldn't be so weak!'

And of course, quitting a habit like smoking can be challenging. One day you might be having a bad day, give into the temptation and pick up a cigarette again. If you do not have acceptance, this could result in painful thoughts and emotions, such as:

'I am a failure.'

'I am weak.'

'I should have been able to do better.'

'I knew I wouldn't be able to do this.'

'Why can others do it but not me?!'

'I know I'm going to fail again!'

Unfortunately, all these negative thoughts can lower your mood and make you feel down and anxious, which may in turn make it harder to stay focused on the task of quitting. It is also easier to give up on your efforts altogether when you are overwhelmed by feelings of anxiety, helplessness, failure and anger. You may think: 'Well I tried it and it didn't work. I'm giving up!'

With acceptance - your thoughts could look more like this:

'Well, whether I like it or not, I am addicted to smoking. Let's see what I can do about it now.'

'No point wasting energy on what I could have or should have done. What's done is done.'

'I am a human being and we all make mistakes.'

> 'I can learn from the past and change the future. But I can't undo the past or the fact that I am a smoker now. Fighting it will only make me feel worse.'

It goes without saying that with acceptance you would have a more peaceful, calm and contented mind. You may find it easier to learn from mistakes, make positive changes for your life and forgive yourself for not being perfect.

If you were to have a bad day and pick up another cigarette at some point, your thoughts might be:

> 'Oh no, I shouldn't have done this. But it is done. I have had a difficult day. Now back on the horse!'

You might even spend some time exploring how to prevent this next time you have a moment of weakness:

> 'Here's the plan. Next time I have a moment of craving or feeling stressed and wanting to reach for a cigarette, I will distract myself by calling a friend and having a chat! Or I might relax on the couch with a bowl of cereal and my favourite TV show.'

This means that instead of wasting time and energy on self-blame, you have accepted that moments of weakness are possible, and you have made practical plans to manage them.

As you can see, having self-compassion is a bit like being on your own team and supporting yourself through your challenges, rather than constantly beating yourself up, opposing yourself and

The Practice of Self-Compassion

Remember the remote control? We learned about ways to not be impacted so much by people's negative judgements. We learned that other people can be wrong, and you don't always have to believe that what they say or think about you is absolute truth. In a similar way, other people can be blaming or non-compassionate. And just because they treat you with blame or lack of compassion, it doesn't mean that you don't deserve compassion. As we grow up, many of us experience non-compassionate treatment by those around us - perhaps by certain adults or other children. As we don't know any better, we interpret the non-compassionate behaviour of these people as a statement of our own worth. So you might think 'if I had been a bit smarter, a bit more lovable, a bit better behaved or just a slightly better child, perhaps I would have been treated better.' Perhaps it is time to switch those beliefs around and begin holding the remote control in your own hand a bit more firmly. Let's try a little exercise:

First, recall a past memory where you were treated with lack of compassion. Imagine walking through that story again, as if it were happening all over again right now. Except, this time, walk through the story with the help of your own adult self. Yes, imagine your current self, walking into the story and supporting your past self. Or if you prefer, imagine the help of another person that you love and trust. This person is there to help guide the child, and to make them feel loved and safe.

Help the child to switch from the belief that 'I am being mistreated because there is something wrong with me' to 'I am being mistreated because those around me haven't learned about compassion, or about not comparing people or perhaps because they are too busy grappling with their own mental health issues to recognise my needs. It is no one's fault. Everyone is struggling. I'm not mistreated because I am deserving of it. You don't have to be perfect to deserve compassion. I am good and deserving of love.'

Now imagine giving the child the love they need. The sky is the limit, give the child a cuddle. Buy them an ice cream. Play some fun games together. Show them that if they make mistakes, you won't snap or punish them. Show them your love however you see fit. Take your time and enjoy this experience.

In the end, pay attention to your body. Do you feel any emotional left-overs? Switch from thinking and imagining to the body, and practise emotion exposure around whatever you are feeling. Take your time.

Now reflect on the following points and questions:

Is it not true that you are closer to yourself than any other human being could ever be? Are you not the only person who can feel what you feel, experience what you experience and think what you think? Sure, others can understand you or share similar feelings with you, or even be impacted by your thoughts and feelings. But could they actually experience and feel what you experience and feel? Is it not true that at the end of the day, their experiences are theirs, and yours are yours?

You may be the only person in the world who knows certain secrets about yourself, and you can keep these secrets as long as you decide to do so. You can lie to others, but you can never completely lie to yourself. A part of you always knows the truth.

You have been there for yourself as far back as you have been alive and will continue to be there as long as you live. Since your earliest memories in life, your thoughts and feelings may have changed; the way your body looks and feels certainly has. But isn't it still you who experiences and feels these things? Only you are in your own shoes.

If you are a person who tends to be kinder to others than to yourself, don't you think that you need the same level of kindness as others do? Can you forgive yourself for your shortcomings or mistakes, just as you would forgive someone else in your shoes? If you have a friend this close to you, wouldn't you treat them kindly? Wouldn't you feel love towards them? See if you can feel love towards yourself. Take a moment and relax into that love.

Pay attention to the sense of being you. How does it feel to be you? Sit with that feeling for a while, without thinking about it or analysing it. Just concentrate on the feeling of being you.

Artwork Ⓕ

Finish this chapter by creating an art-work, by yourself or together with your study group, around the topic of self-compassion or blame.

Chapter 8: Anxiety

Revision

Close your eyes and remember what you learned in the previous chapter, as well as how you've gone with practising it since. Don't pressure yourself to remember everything. Just allow the remembering to naturally happen at its own pace.

Fear, Anxiety, Worry

It is normal to experience fear when there is a risk to our safety. For example, when crossing a road, fear means that we will watch out for the oncoming traffic. Fear stops us from doing unsafe things like sitting down and having a picnic in the middle of a highway! So yes, fear is a helpful thing and, like any other emotion, has a function to play in our lives.

But what if our fears become too intense? What if we start to experience them a bit too often, or when they're not needed or helpful? In this chapter, we will learn about unhelpful fears, anxiety and worry, and ways to overcome them.

Worry

Worry is a familiar feeling that causes so many of us much psychological pain. Worry is the fear of negative future possibilities. It can be very unpleasant and unsettling. As with any fear, there may be times when our worries are reasonable and in line with present realities. For example, it's normal to feel a level of worry if you are waiting to hear the outcome of an exam that is going to play a huge role in your future life direction. Sometimes feeling worry for a brief period can be helpful. It can help you think of potential risks and find ways to prevent future problems. But like any other emotion, problems begin when you start experiencing worry a bit too often, or too strongly. Worrying thoughts could turn into persistent mind chatter that stick around and won't leave. And a mind that's addicted to worrying never runs out of material! A worrying mind can always find countless things that could go wrong in the near or far future.

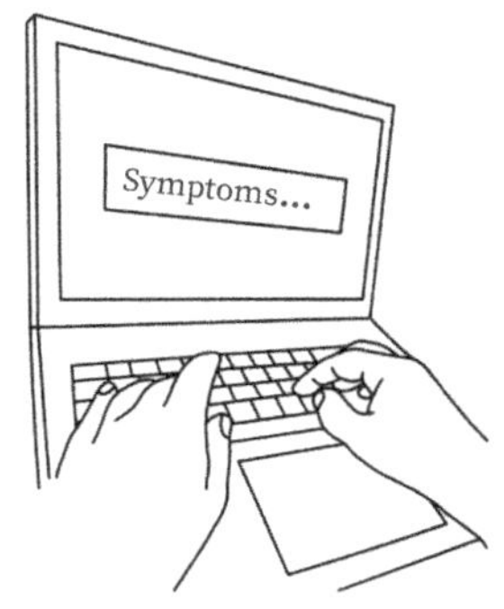

Let's look at an example of unhealthy worrying. Maryam worried about one day being diagnosed with a serious illness. She went to the doctor's for check-ups more often than needed. She also spent a lot of time on the internet, researching different illnesses to make sure she didn't have their symptoms.

Unfortunately, no amount of reassurance from her doctor quite got rid of her worries. Because, deep down, her mind always found a

way to ask questions like 'What if the doctor missed something?', 'What if it's not that problem, but another problem?' and so on.

Here are some errors in Maryam's thinking:

1. When real life problems arise, you're usually given an opportunity to act and do something about them. For example, if Maryam was to contract a serious illness at some point in the future, it would be at that point when she would have a chance to:

   - know the details of her illness

   - learn what treatments are available to her

   - act on her options: receive treatment, work hard and try to get better

   But while worrying about something that hadn't happened yet, none of these options were available to Maryam. Her worries weren't based on a real-life situation. They were based on vague possibilities in some unknown future. She didn't know what illness her future self would supposedly have, if any at all. She didn't know how serious her illness would be or what treatment would be available to her. She could not act as she knew nothing about the supposed illness of her future self. This lack of opportunity to act would have rendered Maryam helpless. This helplessness in some ways makes worrying more uncomfortable than real life problems which we can battle and do something about.

   Please note: at times there are practical things that can be done in the present which could help improve future outcomes. For example, Maryam could learn ways to improve her general health, make better lifestyle choices, use active thinking to create changes to any aspects of her life that may put her at risk of illness and so on. Unfortunately, though, a worrier's 'what if...' thoughts are unlikely to be content with an improvement to chances. Worry thoughts will want a guarantee that nothing bad will happen in the future and, well, usually no one can guarantee that. So if your worry thoughts are not content with an improvement to chances, it is a good idea to do something about them.

2. Let's say you were on a mission to eat a big cake. Which would be easier: to somehow fit the whole cake into your mouth, or to cut it up into smaller pieces and eat one piece at a time? There is great relief in focusing on the present moment. Focusing on the present moment means taking things as they come, in smaller bite sized chunks. It means dealing with just the problems of today, just the challenge that you are faced with right now. People who go about life without excessive worrying have the chance to deal with life's challenges one step at a time, and in smaller, easier to manage sections. But worriers don't give themselves that chance. Worriers tend to see all the possible problems that could happen in the future as a big chunk of 'bad' stuff and as a result they would feel overwhelmed, as if they were trying to manage years' worth of horrible stuff all in one go. In reality, you just need to find a way to get through today - no, in fact, let's step one level closer. You just need to find a way to get through this moment. And then the next. And then the next. Even if you have physical pain,

financial struggles or emotional grief, you just need to get through today this moment.

And when tomorrow comes, tomorrow becomes today and again you just need to deal with today. So in a way, you could say that the future does not exist. Only the present moment exists. The future is only a thought based idea. By focusing on what is happening right now and only right now, you can get through each day and each moment with a lot more ease. When difficult periods come, stay present and soon they will give way to easy, comfortable periods.

When we're in a real battlefield against real life problems, we often develop a strength because we're focused on just what is happening in that moment, while pushing through real life tasks. As a result, we find the strength to deal with every moment as it comes. But when we're worrying, we're not given that same strength and focus. We're trying to eat our big cake all at once. Our focus is on the fear of millions of bad possibilities as if they were all happening at the same time. So we feel overwhelmed, weak, helpless and confused.

3. If you think about it, at the end of the day, all of our fears boil down to one main fear: the fear of suffering, whether it's physical suffering or emotional suffering. Every fear boils down to the fact that we don't want to suffer. An error involved in Maryam's thinking is missing the fact that by constantly focusing on her worries and fears, she was in fact living a life tainted by the very thing that she was hoping to avoid. She was using her fear of one form of suffering (illness) to create

another form of suffering (worry). She didn't have to suffer from illness right now. While she was still healthy, she had the chance to be free from suffering. But unfortunately, her worries meant that she never got a break from suffering. Every day was tainted by it. So can you see the irony? Maryam was creating for herself the very life she was afraid of, a life tainted by constant suffering.

But imagine if Maryam was to make a decision to let go of her worry in this moment, and instead deal with any future problems if and when they arose. This way she could enjoy many calm, anxiety-free moments in her life. Her fears may or may not one day come true. But in the meantime, she could be enjoying life. She could allow her future self to deal with any problems that may arise. Why deal with them now, when they're not real?

4. Yet another error involved in Maryam's thinking is forgetting that her future self is just as capable as her current self in overcoming life challenges and difficulties. Like most people, Maryam had overcome problems in her past and experienced illness and pain. As her challenges were taking place, she was strong and managed to stay focused and get through them. She made decisions and figured out the best course of action. She coped with any pain as it was happening and got through it.

   In fact, if you consider point number 1 on this list, you may agree that her future self would be even more equipped than her current self to deal with any future problems.

   While worrying, we often forget that if problems

were to arise, we would be capable of dealing with them. If you could do it in the past, you can do it again in the future. So why not leave any future problems to your future self and let them go for now?

Tip: if you don't trust your ability to overcome challenges, remember to use emotion exposure around the relevant emotions (these emotions may feel like fear, lack of security, vulnerability or weakness).

Tip: if Maryam worried about her family's capacity to deal with future problems, she could apply most of the above rules to them also. They too could find the strength to cope with difficulties if they focused on being centred in the present moment. So it's best to teach her family to also leave worrying aside, and allow their future selves to find ways to deal with any possible difficulties.

5. Finally, a common thinking error is that worrying is somehow beneficial for us. We think that, for one reason or another, we need to keep worrying in order to survive. Let's explore some of these thoughts and beliefs:

   'Worrying keeps me motivated and pushes me to achieve' – in the long run worrying can in fact lead to exhaustion, tiredness and loss of motivation and drive. A healthy motivation to achieve can exist without worry, as a simple outcome of wishing to live well or achieve your goals. If worry has been your driving force for sometime, you may have lost touch with your real needs or wants. Only by reducing worry and fear will you be able to gradually rediscover the real driving forces within you that can motivate and animate you.

'If I stop worrying something bad will happen' – this is just a thought error, as demonstrated by the many people who live without a tendency to worry, and with no 'bad outcomes'. If you have this belief, test it by observing the worry-free type individuals around you. See if 'bad things' happen to them, any more than they happen to worried people.

'Worry and over thinking will help me solve problems better' – worrying often comes from a place of passive thinking. While worrying, the person often gets entangled with repetitive thoughts, saturated with uncomfortable emotions. They might get confused because they can't focus. As you can see, thinking from a place of constant worry is rarely helpful to problem solving.

Exercise

Maryam's story is similar to the kind of worries that many of us experience. Different people may worry about different things, but the essence of most excessive worrying is the same.

Write down some of the things that you tend to worry about.

.... Ⓟ

....

....

....

....

....

Have a think about the thought errors that we just saw attached to Maryam's worries. Do they apply to your worries?

Now, can you make a conscious decision to let go of your worries? Make a decision to leave future problems to your future self. The future you can deal with them one day at a time. Remember, your future self is just as capable to deal with these as your current self, if not more capable. For now, choose to enjoy life.

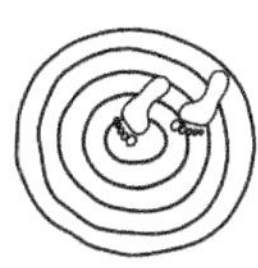

It may be a good time now to practise emotion exposure around the emotions of worry. Keep in mind that at times your mind might tell you that what you're feeling is reality and not an emotion. The key to remember is that if you have pleasant or unpleasant feelings towards any life circumstances, you are feeling an emotion. It doesn't matter how real the circumstances may be. Emotions can come up in reaction to many different things, which includes very real life situations. Such as a friend rejecting you, financial struggles, the loss of a loved one, being fired from a job, conflict with your partner, physical pain and illness and so on. Practising emotion exposure can help you cope better with these real-life situations. If you feel an emotion, regardless of how real the source may be, notice how the body feels and practise emotion exposure. Once the emotion is lifted off, you may find that you can look at your life problem with new insight and an increased ability to cope.

So now, try to think of something that is worrying you at the moment. As you think about it, notice the emotions that come up and place all of your focus on where you feel them. Don't get distracted by all the worry thoughts. Keep your attention on the part of the body where you feel the emotion.

Worry Time

If you still struggle to turn off your worry thoughts, you may have developed a habit of constantly worrying. Habits take a bit of extra time and effort to change. You can't make them disappear overnight. A good exercise to practise is 'worry time'. Worry time can help you break the habit of getting entangled with worry thoughts and stop these thoughts from passively running through your mind all day long. This exercise needs a bit of discipline and focus for a few days. But it will be well worth the effort!

> “Focusing on the present moment means taking things as they come, in smaller bite sized chunks. It means dealing with just the problems of today, just the challenge that you are faced with right now.

Here is how it works: First decide on a time of the day that you can allocate as worry time. During this time, you are allowed to worry as much as you like! However, outside of that time frame, no worry thoughts are allowed. If a worry thought enters your mind, you can write it down or take a mental note of it, and leave it for worry time. This exercise helps you develop the ability to not allow worrying into every moment of your day. It helps you experience moments of relaxation and peace. It helps you quit worrying, just like you would quit smoking or any other habit! And just like quitting smoking, it requires discipline but gets easier as time goes by.

Now take a minute to think about a good time of the day or night that you could allocate to worrying. It can be at the beginning or end of your day, or right in the middle, depending on your lifestyle.

I will practice worry time at this time every day:..........................

You can allocate 15 to 30 minutes (or longer if you prefer) to worrying each day.

The length of time I will allocate to worry time is: ....

Note: *you can adjust the above if, after practising worry time, you decide that your needs are different to what you decided here.*

While having your worry time, try to practise active thinking. You may like to write down your thoughts. After your 15 to 30 minutes is over, bring your attention to your body and practise emotion exposure around any left-over emotions.

Interesting to Consider:

Does practising an exercise like worry time create experiential avoidance (see chapter 2 for a recap on experiential avoidance)?

How is it that we talk about the harmfulness of experiential avoidance, but suggest an exercise that involves saying 'no' to your thoughts at certain times of the day? Well, there is an important difference between the two. When resorting to experiential avoidance, you somewhat lie to yourself. You pretend that your thoughts or emotions don't exist, when in reality they do. You might try to feel emotions that are not true to your current state.

But when you practise worry time, you are not lying to yourself. You acknowledge and notice your thoughts and emotions, but you make a conscious decision that this is not the right time to allow your mind to elaborate and go deeper into these thoughts. You practise mental discipline and decide to come back to the thoughts at a different time. By doing so, you are gradually breaking a harmful habit, the habit of automatic negative thinking. You begin training your mind to do something a little different to usual. Something that perhaps you're not used to doing: taking a break and enjoying life. So, to put it simply, experiential avoidance is being dishonest with yourself, while worry time is training your mind to break out of a harmful habit, while still being honest with yourself.

Fear of Fear

At times, the cause of our anxiety is a fear of our own fears! After one or several uncomfortable experiences with anxiety, some people begin worrying about the possibility of having another anxiety attack. So fear becomes like a cycle that creates and recreates itself.

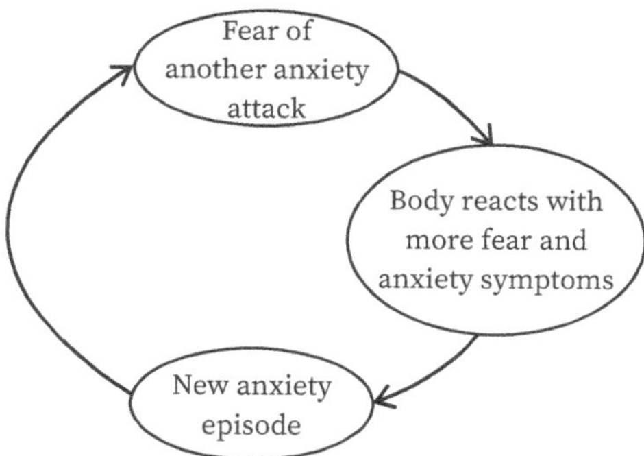

Being afraid of your own thoughts or emotions is the perfect recipe for keeping you in a constant state of anxiety. If you go about your day, constantly having the dread of anxiety on your mind, chances are that you will eventually recreate the experience of anxiety simply through your focus on the concept of 'anxiety' and your fear of it. Your fear of anxiety is the only thing that is causing more and more anxiety attacks. There is no other reason for your repeated anxiety episodes. You may even fight to push away any thoughts about having anxiety attacks all day long. But then we know what happens when we try to fight our own thoughts or emotions: experiential avoidance. Your fear will still be

there, deep down, and it will resurface from time to time. How can you find inner peace if you have to constantly run away from your own thoughts or emotions?

So what's the solution? You probably already know the answer. Just like any other fear, avoidance will not help here. Exposure will. You need to stop 'running' from your own thoughts and emotions and face them! So begin noticing how your body feels when you feel afraid of fear and anxiety. Practise emotion exposure around these emotions.

Once you are ready, you can relax a bit and if anxiety comes, allow it to come in. Remember that this is just an emotion. Notice which parts of the body are impacted by it and practise emotion exposure again. Continue practising this routine. With time, you may notice that your fear subsides, and you spend less and less time thinking about it.

Obsessive Compulsive Tendencies

Obsessive thoughts are persistent and pushy ideas that keep going through your mind, causing you to feel an internal pressure to perform certain actions. For example, if the thought 'have I locked the door to my house?' keeps going through your mind, even though you have checked the door a few times already, you are experiencing obsessive thinking. Or if you feel an internal urge to repeatedly convince yourself of certain worrying ideas or outcomes, almost as if a part of you is setting out to hurt you, you may be experiencing obsessive thinking. These obsessive thoughts might create an internal urge to stick to certain rules, for example to repeatedly wash and clean, count things, or perform various rituals. You may wash your hands several times, but they still don't feel clean enough. You may be assured that certain worries or concerns aren't real, but it still feels right to keep thinking them anyway. It feels like if you stop or break the rules that are dictated by the obsessive thoughts, you risk feeling very uncomfortable, anxious or experiencing other unpleasant emotions like disgust. So you don't break the rules. You just do what the obsessive rules tell you and then you feel better... for now.

At times obsessive thoughts attach themselves to our decision-making processes. Just as obsessive thoughts cause you to wash your hands many times and still wonder if they're unclean, or check the lock many times and it still feel like it may not be locked, for some people decision making becomes an obsessive process. No matter how many times they have gone through all the options and outcomes in their head, they still feel as though they need to check everything again. What if they are about to make a mistake?! So they go through a never ending loop of checking and rechecking all the facts, all the options, all the consequences. And they never seem to be quite happy with any decision. Because let's face it, there is always the possibility of making a mistake. No one can guarantee the future. So they feel stifled and can't go forward. Notice how this is also a form of obsessive thinking.

Those of you who have experienced obsessive tendencies know exactly what we are talking about here. Those of you who haven't, can use the contents of this section to learn about friends or family members who do experience these tendencies. But as always, don't pressure them to overcome their fears. Instead, you could encourage them to seek help or read this book for themselves.

Just as with other fears and anxieties, we may try to soothe the uncomfortable emotions resulting from obsessive thinking using avoidance. We avoid discomfort by doing exactly what it is that these thoughts are telling us to do: check the lock, clean, count, believe in the worries or repeat whatever ritual we feel we need to repeat. But just like it is with other fears, avoidance is extremely unhelpful to the process of healing obsessive compulsive thoughts. In fact, constantly giving into everything that these thoughts demand may lead to the obsessive compulsive tendencies getting stronger or impacting new areas of our lives over time. Just as we said about fear of fear, being afraid of our own thoughts is the perfect recipe for keeping us in a constant state of anxiety. We can't find inner peace if we have to keep running away from our own thoughts or emotions.

Exposure therapy is an effective method for combating obsessive compulsive tendencies. The answer is not to keep these thoughts quiet by immediately giving them everything that they demand and never breaking the rules they have set for us. The answer is to stop avoiding, and practise gradual exposure, even if in the immediate sense it is not comfortable.

If you suffer from obsessive and compulsive tendencies, take a moment to create a gradual and practical exposure plan. Here are some ideas you could try:

– Take a bit longer than usual before you perform the task, so that you get a chance to face the emotions that it brings up. For example, before you rush off to wash your hands, take a moment to sit with the emotions that result from your unclean hands. Don’t worry, you can wash your hands after this.

- Imagine the possibility of not performing the task. Again, don't worry, this is just an imaginary exercise, you don't have to push yourself beyond your limits. You are just considering that possibility in your mind in order to give yourself a chance to sit with the emotions that come up.

Keep practising these exercises on a regular basis and don't give up if it takes a while to notice any change. Exposure will gradually help you feel calmer and less stressed by the obsessive thoughts.

Active thinking is another helpful tool for combating obsessive compulsive tendencies. Taking the time to actively explore and understand your own thoughts, beliefs or concerns related to the obsessive compulsive tendencies may help you see the situation differently and develop a new perspective. Although this new perspective may be on a purely logical level at first and may not create any immediate changes to your emotions or behaviour. The strong emotions, such as anxiety or disgust, which you may be feeling are in the body and you may need to practice emotion exposure to help shift them overtime.

What might also be helpful to consider is that your obsessive compulsive tendencies may have at first originated from very legitimate concerns, but that the intensity of the emotions that have been generated around those legitimate concerns have now resulted in unhelpful patterns that are harming you, rather than benefiting you. For example, your need to clean excessively may have started from a need to protect yourself from certain environmental contaminants. But now, this need is no longer serving your health and may even be harming it, for example, through the excessive stress that it's causing you or a dermatitis on your hands which have resulted from washing your hands too much.

You can begin the process of active thinking or planning your exposure therapy steps by making some notes below:

.... Ⓟ

....

....

....

Posttraumatic Stress

At times, when people undergo a traumatic experience, they may notice some changes to their thoughts and emotions in the aftermath. First, let's see what we mean by trauma. Trauma can include any experiences that are deeply distressing or disturbing, or that threaten your safety. Examples are experiences of war, assault, motor vehicle accidents or any form of abuse. Some symptoms that you may experience following trauma are:

- Mental flashbacks to what happened or vivid memories of the event, as if it is happening again in your mind
- Nightmares or insomnia
- Fear and anxiety

- Strong emotions in the body
- Issues with memory or concentration

These symptoms might last for only a short period of time, while you are still processing what happened. But they could also turn into a long term issue, and our old friend, experiential avoidance, plays an unhelpful role here. Experiential avoidance means that you are now stuck in a never-ending loop. The more you try to forget or push away the memories, the more they try to come back to you. You may start experiencing an urge to constantly keep busy or distract yourself because you need to try so hard to not let in the uncomfortable memories and emotions.

Remember the story of Jasmine and the monster in the box? The memories of your traumatic experience, along with the uncomfortable emotions that come with it, may feel like a monster that you need to keep avoiding. But you can start small and gradual. There is no need to overwhelm yourself. Start by practising emotion exposure on a regular basis, as you notice any emotions that are related to your trauma. Or when you have bad dreams. Allow your body to gradually guide you into processing the memories. Allowing your body and dreams to guide you is a good idea, as it will make it easier to process your memories at a pace that you are ready to process.

Also remember to practise active thinking, write down your thoughts and explore alternatives to any thought errors you find. What did the trauma do to the way that you see the world or yourself?

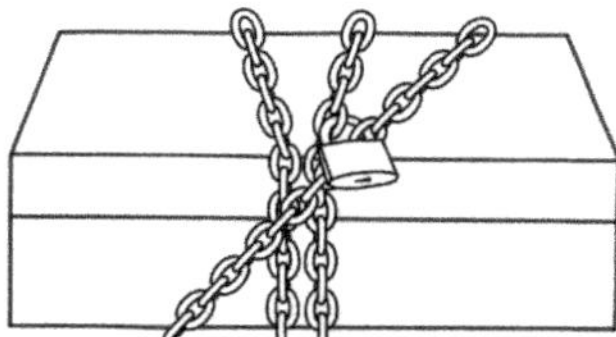

This process may take some time. There is no rush, take it one day at a time. Your goal is not to forget or wipe those memories. That won't be possible or helpful. Your goal is to change your relationship with those memories, to be able to remember without experiencing strong emotions. To be able to remember them as memories that belong to the past, and nothing else.

You can begin the process of active thinking around your memories of trauma by making some notes below. Remember not to overwhelm yourself, and start with smaller, easier steps:

....Ⓟ

....

....

....

....

....

....

A Good Place

Let's finish this section by once again visiting the 'good place', which you created in chapter 4. Consider the following question:

If you had a magic wand that could suddenly take you to a place where there would be no pain, suffering, anguish, stress or anxiety, what would it look like? What would be its characteristics? Now let your imagination go free. Enjoy this place, explore it. Get to know it. This place can be realistic or abstract. Create it however you like it! Take your time.

Now bring your attention back to your body. If you are feeling any uncomfortable emotions at this stage, practise emotion exposure for some time.

Chapter 9: Task Management

Revision

Decide if the following statements are true or false.

The best way to combat obsessive thoughts is to avoid the uncomfortable situations that trigger them.

True ☐

False ☐

Incessant worrying can help us deal better with future problems and emergencies.

True ☐

False ☐

Your future self is a lot better equipped to deal with future problems. So, allowing your current self to worry about unknown future scenarios is a waste of your time and energy.

True ☐

False ☐

By worrying, you experience suffering on a daily basis. This is ironic, since we often worry because we don't want to suffer.

True ☐

False ☐

Task Management

For many people, unfinished tasks, unachieved goals and work that never seems to end are great sources of stress. If you find that unfinished work is forever competing with your drive for life, happiness and life satisfaction, this chapter is for you.

You finally have a day off. A day to yourself. Except that, taking one quick look around your life, here is what is staring you in the face:

> That messy cabinet that you never organised
>
> Those friends and family members you needed to contact and never did
>
> That job you wanted to apply for
>
> That course you wanted to study

And so on. Of course, these are all in the 'too hard basket' and there is no chance of you doing any work towards them. Yet they are always 'there', reducing the joy in your spare time.

Today's chapter is about clearing the clutter in your life, about getting those pesky old jobs done, so that you can make room for peace and happiness. Take a moment to make a list of all the things cluttering your life - all your unfinished tasks and unachieved goals:

....

....

....

....

Reassess Your Goals

First, let us spend some time reassessing the items on your list. Many of the goals in your life may have been a result of fears, concerns or needs that you had before you started this book. For example, some of your goals may have resulted from:

- Various thought errors
- Lack of acceptance
- Fears created by living in a world of comparisons, competition and a need to finally become 'good enough'
- Fear of being judged negatively by others
- Past emotions that you have now processed and cleared

And so on. Since we started this book, you have come a long way, learning about yourself and in many ways shifting your views of the world around you and within you. So, a lot of the emotions and thinking errors that influenced your goals in the past may no longer be there. Use your skills in active thinking to reassess each of the goals on your list: ask yourself, will pursuing this goal help to improve my life or the lives of those around me? If there are goals that no longer apply, cross them off your list. Your peace of mind and happiness are important. So, don't be afraid to get rid of unhelpful goals, and notice how much lighter you feel as a result!

If you notice that unhelpful emotions are still making it difficult to let go of certain unnecessary or unwanted tasks, close your eyes and practise emotion exposure around those emotions.

Understanding the Barriers

So, what causes so many people to end up with such an annoying build-up of incomplete tasks and unachieved goals? The answer is simple: passive thinking! How does passive thinking lead to this? Let's demonstrate with a story:

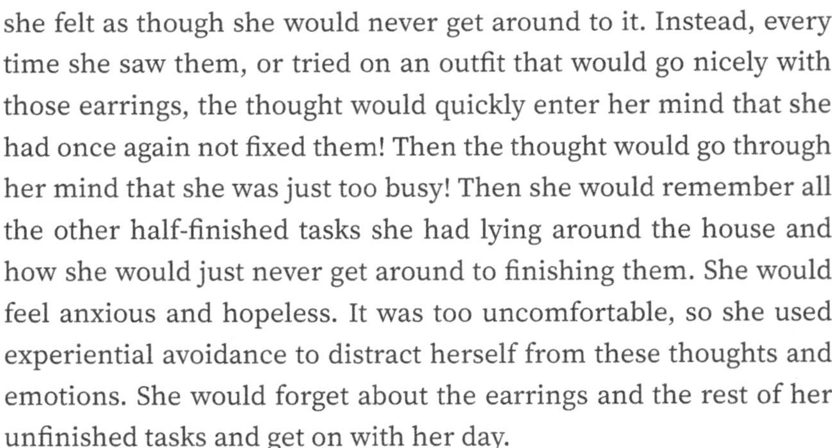

Ashley had a pair of diamante earrings. They were her favourite pair. Unfortunately, a few of the diamantes had fallen off and needed to be glued back on. She knew she needed to eventually glue them on as she wasn't willing to say goodbye to her favourite earrings!

However, being a busy person, she felt as though she would never get around to it. Instead, every time she saw them, or tried on an outfit that would go nicely with those earrings, the thought would quickly enter her mind that she had once again not fixed them! Then the thought would go through her mind that she was just too busy! Then she would remember all the other half-finished tasks she had lying around the house and how she would just never get around to finishing them. She would feel anxious and hopeless. It was too uncomfortable, so she used experiential avoidance to distract herself from these thoughts and emotions. She would forget about the earrings and the rest of her unfinished tasks and get on with her day.

One day, Ashley decided to start practising active thinking and actually look at why she was not getting around to fixing the earrings. She found a few interesting points:

1. Ashley realised that fixing the earrings would actually take no longer than a minute or two. In reality, this did not have to place a large strain on her time, and she could easily manage it. In her passive thinking mode, she had turned this into a difficult mountain of a task, while in reality it was far from it!

2. She then realised that in her passive thinking mode, she had also ignored the fact that she needed to set some short-term goals to get the task done. More specifically, she needed to buy the glue next time she was at the supermarket! It was simple. She just added the glue to her shopping list for next time she was in the shops.

3. Once the glue was purchased, she simply needed to schedule a time to glue on the diamantes, rather than constantly feeling guilty and anxious about it. She could easily find a few minutes to do that.

4. Ashley realised that most of the items on her list were similar to this one: they just required a bit of active thinking and simple planning. Getting them done, though, made a massive difference to the quality of her life.

5. Perhaps, most importantly, Ashley needed to focus on one task at a time to avoid feeling overwhelmed. Each of the tasks on her list were simple enough to do. But when Ashley thought of all of them at the same time, they seemed unachievable. You see, in her passive thinking mode, Ashley was missing the fact that she needed to do the tasks on her list one at a time. So why was it that when she looked at them collectively, she felt that they all needed to be done at the same time and right there and

then? It's like standing at the bottom of a ladder and thinking 'how on earth will I jump all the way to the top?' Well, you don't have wings and can't jump all the way to the top! So the task can feel impossible. But you don't need to jump all the way to the top. You just need to take one step. Then the next step. Then the next step. Before you know it, you will be at the top! So, when looking at large, overwhelming jobs, remind yourself that you only need to do one task. And then another. And then another.

Understanding Goals

Some of our goals are important and time consuming, like achieving a career dream. Others are small and humble, like cleaning up the pantry, or filling in that one page application form that's been sitting on your desk for the past few months. Regardless of the size of your goals, it's a good idea to learn about them and know how to manage them.

There are two types of goals. Distal goals and proximal goals. Distal goals are bigger overall goals, which are more long term. Proximal goals are the smaller steps needed to achieve a distal goal. Proximal goals are practical and immediate, and pave the way for the distal goal to be achieved. For example, if your goal is to organise a dinner party with your friends and family, these would be your distal and proximal goals:

Distal:

to organise an enjoyable dinner party with good food

Proximal:

to invite the guests

to decide how much food is needed to feed all the guests

to decide on a budget

to decide what food will be served

to shop for all the ingredients

to set up the dining area

Both distal and proximal goals are important and necessary. Distal goals give us hope and motivation to work through hard or boring tasks. They provide direction and stop us from becoming distracted. This means that by showing us the end goal, they stop us from jumping from one thing to another. Proximal goals, on the other hand, provide the means to attain the distal goal. They are small and achievable. Without proximal goals, the distal goal is nothing but a dream. Below is an example to show the importance of both distal and proximal goals.

Lee wanted to become a personal trainer. Here's why he needed to pay attention to both his distal and proximal goals:

- **The distal goal** was needed to remind Lee what his ultimate aim was. If he had forgotten about his distal goal, he may have jumped from one thing to another with no real direction and spent his time focusing on many unrelated things. Maybe he would stop training or let go of his goal altogether. But Lee knew that the classes he enrolled in and plans he made, were to ultimately pave the way for him to become a good personal trainer. Thinking of his ultimate goal also gave him hope and energy to tolerate the challenges along the way and stay focused.

- **The proximal goals** were there to tell Lee what he needed to do on each given day. They helped him realise each of the steps needed to achieve the distal goal. For example, he knew that, on a certain day, he would have to pick up the phone and enrol in a personal training course, or, at another time, he needed to read a book about sports science.

Unfortunately, passive thinking often means that we don't have clear distal or proximal goals. We may have no distal goal at all, or a distal goal that is not clear enough. This means that our thoughts around what we want to achieve in the long-run are confused or full of contradictions. Passive thinking can also result in a broken, incomplete or non-existent proximal plan. That's exactly what we saw in Ashley's story. Passive thinking had caused Ashley to not think through her proximal goals clearly, so she wasn't able to put them into action to fix her earrings.

Now return to your own list and identify your distal and proximal goals. As you think about your proximal plans, allocate them to certain times or days, where possible. For example, you may write something like:

'I need to organise my paperwork cabinet. This is a distal goal. Below are the proximal steps needed to achieve it:

1. Dedicate Thursday afternoon to this task

2. Buy paper folders first thing in the morning
3. Divide up the cabinet into smaller subsections
4. Allocate groups of documents to the relevant subsections

Give it a go with your own list now.

....Ⓟ

....

....

....

....

....

Take a minute, close your eyes and see if you can make a conscious decision to put in the hard work towards decluttering your life. It may be hard work to begin with, but wouldn't it be nice to no longer have that list competing with your peace of mind and relaxation?

Emotions and Task Management

Overwhelming goals, incomplete tasks and work in general can be common causes of strong, uncomfortable emotions for many people. We often have unpleasant emotions attached to our to-do lists. And since humans like to avoid uncomfortable emotions, we tend to avoid our to-do lists!

Here are some common thoughts that can come up when we look at our to-do lists:

I'm not good enough.

I'm a failure.

This is too hard.

I'm too tired.

I can't do it.

There is too much to do here. It will never end.

I don't know where to start.

I hate doing this task.

And of course, with these thoughts, there will often come a range of emotions. Remember, when you dislike doing something, you are also feeling an emotion towards it. So, whenever you feel that you don't like doing a task, treat it like an emotion in the body.

Close your eyes, notice the emotions that you feel around your to-do list. Do you feel these emotions somewhere in your body? Practise emotion exposure around them. Take your time. Remember, your job is to just stay with the emotion and feel it. Not to try to fix it, control it or soothe it. As uncomfortable as it may be, avoid the temptation to push it away. Keep your attention still.

Now take another look at your to-do list. Notice if any other emotions come up. If so, close your eyes and practise emotion exposure again. Repeat this a few times.

Reward Yourself

Another point to remember is that it's a good idea to include a reward for yourself as you achieve more and more of your goals. Rewarding yourself will help with creating motivation and discipline. In the long run, it can help with creating more positive feelings towards work. So, don't skip this step. Feeling good is important.

Imagine being a parent trying to teach your child to clean up their room every day. Sure, you could motivate them with pressure or negative emotions like 'clean up your room because it's your responsibility', or 'clean up because I said so', or 'clean up, otherwise I'll take away something you like'. These methods may work. But can you see how, in the long run, they don't do anything to make your child actually like their chores or want to do them? Now imagine saying to them that something they like doing, like their TV time or their favourite snack would be the reward for doing their daily cleaning. If done right, this method can help create a bit of excitement around getting the chore done and reaping the reward. All of a sudden, the joy of the outcome overshadows the difficulty of the work. You can go one level further and even turn the work into a game or a fun challenge. The more positive emotions you manage to associate with the work or the outcome, the more success you can expect to have with your child.

Now imagine that you are both that child and the parent. You are going to pick some of the things you enjoy and use them as rewards each time you achieve a goal. For example, if you want to get 30 minutes of exercise each morning, schedule the exercise right before having a relaxing cup of tea and reading your morning news. Now act as a fun, kind and assertive parent who will enforce this discipline. Looking forward to that cup of tea becomes the reward that pushes you through the challenge of the exercise. Before you know it, you may enjoy the exercise enough that it becomes a reward in itself. But to get to that point, you may need a secondary reward to push you through the physical discomfort and mental resistance. Remember the person in our earlier story who was organising their paperwork cabinet? They could reward themselves with a favourite TV show after they have achieved their goals for the day.

Now return to your list and decide on rewards for yourself wherever you see fit.

Tip: Make sure your reward is in proportion with the size of the task you give yourself. A one-hour break may be a good enough reward after a morning of chores. But it may fall short if it's the only reward you give yourself after weeks of hard work. At the end of the day, you are the best judge. Just remember that your reward should excite you enough that you see a light at the end of the tunnel of your hard work. It should instil hope and joy.

An important point to remember: From time to time, it is important that you take another look at your list and review your achievements. You may have had success with some items on your list. But there may be items that need more work, meaning that your proximal goals may need to be improved, a better schedule may need to be planned or a different strategy may need to be tried.

Please also remember: Your success in completing your list is not about a perfect plan every time. It is about your willingness to try, fail at times, and then try a different approach. What determines your success is your determination and willingness to keep going and not give up.

Plan

So, you are planning to study, organise your tax, prepare to give a speech to your community group, clear the clutter in your house, write a short story, or complete a work project. But every time you approach the task, you feel overwhelmed, you don't know where to start, your mind gets flooded with so many ideas, or no ideas at all. Eventually you leave the task and begin procrastinating.

There is one common mistake that can lead to this problem: poor planning. Or often no planning at all. We are often in such a rush to start the job that we forget to take a minute to think. We don't practise active thinking around what we need to do and how we need to do it. Plan before you do anything else. If you can help it, don't even approach your desk, workstation or study area until you have done some planning in your head or on a piece of paper. The importance of planning may seem obvious, but many people fail to start or complete their goals because they overlook the planning stage. Here are some tips to help you with this step:

1. **Actively think about your main objectives** - Write them down

on a piece of paper if you need to. For example, if you are planning a speech, write down the main points that you are hoping to communicate to your audience. If you are organising your pantry, take a good look at all the food items that need to be organised. Break it down into smaller parts or steps.

2. **Decide on the order of what needs to be done** - Sometimes a bit of active thinking will help you prioritise those things that need to be done first. For example, Ashley needed to buy the glue before she could fix her earrings. It may seem obvious, but passive thinking means that she was missing this obvious fact.

   But at other times, there is no clear order of priority. In that case, it wouldn't matter too much which of the items on your list you start off with. What would be the best item to start off with in those cases? The simple answer is to start with the task that gives you joy. Start with the task that you feel like doing the most. Why is that? Because doing this creates the least resistance, it's the step that gives you the most motivation, it's the step that generates the energy you need to get through. While doing this, try to stay in the present moment and not worry too much about the other tasks. Because at some point during this process you will probably be able to identify the next task you feel like doing, the next step that motivates you. The same could happen for the other items on your list. You may find that a task that at one point didn't motivate or inspire you, will do so at a later stage. So why not go with the flow of your inspiration and motivation so that you can journey through your to-do list with more ease and positive emotions.

3. **Notice when your attention wanders off** - if you notice an urge to procrastinate, you have most likely just hit an obstacle. Our automatic reaction to obstacles is often avoidance. But if you are aware of this, you can choose to react differently to the obstacles from now on! Catch yourself in the act, and instead of avoiding, pay attention to the obstacle that you have just faced. Write down what the obstacle is if you need to. Then practise active thinking around it: are there any ways to deal with this obstacle? Is there someone you can talk to, to bounce ideas off, or to get some advice from? Or perhaps you can take a completely different approach and see the task at hand from a different angle. Focus on the obstacle for as long as it takes to resolve it. Writing or talking to a friend could help you with active thinking here. If a solution doesn't come to you easily, it doesn't mean that you have to give up. Or if it's not necessary to get this part of your work done right now, leave it for a later time and focus on another area of your work. If your obstacle is an emotional one, don't forget to practise emotion exposure.

> “ **Plan before you do anything else. If you can help it, don't even approach your desk, workstation or study area until you have done some planning in your head or on a piece of paper.**

Practise the above steps next time you need to plan for a task.

Mindfulness in Work and Study

Many of us can relate to the story of the following student. Grace has an exam in two days' time. She needs to get through a thick text book and has a long way to go. She's feeling stressed. Every few minutes, she looks at how much more there is to do, checks all the unfinished tasks and feels overwhelmed. She then tries to return to the page she was reading, but the feeling of anxiety makes it hard for her to concentrate. Grace is experiencing worry due to not focusing on the present moment.

Today Grace decides to do things differently: She first practises emotion exposure on her worry and anxiety. As we learned in the previous chapter, the solution to worry is to focus on the present moment, and to leave the future to your future self. So, Grace reminds herself that she will achieve the best results by focusing on the present page, and not thinking too much about all the other pages that need to be studied. She will get to them one at a time. Each time her attention begins to wander off to her unfinished tasks, she gently brings it back to the task at hand. Over and over again. Before long, Grace begins to develop an interest in the topic she is reading about and this increases her focus and speed. She achieves a lot more today.

Let's practise the skill of focusing on the task of the present moment, rather than worrying about the future. You have 1 minute to draw one hundred circles in the blank space provided. Even though your time is limited, your aim is to stay focused on only the circle that you are drawing at each given moment, as opposed to worrying about running out of time. Please note that planning and worrying are not the same. You can plan your time, but then calmly focus on just the present moment. Worrying is emotional and causes you to have less focus on the present moment. In this exercise, planning can help you decide how much time you have for each circle, or how fast you need to draw. But as you draw at whatever speed you need to, you can be completely focused on the circle that you are drawing.

This may need a bit of practice. Initially, you may notice your mind wandering to thoughts like 'I'm running out of time!', 'What if I fall behind?' and so on. If you notice similar thoughts, gently bring your attention back to the circle you are drawing. In that moment, no other circles exist. Okay, are you ready? Let's start!

Use a kitchen timer or the timer function on your phone. Set it for one minute and go! Ⓕ

How did you find this task? Did you manage to focus on only one circle at a time? Could you relax and enjoy the process? Now can you see how the same principle can be applied to washing the dishes, sweeping the floor, watering the garden, studying for a test or any other task?

Activity Ⓕ

Now grab a piece of paper and create a banner to place near your workplace, be it by your computer, in your workshop, in the kitchen or in your toolbox, to remind yourself to practise mindfulness as you work.

Mindful Walking

Let's begin the process of mindful living and working by doing a gentle walking exercise. Stand up, find some space in the room and begin walking around. As you walk around the room, become mindfully aware of the feelings in your body. Notice the sensation of your feet touching the ground, and then lifting off. Notice the feeling of your muscles tensing and relaxing. Notice the air moving against your skin. Every little sensation as you walk. Try to maintain mindful awareness for as long as you can.

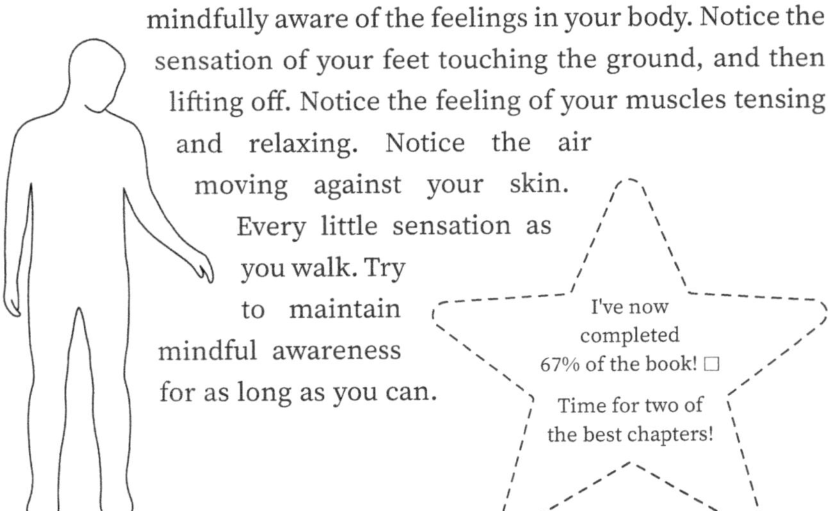

Chapter 10: Communication

Revision

Close your eyes and remember what you learned in the previous chapter, as well as how you've gone with practising it since. Don't pressure yourself to remember everything. Just allow the remembering to naturally happen at its own pace.

Islands

> In this chapter, we will be using the word 'partner' from time to time. Please note that what we mean by 'partner' here is anyone that you might communicate with. This includes your family members, friends, co-workers or community members.

Today we will learn about relationships and about healing them through healthy communication. Relationships are important to our mental health. Do you feel that you live in a compassionate, warm world where you are connected with others? Do you feel that you can be who you are and still be safe in your relationships? Or do you feel isolated, alone and disconnected from others around you? Communication is an important tool that can help us make our relationships healthier and more secure.

Imagine an ocean full of little unique but isolated islands. Each island is separated from the other islands by large bodies of water. Those who live on the islands have no real way of knowing what the other islands are like. They can assume and imagine, but they can't truly experience it. They look at the other islands as lands full of mystery and unknowns. Until, one day, someone invents a boat! The boat helps these people to travel across the ocean to the other islands and get a glimpse of what they are really like. No more assuming and imagining, but a closer experience of the reality of the other islands!

Each one of us is like one of those islands. And the boat is communication. Without communication, the other islands remain a mystery. We might feel isolated and alone. We might fear the other islands or think they are very different to us. We rely on our assumptions and imagination when trying to understand what those islands are really like. Are they friendly or not? Are they beautiful happy places? Or lands full of anger, aggression and suffering? Will they welcome me or hurt me, if I approach them? At times we imagine the worst. But it's through communication that we can finally get a glimpse of what's really on the other islands. We don't need to imagine or assume any more. We can understand the reality of the islands around us.

What is communication? It's the process of sharing our thoughts, emotions, needs or other information with others. Communication can be through talking, but it can also happen through body language, tone of voice, writing, art, music and so on. It's what connects us with every living being around us. When a baby cries to show that they need something, when a dog wags its tail in excitement, when a cat raises its tail to show friendliness or when your angry neighbour throws his hands in the air in protest - these are all forms of communication. Whether or not we are interested in communicating with others, we are continually sending messages to them in many different forms and so we are, in effect, communicating. But the most complex form of communication is through the use of language. Words can help us communicate very complex ideas. They can also create misunderstanding and confusion. This is why we will be focusing on mastering the art of language-based communication in the next two chapters.

Sifters and Moulders

When it comes to attitudes towards relationships, there are two types of people: Sifters and Moulders.

Sifters spend their lives looking for people they can trust. People who won't make mistakes. People who won't hurt them. They sift through relationships, testing, checking, and being disappointed each time a behaviour suggests that a person isn't to be trusted or doesn't care about them. They then disconnect from that person and move on to another. Sadly, sooner or later, most relationships disappoint the sifter. There are two main reasons for this:

1. **No relationship is perfect** - when people are under the influence of emotions and thought errors, they can act in ways that can hurt others. In an emotional state, people see the world through the lenses of their emotions. So they act in ways that they normally wouldn't.

2. **Misunderstandings are very, very common in relationships** - they are much more common than most of us realise. People are very different from one another. Behaviours and words mean different things to different people. When we interpret

other people's behaviour using our own world view, we miss what they actually mean, feel or intend. Without effective communication these misunderstandings can stay hidden and never be resolved. We can go through our lives and never even find out about them.

So sadly, sifters can often feel lonely and disappointed or struggle to trust others. At times, they may give up on relationships altogether.

Moulders focus on improving relationships through communication. They put in the hard work to gradually mould their relationships into the healthy happy connections that they desire. By working on the quality of their relationships, they learn about themselves and about others. They see people as essentially good, and see their behaviour as the result of complex processes of thoughts and emotions. So they seek to understand others. Using reasoning and communication they try to find common ground with others. As a rule of thumb, moulders don't give up on relationships too easily. When possible, they try to make relationships work. They don't expect relationships to be perfect or free from issues. So moulders have a better chance of ending up with deep, meaningful and fulfilling relationships in their lives.

Note: to be a moulder doesn't guarantee that you can salvage every relationship. Communication is a two-way process. Which means that both parties need to be willing to communicate and work on the relationship. People are free to choose and make decisions. You can only decide to do your part. The other person's decision is theirs to make. So, they might decide that they don't wish to communicate or mould the relationship into a healthier one. If that's the case, it's important for you to be accepting of the other person's ultimate decision. The reality is that if, at the end of the day, the other person has no interest in communicating with you to improve your relationship, and if staying within the relationship in its current form is harming you, then it's okay to sift. It's okay to disconnect from that person, until and unless they decide to give your relationship a chance at some point in the future. In the meantime, the best you can do, if you get a chance, is to gently educate them about the rules of healthy relationships. Sometimes, people do change over time. So it's okay to give people another chance. The rule of thumb is, work hard to improve your relationships. But if the other person is not willing to allow communication, then it is okay to choose your happiness and walk away.

Also note: moulding doesn't mean that you give the same energy and attention to every relationship. We all have limited time and energy. It's natural to work harder at moulding those relationships that are closer to our heart, or the relationship with those people that for various reasons we have to interact with more often.

Putting it into Practice

What makes people sift, rather than mould? Why would people rather end relationships than try to improve them? You guessed it. It's usually because of our old friend again: Avoidance! Communication can be difficult, emotional and uncomfortable. Sometimes we don't want to hear what the other person really thinks, or we don't want to share our thoughts with them, and we know that humans usually like to avoid uncomfortable things. But just like the areas we've looked at in the previous chapters, avoiding communication causes us harm in the long run. So it's best to manage our emotions using the methods we've learned in this course, instead of resorting to avoidance and sifting.

Let's practise this a bit now. First, write a list of some of the people in your life that you need to communicate with for one reason or another. You may need to communicate about big issues, like the overall quality of your relationship with your partner or parents. Or, it could be about a small irritation, like the fact that your roommate keeps leaving the bathroom lights on.

.... Ⓟ

....

....

....

....

....

Now consider communicating with one or several of the people on your list. You can use your imagination to picture yourself communicating with them. Are any negative emotions coming up? Any emotions that would make you avoid or delay communicating? These emotions could feel like dread, fear, anxiety, anger, shame and so on. Where do you feel these emotions in your body? Close your eyes and practise emotion exposure around them.

At this stage, please don't concern yourself too much with how to communicate, or what to say, or not to say. We'll learn about this later. For now, just concentrate on the emotions in your body.

Once again, imagine communicating with these people. Are any uncomfortable emotions coming up again? Close your eyes and practise emotion exposure one more time.

Please continue working on these emotions if needed. Every time you feel it's important to communicate with someone in your life, but you notice emotions causing you to avoid or delay it, remember to practise emotion exposure. Once those emotions are alleviated, you may find it a lot easier to begin communicating with those people.

An Art

Communication is an art and should be treated as such. Just like playing the piano or painting, there is always room to perfect your art. And just like creating art, if you use your creativity, patience, active thinking and attention to detail, you can create a more delightful outcome! At times there may be no simple or straightforward way of communicating with someone. So treat it as a creative art project. Use your creativity to find innovative ways to communicate.

Also, just like mastering an art, there may be some hard work needed at certain stages. You may need to learn certain skills and may need to try - and when you don't succeed, try again. But in the end, as your hard work pays off, communication can result in a more enjoyable life with more meaningful relationships. So it is worth the effort!

The 3 Relationship Types

What makes some relationships healthy and long lasting, and others fragile or full of problems? What types of communication are healthy? What types tend to be problematic? Below are 3 types of relationships:

Type 1 – no communication

Type 2 – ineffective communication

Type 3 – effective communication

Let's learn more about each.

Type 1

In this type of relationship people don't communicate anything that might make them feel vulnerable, or cause conflict or confrontation. Sure, they might communicate normal day to day things like the weather or what's been on the news with no problems. But when it comes to issues like being hurt by the other person's behaviour, or having any criticism towards them, they don't communicate. If the other person does anything to offend them, they don't say anything. If the other person breaks their trust, they don't say anything. If they disagree about certain things, they don't say anything. This means that the relationship looks calm and peaceful on the surface. Everyone seems to get along.

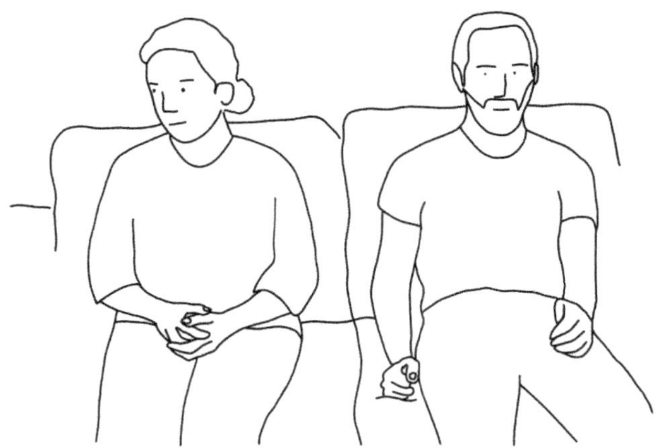

As we learned earlier, misunderstandings are very common and, unfortunately, people in this relationship type rarely get a chance to clear their misunderstandings with one another. So deep down, people are developing grudges, feeling hurt or resentful. Over time, this can result in a gradual loss of affection for one another. They grow apart and stop caring about each other. At times, all of this may be silently happening for one person, while the other person does not have the faintest idea that there is anything wrong. They may think that everything is going perfectly well in the relationship.

But then one day, they suddenly get a huge shock as they become aware of the festering problems in their partner's mind that are now deep and beyond repair. So, if you think that by not communicating, you are protecting the other person, think again.

When your partner finally finds out about your anger, resentment or loss of affection, they will be far more hurt than if they had heard earlier on about their little habits that were getting on your nerves. You're not doing them a favour by keeping them in the dark.

In this type of relationship, our isolated islands never end up reaching the other islands and actually seeing what they're like. People who don't communicate, often assume what it's like to be on the other islands. Assumption is all they have to go by. And assumption is often far from reality. And since at times they have been hurt by those other islands, they may develop a general mistrust towards people.

Why do people become type 1 communicators? There are many reasons:

- **Fear of confrontation** - they may have strong negative emotions around confrontation. These could be emotions like fear, dread, anxiety or shame. If this is a blockage to communication for you, practising emotion exposure and using your active thinking can help you gather more courage to communicate. Face your fear one little step at a time.
- **Keeping peace** - they may have a belief that staying away from conflict and disagreements is the best way to have trouble-free relationships. We have now learned that lack of communication might seem to create more peaceful relationships in the short term, but causes relationship breakdowns in the long term. So, if this is a blockage to communication for you, reminding yourself of this principle may help.
- **Culture and norms** - it could be because of cultural factors and

social conventions. Often the society around us tells us what's okay to do and what isn't. And if confrontation and conflict are not considered socially okay, you might find it particularly difficult to act against the social norms. Culture and tradition can offer us wonderful things.

But if parts of tradition no longer lead to a healthy and happy life for people and the community, would it be okay to change those parts? Could you use the principles of active thinking to bring your culture more in line with what's beneficial for the health of your mind? After all, what is culture? Culture and tradition are a result of hundreds of years of thinking by many people before us. And we know that thoughts can have errors in them.

So, if cultural norms make it difficult to communicate in a healthy way, perhaps you can be a leader in gently bringing in change, by encouraging people to speak to each other. Start by speaking to those around you who are more open to change. Practise healthy communication whenever you find a chance. At times, change can happen slowly. We need to be patient. What is important is that we don't give up!

Type 2

In the 2nd type of relationship, people appear to talk about their differences. But problems don't seem to go away. The same old issues and arguments come up over and over again. So, if people are communicating, why is nothing improving? Why are the islands not growing closer to each other? The answer is that even though communication appears to be taking place here, the focus of it is in the wrong place. Healthy communication should be focused on increasing understanding between the islands. But what if, instead, the communication is focused on quickly feeling better by acting out your anger, resentment or hurt feelings? What if the focus becomes your need to quickly feel better by behaving in the way that your unhelpful emotions are telling you to behave? Unfortunately, this may result in the islands going to war, rather than growing closer to each other. Emotionally driven communication includes blame, hurting back, harsh criticisms, threats, defensiveness, or blocking. Let's learn a bit about them:

- **Blame** is when we are focused on trying to find whose fault it is and showering them with our anger, instead of trying to understand all parties and focusing on a solution.
- **Hurting back** is acting on those angry feelings that want you to hurt the other person. At times this is through physical violence. At other times it's through being emotionally hurtful. You might say things that you know are hurtful to the other person. Or do things to get back at them. At times we might use subtle means like hurtful humour or sarcasm.

- **Harsh criticisms** are also a form of hurting back. Criticisms are okay, if they are made with compassion. If we take care not to attack the other person. Criticism should be used sparingly and only when necessary. If it's important and necessary to criticise someone, it's best to take every care to use gentle words, and to combine your criticism with positive, encouraging statements. But when criticism is used as a way to relieve emotions like anger or resentment, we often don't concern ourselves with how they will impact the other person. We use criticism as punishment. So emotions can make us criticise harshly or unnecessarily.

- **Defensiveness** is about relieving emotions like shame or hurt. The problem with defensiveness is that it causes us to ignore an important goal of communication, which is understanding the other person better. When we are defensive, we're not interested in really hearing the other person. Our main focus is to protect ourselves so that we can feel okay again.

  Please note, feeling defensive is different to communicating your side of the story. When you communicate your side of the story to the other person your intention is to help them understand you, but you are also interested in understanding them. But when you feel defensive you are only focused on protecting your own position. You are trying to reject the other person's side of the story, not understand it. A defensive person finds it too emotionally uncomfortable to truly listen to the other person.

They are in a rush to prove that their side is right and to silence the other person.

- **Threats** are also a method for us to relieve our anger, or to pressure the other person to do what we want them to do. At times we might resort to threats because we are feeling helpless and don't know how to get the other person to hear us or collaborate with us. The issue with using threats in communication is that this method in fact reduces any chances of the other party wanting to collaborate. They will begin viewing you as a person who they need to protect themselves from. They may feel unsafe, stop trusting you and stop opening up to you. Instead of communicating, they are more likely to use unhelpful methods like defensiveness, pushing back and alienating you.
- **Blocking** communication can be done through many means. These include walking out in the middle of the conversation, or saying things that show that you're not interested in hearing what your partner has to say. For example, you might say things like: 'I don't want to hear your excuses', 'Here we go again', 'Stop making a big deal out of everything', 'I don't need to explain myself to you', 'You should know. I shouldn't have to tell you' and so on. These will either result in your partner making more and more desperate attempts to be heard or giving up altogether. Giving up may mean that they will stop communicating with you, and instead start developing a growing internal resentment towards you, gradually drifting away and losing interest in your relationship.

So blocking communication with others is never a good idea. If you have blocked communication with someone before, it's not too late to invite them to open up to you again. If, during communication, you are tempted to block, remember that what's on the other person's mind won't disappear just because you manage to ignore it. Communication can be painful, and we may need to be brave in facing the reality of what's on the other person's mind.

Type 3

This is the kind of healthy relationship that we should aim for. While people in the type 1 and 2 relationships can drift apart over time or end up with more and more conflict, type 3 relationships gradually deepen and improve. These people grow closer to each other in time and enjoy each other's company more. Conflict can reduce over time and understanding can increase.

What does it look like? People in this relationship type communicate their thoughts and emotions with a true interest in understanding the other person, as well as helping the other person understand them. Once they understand each other, they try to find solutions that everyone will be happy with. They show courage by facing conflict in order to truly understand others and their intentions. They assertively communicate their needs and ideas. At the same time, they truly listen and try to clear out misunderstandings. They stay away from mind games or emotionally charged behaviour.

Please note: conflict and disagreements are not harmful to relationships. They are a sign that two different islands, with two different understandings of the world, are trying to 'get' each other. So, don't be afraid of arguments. An argument that is prolonged is also not a sign of problems. It may take time for these islands to finally get each other and find common ground. It's your approach to communication that is the sign of a healthy relationship, not how quickly you resolve arguments.

Reflection

Think of some of the more important relationships in your life. These could include your relationships with your partner, child, parents, a close friend and so on. Is your communication with these people type 1, 2 or 3? Or a mixture of these?

Reflect on the possibility of changing your communication to be more in line with type 3. You may wish to close your eyes and imagine what that would look like. What changes need to take place for this to happen? If any emotions are getting in the way, practise emotion exposure.

Active Thinking and Communication

The first step to good communication starts with active thinking. We first need to be clear about what's on our mind that we are wanting to communicate. So before you rush in to say those few words that are going to open the floodgate to a screaming match, stop and pay attention to your thoughts. Before you say anything, notice what it is that you're trying to say and what outcome you are hoping for. As you may remember, writing is a helpful tool when active thinking. You may want to start by writing down your thoughts. If you prefer not to write, give yourself a bit of time to concentrate and notice your thoughts. Communication often fails because we're not very clear on what our thoughts are. Let's look at an example. Michael was diagnosed with a heart condition and since being diagnosed, he had been feeling very anxious. After practising active thinking, he realised that a few important questions had been on his mind. The questions were:

- What physical activities can I do, and what activities are harmful to my heart condition?
- What can I do to prevent a relapse?
- What are my chances of making a full recovery and feeling like my old self?

And so on... Because he didn't know the answers to these questions, he had been making all kinds of assumptions and expecting the worst!

Michael realised that because he hadn't paid attention to the questions on his mind, every time he had seen his doctor he had been distracted by other issues and hadn't asked the right questions. Now that he noticed the questions on his mind, he knew what to ask from his doctor at the next appointment. Once he communicated these questions and received the answers he was after, he began feeling much less anxious. Without active thinking, Michael could not have communicated the right questions or received the right answers.

Now return to your list from the beginning of this chapter. Pick one person from your list and while practising active thinking, write down the points that you want to communicate to them. At this stage, don't worry about how you might say what you want to say. We will learn about that later. Right now, just let your mind go loose and write down whatever comes up.

....

....

....

The next step is to organise your points. Take another look at what you've written. It's important to communicate only one point at a time, and in an order that will make sense to your partner. Mixing different ideas together and jumping from one point to another will confuse your partner. So separate your different points. Group together those points that are related to each other. Then, you should place your points in some kind of order. You can use the following two strategies to organise your points:

1. Organise your points in an order that would make sense to **your partner.** Remember they're not inside your head. Make sure they understand how your mind works and how your various points relate to each other.

2. Organise your points in order of what is important to you. First say the issues that are bugging you most. Get them off your chest and discuss them until they are resolved. Then bring up the less important issues.

Activity

Let's take a look at the following comments made by a woman to her partner:

'I think you're very distracted. Like remember the other day when I asked you to pick up a watermelon from the shops and you came home with a bag of tomatoes instead? We needed tomatoes for the soup, but if you had asked me first, you would have known that we already had enough tomatoes in the fridge. And speaking of the fridge, I can't believe you still haven't fixed it. You promised to fix it. You never carry through with your promises. I bet if your ex had asked you to fix her fridge, you would have done it in a heartbeat!'

How many different points do you see in this paragraph? How many different thoughts, emotions or concerns is this person raising at the same time?

....Ⓖ

....

Can you separate and group the main points, then think of a good order for this person to communicate their main concerns to their partner? Take a few minutes to do this.

.... Ⓖ

....

....

....

Now have a go at doing the same with the points that you're planning to communicate to your own family member or friend. Separate out the main points and decide on a good order to present them in.

.... Ⓟ

....

....

....

Structuring Your Ideas

As you actively think about what you're about to communicate, it's helpful to split your ideas into the following 4 sections:

1. **Facts** - what is it that you're seeing or noticing? You might describe the situation or point out the details of the scenario. Observations are not about your ideas or thoughts. They're not about opinions. They're simply describing the facts. So, it's best to not mix up your thoughts and opinions with the facts. You can simply say things like: 'there were 5 people there', 'the

shoes were blue', 'lunch was ready at 12:30pm'. During disagreements, sometimes it's a good idea to try to establish the facts before you move on to your thoughts, emotions or wishes. See if you and your partner can agree on the details of the situation first. Establishing the facts is important. This is where people often start the communication on the wrong foot and misunderstandings start to be created.

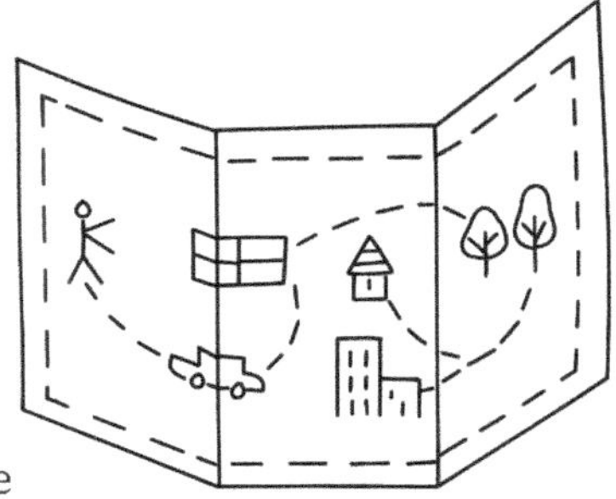

On a related note, you might be surprised to know that often our emotions and beliefs can impact the way that we remember facts. It's not surprising, then, that people so often remember the same incident in different ways. This little rule is the cause of so many misunderstandings in relationships. Each person remembers the events differently and so we build the rest of our communication based on different understandings of what actually happened. Then we are surprised that we can never agree on anything!

One of the issues that this causes is that as people try to communicate, they feel that the other person is being dishonest and lying about what actually happened. Sure, there are times when people lie or twist the truth for various reasons. But more often than not, that's not what's happening. More often than not, it's not that people are being deliberately dishonest. Rather, it's their emotions and your emotions that have influenced both of your memories about what actually happened. And that's the reason for people's stories being so different. Don't take our word for it. Put what we are saying to the test and start checking your memory of events against other people's. See how often your memories are different. So, before you interpret what the other person says as dishonest, make sure it isn't a misunderstanding.

2. **Thoughts** - this is where you can describe what you think about the situation. Your ideas, opinions and beliefs. Thoughts are not facts. They're your point of view about the facts. So it's important that when you're describing your thoughts you describe them as your thoughts and not as pure facts. Don't say things like: 'You're wrong'. This implies that it's a clear fact that your partner is wrong. The problem is that your partner will immediately become defensive, trying very hard to prove to you that they're not wrong. Instead say: 'That's not how I see it' or 'I don't quite agree'. This way you can express your opinion in a non-threatening way, and your partner will be more likely to listen without being defensive.

   An important reason for speaking about your thoughts with your partner is to remove any thought errors that you or your partner may have. That way you, can correct any misunderstandings your partner has, or let them clear up your misunderstandings.

3. **Emotions** - when you speak about emotions, try to be clear that they're your emotions and not facts or logical thoughts. We've learned that emotions don't always match logical thoughts. For example, logically you may know that your partner has never done anything to

intentionally hurt you. But your emotions may make you feel that your partner has said or done something with the intention of hurting you. So it's important to be clear to your partner that it's your emotions that make you doubt their intentions, and not your logical thoughts. This is an important distinction to make. If your partner thinks that the issue is with logical thoughts or facts, they will keep trying to prove things to you on a logical level. And then they get frustrated when their logical arguments are met with your emotions that are, well, not very logical. No matter how hard they try, their logical arguments won't quite get rid of your emotions. Can you see how quickly the argument would escalate into an unhealthy emotional storm? So if it's an emotion, be clear and let your partner know that it's an emotion. Your partner could also be communicating from a place of emotions without you knowing it. If you suspect this may be happening, ask them questions to help clarify this.

4. **Wishes** - it's important to be clear about the purpose of your communication. Do you just wish for your partner to understand you better? Are you asking them to change a certain behaviour or approach? Are you asking that the two of you work together to find a solution to a problem? If you're not clear about your reasons for discussing an issue, all kinds of unexpected misunderstandings could be taking place and you may not even know about it! Your partner may think that you're just complaining for no good reason, or may completely misunderstand your reasons. Let's take a look at a misunderstanding that took place between a couple because they weren't clearly communicating their wishes and motives:

Jane: You went and made yourself a cup of tea and didn't offer me one. Why don't you think about me for once?

Tony: I'm sorry, I'll go and make you one now.

Jane: No, but why didn't you ask me? This isn't the first time you've done this. It feels like I don't exist.

Tony: I won't do it again. I don't know what you want me to say. I already offered to make you one now. Are you just trying to pick on me?

What this couple is missing is that they are not on the same page about what Jane is asking for. Jane is not so concerned about the practical outcome. To her it's not about getting a cup of tea. She is more interested in understanding Tony's motives. She keeps repeating her question, not because she is picking on him, but because she is hoping to understand his mentality, because at the moment, she is seeing Tony's behaviour as a sign of neglect. She sees it as a sign that he doesn't care about her. She is desperately hoping for some information that tells her he does care. Tony might be unaware of Jane's wishes and motives because, if he were in her situation, his own wishes and motives would have been completely different. He might not generally worry about others neglecting him or not caring for him. So if he had been in her situation, he would have been happy with a simple 'Sorry, I'll go make you a cup of tea now' response!

How could this have been prevented? Let's repeat the scenario, but this time with Jane describing her wishes more clearly.

Jane: You went and made yourself a cup of tea and didn't offer me one. Why don't you think about me for once?

Tony: I'm sorry, I'll go and make you one now.

Jane: Thanks, but it's not so much about the cup of tea for me. It's more about understanding you better. I feel a bit neglected and not cared for. Can you help me understand if I'm right or wrong to feel that way?

Tony: Oh, sorry if it looks like that. I didn't do it because of not caring. I did it because growing up in my family, everyone just grabbed their own cup of tea or food. It's a habit. I was never in the habit of asking the other people in the room. I feel like a cup of tea and so I go and grab one. But I'll definitely try to remember next time.

This communication helped Jane understand that when Tony did not offer her tea, it was not because he did not care for her. It came from a place of habit and cultural norms. So, be clear about the aim of your discussions. Don't just stop at a discussion about what's wrong. If you are too focused on what's wrong and don't point out what you're hoping to achieve out of the discussion, you run the risk of making your partner feel that you're just complaining, punishing or blaming.

Practice

Now let's go back to the points that you are planning to

communicate to your family member or friend. You have already done the following two steps:

1. Active thinking around your ideas
2. Organising your ideas, making sure that you stick to one idea at a time

Now try the following step:

3. Formulate your ideas by separating observations, thoughts, emotions and wishes

.... Ⓟ

....

....

....

....

....

....

Active Listening

Listening effectively has at its core a sense of curiosity and an urge to really 'get' the other person, resolve pain and meet mutual goals. While communicating, there are times when your partner says things that are key to understanding each other better. This includes those times when:

- What they are trying to explain to you seems very important to them (you can see that through the intensity of their emotions. Or through the fact that they keep coming back to this point and repeating themselves).

- What they are talking about is important to you (e.g. if they are trying to answer a question that you have. Or if they are elaborating on a matter that is significant to you. Or if you are not quite sure that you are understanding their points).
- You have a sense that there is a misunderstanding, or you seem to keep missing each other's points.

It is at these times that active listening becomes a helpful tool. Active listening has 3 stages:

1. Paraphrasing
2. Clarifying
3. Feedback

Let's take a closer look at each.

Paraphrasing

While paraphrasing, you repeat what you think your partner has said in your own words. First you listen carefully to their points and then use your own words to say what you understand them to be trying to say to you. It may look a bit like this:

'So, are you saying that you are angry at me for working long hours?'

'I'm hearing that you feel I care more about my other friends than you. Did I understand your point right?'

‘Do you mean that when I suggest that we declutter and tidy up the house, you take that as a criticism?’

Paraphrasing can help with a few things. Firstly, it allows your partner to clear up any misunderstandings. You will allow them to hear what you think they said and correct any misinterpretations. Secondly, paraphrasing helps your partner feel that they are being listened to. And as soon as people feel that they are listened to, they will feel calmer and will be more open to hearing what you have to say back.

Clarifying

Once you have paraphrased what your partner said, your partner may do one of two things:

1. Indicate that you understood them correctly.
2. Indicate that you misunderstood or misjudged what they said.

If you didn't understand your partner correctly, it's time to try to clarify. Your partner might volunteer to give you their side of the story. Or you could ask questions that would encourage them to help you understand, to invite you into their island and show you what it's really like.

As you ask questions, remember to respect your partner's choice in answering. Try your best not to make them feel interrogated or pressured. Communication is a two-way process and it is up to your partner to invite you to their island, just as you invite them to yours. You may ask questions like:

'Can you help me get what I misunderstood?'

'Can you describe what you mean by this?'

'I'm finding it hard to understand your perspective on this. Can we talk about it more?'

'Can you help me understand what makes you think or feel this way?'

'When people say this, they can mean many different things. What are you referring to?'

It is important that you stop and take note of what your partner is saying as they clarify what they actually mean. Remember, your partner might think or feel completely differently to how you would have thought or felt if you were in their situation. It takes real skill to stop here and really hear and understand them. Listen to what they are saying word by word and take their points at face value. Try to place yourself in their shoes and understand their world view (even if you don't agree with it, or if it is very different to your own world view).

Feedback

After you've listened to what your partner has to say, and used paraphrasing and clarifying to understand them better, it is your chance to respond with whatever feedback you may have for them.

Remember: your feedback is only effective once you have ensured that you have understood your partner correctly. If you skip the previous two steps, your feedback may not be relevant to what's actually going on in your partner's mind. This means that you are both just going on about your own stories, without anyone actually listening. And that's where many communication breakdowns start.

During feedback, you can speak to your partner about your thoughts, emotions, beliefs, opinions and so on. You can share your view of what is being discussed, help them understand your side of things and respond to any questions they may have. This is where you get to practise the art of conveying your thoughts without blame, hurting back or blocking.

Effective feedback has three characteristics:

– It is immediate

– It is honest

– It is supportive

Immediate - once you have heard your partner well and believe you have understood their message, it's best to convey your feedback immediately. Long delays can result in the context being lost and your message losing some of its effectiveness. Also, at times when discussing sensitive matters, delaying feedback can result in increased discomfort and anxiety in you or your partner.

Honest - since the goal of communication is for you and your partner's islands to come closer, so that you can truly understand each other, it's important that you express your thoughts and feelings with complete honesty. Lack of honesty can, in time, result in trust being lost and islands drifting further and further away from each other. Broken trust can be a difficult thing to repair.

Honesty means showing your truth to the other person. This can include expressing yourself when you disagree with your partner, or if you feel uncomfortable with something they have done.

Supportive - keep in mind that the aim of your honesty is to create mutual understanding, not to hurt your partner in any shape or form. So, take care that your honesty doesn't turn into brutality. Consider the gentlest way to express any feedback that may be difficult for your partner to hear. Use your knowledge of your partner's sensitivities and tendencies to help you communicate in ways that will create the least amount of defensiveness or emotional hurt.

Also, when expressing your honest feedback, keep it relevant to what is being communicated. There is no need for an uncensored expression of all of your thoughts if they are not helpful to increasing understanding around the matters that are being discussed.

At times during your feedback you may also communicate your emotions. Describe your emotions rather than attacking with them. You may use sentences like 'I feel sad, hurt, upset', etc., rather than 'you are making me feel sad, hurt, upset', etc.

In the next chapter, we will further dive into the exciting world of communication. Are you ready to lift your communication game even further?

I've now completed 75% of the book!

☐

Chapter 11: Fine-Tuning the Art of Communication

Revision ⓖ

Decide if the following statements are true or false.

People are like islands. The job of communication is to stop the islands from guessing what is on the other islands, and instead seeing for themselves what is really there.

True ☐

False ☐

If communication becomes difficult in a relationship, there is no point trying too hard. It is best to stop talking about things or, if necessary, end that relationship.

True ☐

False ☐

Communication can be hard work, and we may need to practise, be patient and use our creativity.

True ☐

False ☐

Healthy relationships are those in which people do not argue, and do not bring up problems or disagreements.

True ☐

False ☐

The goal of communication is to get a quick relief from emotions like anger, hurt or shame, by acting on these emotions (e.g. by blaming, hurting back, or focusing on self-defence).

True ☐

False ☐

Good communication is focused on understanding the other person and helping them understand you.

True ☐

False ☐

In the previous chapter we learned the following important steps to good communication:

1. Notice your own thoughts that you want to communicate (active thinking).
2. Organise the thoughts that you want to communicate in an order that makes sense. This includes not saying too many ideas all at once. Separating and grouping your different points, then saying them in an order that makes sense to the other person. Or in the order of priority - meaning that you decide what points are more important or need to be talked about first and get those out of the way, then move on to the rest of your points.
3. Separate out:

   – Facts

   – Thoughts

   – Emotions; and

   – Wishes

And, finally, make sure the other person is clear about what you are trying to say, and if in doubt, practice active thinking. Have you been able to implement these steps in your communication? Have you come across any challenges?

16 Do's and Don'ts While Communicating

1. **Make sure you address the other person's point** - this may sound a bit obvious, but we often miss it when it comes to practice! If they raise a point, address it. Don't go past it. If they have a question, answer it. If they seem to be misunderstanding something, clarify it. If they have a concern, discuss it.

2. **Put yourself in their shoes** - one half of communication is about understanding the other person. Putting yourself in their shoes means seeing if you can understand how their thoughts work, what emotions they might be feeling and what makes them act or behave in the ways that they do. This will help you ask the right questions, clarify what's not clear, and then have empathy when needed. Here's a thing to remember: people are different. You might at times think to yourself, 'Something is missing. I really don't understand this person'. When you have that realisation, take it seriously. That realisation is your cue to stop and make it your aim to communicate more until you finally 'get' them.

   Here's an important but delicate little detail though:

putting yourself in someone else's shoes means that you try to understand them, not just assume that they think or feel the same way that you would think or feel. This is a very intricate little skill that we need to learn in order to communicate better. We need to stop guessing what the other person feels or thinks, and find out from them instead. We see the world through our own eyes and it's easy to assume that other people think or feel the same way we do. If I would feel jealous in a certain situation, I assume that my friend would feel jealous in that situation as well. If I don't tend to worry much, I assume that other people wouldn't either. If I tend to dislike myself because of how I look or behave, I assume that other people would dislike me too. If I think in a certain way, I assume that other people think in a similar way.

The reality is that people are super different to one another. Sometimes they might think or feel in a similar way to you, but at other times they don't. So always remind yourself of this principle and when putting yourself in their shoes, do your best to actually understand what it feels like to be inside their shoes. Not just assume that their shoes would feel like your shoes! Ask questions like: 'Can you tell me what you actually feel or think in this situation?' or 'What makes you feel or think this way? Can you help me understand you?'

Be particularly mindful of this rule where there are cultural differences - Everything down to the meanings attached to certain words, small body gestures or facial expressions is culturally defined. If you are communicating with a person from a different cultural background or social class, take particular care to stay away from interpreting what is said or done based on your existing knowledge. Always have a learning attitude. Ask, communicate, research.

3. **Be simple and to the point** - only say what is really on your mind, in a clear and simple way. When we act on emotions, it's tempting to hide what is really bothering us, and instead say things that are emotionally charged, while confusing the listener about what the actual point is.

Here's an example. Ava is meant to catch up with her brother on Saturday night. He messages on Saturday morning to tell her that he has just caught a cold and isn't well enough to see her. Her thoughts are: 'I must be a boring person. He keeps making excuses to get out of our catch ups. Maybe he doesn't like spending time with me. I bet he would rather see his friends who are more interesting than me.' Now, she could simply communicate these thoughts and seek clarification from her brother. But instead what she says to him is: 'I'm going to be all alone on Saturday night. I have no one to hang out with. I hate it when people cancel plans last minute. I really expect more notice so that I could have time to organise something else for myself. How bad is your cold anyway? The weather is warm, why would you catch a cold this time of the year?' Her brother won't understand Ava's real concerns based on what she just said. She has said 4 or 5 different points, but none of these points are what's really

> "When putting yourself in their shoes, do your best to actually understand what it feels like to be inside their shoes. Not just assume that their shoes would feel like your shoes!

bothering her. Her brother feels confused. He doesn't know which one of the points to respond to. He also feels that Ava is being unfair and accusing him of stuff. So instead he goes in with his own defensive remarks: 'You're being very unreasonable. It's not like I could predict a cold coming. Why is there always drama with you? People cancel plans, get over it. Plenty of people catch colds in summer. I can't control getting sick!'

Well, of course by this stage not only does Ava not feel better, but her initial hurt has increased due to her brother's new attacks and accusations. He just doesn't seem to get how upset she is! So she attacks back: 'Oh, there is no reasoning with you! You just don't get it. You never care about anyone but yourself.'

As you can see, it's easy for this argument to escalate. An alternative, more helpful, way of communicating would have been for Ava to communicate exactly and only what was on her mind in the first place:

> Ava: 'Something is upsetting me a bit. Can we talk about it?'
>
> Ava's brother: 'Sure, what's wrong?'
>
> Ava: 'I've been feeling a bit insecure about our relationship lately. I feel like you're not very keen to meet up with me. I sometimes wonder if you enjoy hanging out with me.'
>
> Ava's brother: 'Oh, why do you think that? Did I do something?'
>
> Ava: 'Well you've cancelled our catch up plans a few times

lately. I felt like each time there was another reason why we couldn't catch up.'

Ava's brother: 'Well, I was sick the other night. But to be honest, there is a reason I've been trying to get out of our catch ups. I feel at times you can criticise me a bit and I'm feeling insecure myself at the moment.'

Ava: 'I'm sorry. A lot of what I say is because I worry for your wellbeing. I didn't think you would see my concerns as criticism. I will try to stop that.'

As you can see, once they started communicating with honesty and saying only what was really on their mind, the communication took a completely different turn. It was easy for Ava's brother to understand her and to respond to her concerns.

4. **Be specific** - don't use ambiguous, abstract or over-generalised ideas. The more specific you can be in communication, the more you are facilitating understanding. For example, saying 'you don't listen to me!' is too general. It's better to say 'yesterday when I was telling you about xyz, I felt like you weren't listening to me'. This allows the other person to understand and respond to your specific points. Statements like 'you don't listen to me' don't leave room for ongoing rational exchange of ideas about the topic. If your partner uses generalised statements, ask them for examples.

5. **Call it** - you're learning so much about communication in these chapters. Yet, you or your partner could at times break the

rules of communication or use unhelpful strategies. If you notice it, don't be afraid to bring it up. Describe what you think is going on that's halting the process of communication. And then listen as your partner gives their view of what they think is going on. In other words, use your skills in communication to communicate about communication! It's a worthwhile discussion to be had. Communication is like teamwork. Work together to improve the skill.

6. **Correct thought errors** - we know that thoughts can have errors in them. Those thoughts that you and your partner are communicating to each other are no exception. If you notice a thought error, don't be afraid to gently and kindly point it out. Just as you have learned to notice your own thought errors and correct them, notice any logic errors that come into the conversation with your partner.

   As you speak to your partner about these errors, take care to use language that is gentle and doesn't sound derogatory in any way. You could simply say things like 'Have you considered this other angle...?', 'Do you think there might be a chance that what really happened was xyz?'

7. **Make sure you're talking about the same thing** - sometimes in communication the two people may seem to be discussing the same thing, but they are each talking about something quite different. So they just never reach a resolution! Here's an example:

   > Eva: You always let friends walk all over us. You don't stand up to them.

Andre: If our friends mistreat us, I can't be responsible for that! I'm only responsible for my own behaviour.

Eva: You are too nice to people. We need to have boundaries! I don't understand why you don't care enough to do something about this!

Andre: Look, I can't control how other people behave. Other people mistreat us and I get blamed for it?

Do you see the problem here? At first, it may look like they're talking about the same thing and addressing each other's points. But in reality, Eva is talking about Andre's behaviour and Andre is talking about other people's behaviour. Eva is suggesting that Andre needs to change something about his approach. Andre is saying that he's not responsible for other people's actions. At no point, do either of them pause and address the other person's concern.

How could this change? Eva could 'call it'. This means that she could stop and point out that they are each talking about different things and not addressing each other's points. She could then say something like: 'I'm not blaming you for the actions of others. That seems to be a misunderstanding. My concern is about your behaviour, not other people's.' Or Andre could stop and change his points to make them relevant to what Eva is saying. For example, he might say: 'this is how I'm used to behaving. I don't like confrontation, so I try to avoid it, even if it means not standing up for myself. It causes me anxiety to do anything differently.' Once they finally begin talking about the same issue, they can delve deeper, understand each other better and find better solutions. For example, once Eva finally understands the real reason for Andre's behaviour, she could feel more empathy for his challenges and work with him as a team, instead of blaming him for not doing better.

8. **Don't give in to the urge to derail** - we've already learned the importance of sticking to one subject at a time when communicating. But at times, emotions and passive thinking will push us to lose track of what we're discussing. Picture communication as a tree branch. Your job is to follow one branch and get to the end of it. Then if there are other branches, you can get to them later. But derailing means that you never get to the end of your branch, because at every juncture, you go off to a different branch, and from there to another branch and another branch. You find yourself lost and confused after a while. Here's an example of a conversation between a couple:

    Noah: You've got to stop insulting and attacking me for no reason. I can't believe how many insults you threw at me on Saturday, when all I was doing was offering to help take our daughter to her piano classes?

    Ella: You were going to take her to the piano classes in that embarrassing car. Why can't you spend a bit of money and buy a car that doesn't embarrass our family all the time?

    Noah: You don't understand anything about our finances.

> Maybe if you didn't leave everything up to me to do, you'd understand that we can't afford a better car.
>
> Ella: So you're saying that I sit around all day doing nothing? I'm sick of you undermining everything I do around this house!

What would be a good way for this couple to resolve their differences? Firstly, both Ella and Noah could do their best to avoid making inflammatory remarks. Any statement that triggers new emotions within the other person, increases the chances of an urge to derail the conversation into new directions and away from the main concerns. Can you see any points where Ella or Noah could have omitted comments that triggered new emotions in the other person?

Once the derailing started, what could the couple do to help prevent it from escalating? Either one of them could stop and 'call it'. They could say something like 'hang on, we're talking about too many points here. Let's stick to one point at a time'. After that, they could try to identify the main point to focus on. So, for example, Ella could say, 'On Saturday I wasn't just trying to pick on you for offering to take our daughter to her piano classes. There was more to it than that, but we can come back to that later. For now let's stick to the main issue that you wanted to talk about, which is you feeling like I attack and insult you a lot'. Or Noah could say something like 'I know you're unhappy that I'm not buying a better car, and you know that I have my own thoughts about that topic, which I can try to clarify later. But first, could we talk about the way we talk to each other? Is there a way for you to disagree with me without using insults?

As you can see, sticking to the main point takes mental discipline from all parties. If you notice that your emotions are causing you to derail, stop and work through the emotions. If your partner derails, don't fall for it. Bring them back to the original topic. If they are too distracted or emotional to stick to the main topic, give them paper and pen and get them to write down any unrelated matters that come to their mind for another discussion later. You can be assertive and let your partner know that your debate will never resolve in this manner. See if you can get them to agree that you need to stick to one topic at a time if you are to get anywhere. Keep in mind that at times people with very busy minds struggle to stay focused on one topic. Once they at least agree with you in principle, come up with a creative way together to stay on one topic at a time. You could use creative approaches like writing all the ideas on a big piece of paper to help you make decisions on what points to talk about first.

9. **Get into the same team** - while communicating you often have the choice to either bring the other person into the same team as you, making them feel like you are both on the same side and can collaborate, or you could raise their defences and give them the impression that you are two competing teams who need to enter a battle. Which choice do you think is smarter to go with? Of course, if they are in your

team, they will be more receptive to what you have to say. Their emotions will be calmer and less likely to interrupt healthy communication. Instead of feeling defensive, there will be real listening.

So how can you bring the other person into your team? Firstly, don't allow emotions like anger to cause you to say things in a way that you know will trigger the other person. Be especially mindful of hurting their self-image. The moment you have hurt their self-image, you've lost yourself an audience. They will now try to use the rest of the conversation to repair their self-image, trying to get rid of feelings of shame, humiliation, anger or hurt. So, as you talk about sensitive things, be mindful of how the other person may see them. Describe your points in a way that would help them understand your side of the story, rather than being triggered by it. Choose your language wisely. Leave triggering words or phrases out and instead use words or phrases that will communicate the same points in a way that's not so triggering.

Another step to helping the other person get into your team is to find common things that you both want. If your child refuses to help with the chores, nagging them about how irresponsible they are being will push them into the other team. Instead you could say something like 'I'm feeling a bit tired and drained from doing house work and it's getting in the way of me being able to relax and have fun with you. Could you help out after dinner and then we can play a board game together?'

Saying things like: 'You're tired? So what? I'm more tired!', 'You think I was mean to you? Well what about the other day when you were mean to me?' will push the person into the other team. They will feel like they need to do everything they can to prove you wrong and make you hear their points. Jumping into the same team means that instead of tit for tat, we can acknowledge our common issues that need work. So, you might say 'So we are both tired and have very little time for rest. What can we do about that?', or 'Do you agree that we've both been a bit mean to each other lately? How can we change that?'

10. **Be opportunistic** - notice opportunities for communication and act on them. For example, if someone reaches out to talk to you about something you did which has upset them, this is an opportunity for communication. There may be a misunderstanding that needs to be corrected. They may need to understand your position better. Or you may need to understand theirs better. It's not personal. Don't be offended. They are not trying to hurt or disrespect you. They are trying to connect with you. So be happy about this opportunity. In fact, if they only hint at the idea that they are upset with you, or are unhappy with something you've done, grab that opportunity and find out what's on their mind. Maybe they don't have the communication skills to talk to you more openly. But now you do have those skills. So, don't let things go unsaid. Invite them to open up and be honest. Even if it's painful to hear what they have to say, it will be worth it in the end. Don't allow the emotional pain to cause you to avoid. It's also worth mentioning that sarcastic remarks are often a sign that the person has something on their mind but doesn't have the

courage to say it openly. Don't let the moment pass. Ask them what they meant by their sarcastic remark.

11. **Let them tell you what they feel** - during communication, each person has the highest authority to talk about their own thoughts, emotions or other inner processes. What we mean by that is that you are in the best position to tell others what you think, feel, believe or want. And your partner is in the best position to tell you what they think, feel, believe or want. It's not your job to tell them what is on their mind, and it's not their job to tell you what is on yours. If you say things that suggest that you know better than them what they are thinking or feeling, you are essentially taking away their power to trust their own judgement. Or you're telling them that you don't trust them enough to tell you what's going on for them. Ask questions like 'How do you feel about this?', 'It seems like you're feeling a bit worried. Am I right?', 'Why is it that you seem to not like it when I ask you this question?' Don't make statements like 'I know you think this way', 'I know you feel that way', 'You react negatively because you're trying to control things', 'You act all high and mighty because you think you're better than others'. Give them the respect and trust to tell you why they acted in a certain way, or why they said certain things.

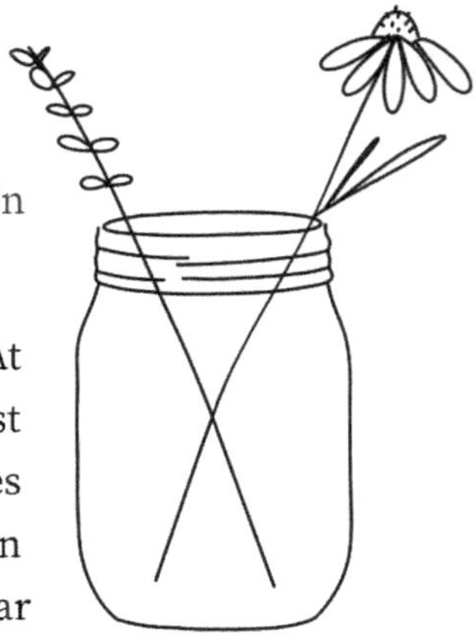

    There is one exception to this rule: At times you may have genuinely lost trust that your partner communicates their thoughts or emotions in an honest way. If this is the case, be clear about the issue. Instead of passively discounting everything they say, speak to them with honesty about your reasons for losing trust in their integrity. That way, you can open the gates of communication around this trust issue.

12. **Say 'sorry'** - don't be afraid to admit to being wrong. While communicating, if you notice you have been wrong, over even a small detail, don't hesitate to acknowledge it. If necessary, apologise. Being wrong is human. During a disagreement, its common for both parties to make the occasional communication error when under the influence of emotions or misunderstandings. So, when you notice yours, own up to it. This will not make you 'the wrong one', or make the other person 'win' the argument. On the contrary, it may: a) help them feel that they are communicating with a fair person; b) help lower their defences and so make them a lot more receptive to all the other points you may have to say. Maybe they will also find the courage to say sorry back to you where they have been wrong. If, at times, the other person tries to take advantage of your genuine apology, call it! This may be food for a new topic of discussion with the person.

13. **Notice subtle things** - the art of communication is full of intricacies. At times things are not what they appear to be at all. You may be convinced that you understand a behaviour or a statement. But investigation shows very subtle but very important differences to what you had understood. So, look for subtleties. Investigate things with a fine-toothed comb! Here's an example. Two

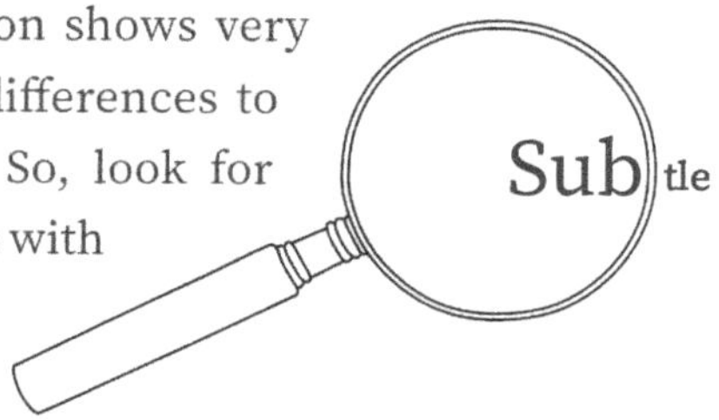

friends, Kym and Asha, were having a meal at a restaurant. Asha realised that she had forgotten her wallet. Of course, Kym offered to pay for her meal. But while offering, she made it clear, several times, that it was a loan and that she needed the money back soon. Asha felt hurt, but because she knew the rules of healthy relationships, she talked to Kym about it. Here is how their conversation went:

> Asha: I felt hurt that you kept bringing up that you needed the money back.
>
> Kym: Sorry. It's just that I'm having a lot of financial issues at the moment, so I've been feeling a bit anxious about money.
>
> Asha: I'm sorry you're feeling stressed about money at the moment. What actually upset me, though, was that it sounded like you doubted that I would volunteer to pay you back. Of course I'll pay you back as soon as possible.

Can you see that Asha skilfully noticed that the conversation was about to go in a different direction to what she had intended, as Kym had not understood Asha's actual concern. So Asha was able to clarify and redirect the conversation.

> Kym: Oh no, of course I know that you would intend to pay me back as soon as possible. It's not that at all.

Kym is really clever here in first setting Asha's mind at ease, reassuring her that she had no doubt that she was planning to pay her back. Then, she went on to clarify her earlier behavior...

Kym: I just thought that you might forget because I have a terrible memory myself and I'm always forgetting to pay people back when I owe them money! I just assumed that you might forget as well.

Asha: Oh okay. That makes sense. It hadn't occurred to me that you would be concerned about that.

Asha listened well and quickly understood Kym's point. It wasn't personal. In her moment of anxiety around finances, Kym had panicked, thinking that Asha might forget to pay her back. Of course, if it wasn't because of their skillful communication, this incident might have put a strain on Asha and Kym's friendship.

14. **Don't get caught up in communication games** - emotions can cause us to play all kinds of mind games during communication. These games are rarely helpful. Here's an example of a conversation between a couple:

    Fiona - We are fighting every day. If we want our marriage to survive, we need to be able to sort out our differences.

    Doug - You never wanted to be with me in the first place. If you want to leave me, you can just leave. No one is stopping you.

    Fiona - But I'm saying that I want to fix our problems, not leave you.

    Doug - I know what you really want. I bet you've met someone better.

    Communication games often involve one party intentionally

twisting what's being said, usually because of a defensive, emotionally charged stance around the subject. Communication games are different to genuine misunderstandings. There is an unwillingness to hear the other person and an intentional manipulation of what's being said. There could be many reasons for this kind of behaviour, including angry and passive aggressive emotions. In simple words, they are too angry or hurt to want to hear you. At times, what you're seeing is the result of a person who has such a negative self-image that they feel a strong urge to defend themselves by deflecting.

As you can see, this would make it nearly impossible for the two people to ever reach a resolution. Instead of the two islands getting closer to each other, they start to mistrust the boat of communication. They start to believe that the information communicated can't be trusted. Over time, this will encourage more and more game playing.

How could this problem be resolved? Well, as a first step Fiona needs to stop and 'call it'. She would need to openly speak about the communication block that's affecting them. She could then inquire about the deeper issues that are causing her partner to play these communication games. As a final step, the couple could set a new rule that, from that point on, they would only say what they mean and would take each other's statements at face value. What their partner says is what they mean. This is is an important rule that can gradually establish a new pattern within relationships where there are no hidden meanings behind words. What you mean is what you say. If both Fiona and Doug committed to trying to practice this new rule, gradually communication could become simpler and easier between them. Of course, for people who have lived a lifetime learning that words have double meanings, or have learned to sooth their emotions by resorting to communication games, these habits may take time to wear off. Speak to your partner about these each time they happen again so that you can gradually mould your relationship into one that can create trust and safety for both.

15. **If someone breaks your trust, don't stop talking to them** - people who have been hurt in the past, often develop a theory to explain why they have been hurt. The theory could be that people hurt you because:

    They don't care about you.

    They look down on you.

    They don't have your best interests at heart.

    They are selfish and only care about themselves.

    They are humiliating you or laughing at your misfortunes.

    Or, on the other hand, you might think that there is something wrong with you that has made you a target. For example, you might think that:

    You are weak.

    You are unlikable.

    You are uncool.

    You are too different from others.

These are just a few of the explanations you might have found for the wrongs that others have done to you. However, these theories are often far from the truth. The reality is that people are all so different and the reasons for their behaviours are diverse. Even two individuals who have broken your trust in exactly the same way may have had two completely different reasons for their behaviour. Understanding their reasons can help you understand that other people may not always view you in the way you have been conditioned to believe.

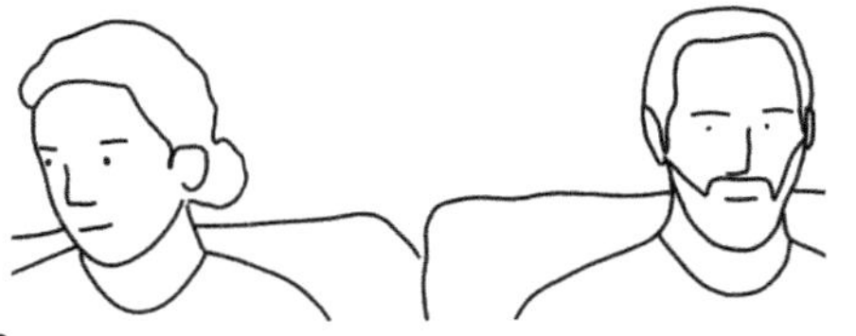

It may be tempting to stop communicating with a person who has broken your trust, but for the sake of your own mental health, try to resist making a habit of doing this. Find out why they did it. Find out how their mind works and what caused them to behave that way. It's easy to assume that they hurt you because of whatever old theory you have about yourself or about them. But there's always a chance that what really happened was not exactly what it looks like, or that there is a lot more to the story than meets the eye. Communicating with people who have broken your trust is also important because, if you don't, you run the risk of doubting your own ability to judge who can and cannot be trusted. You essentially lose trust in your own judgement. You may even begin to feel that you can't trust anyone at all.

Please note: this doesn't necessarily mean that you have to give your trust back to the person. If, after thorough communication using all the skills you've learned in this course, you are still firm in your belief that you should not trust this person, then at least you can walk away with a greater understanding of them or a better feeling about yourself.

16. **Don't give them the impression that you agree, if you really disagree** - this one might seem a bit harmless. You're kind of tired of talking about the issue and want the conversation to be over. Or you can't be bothered arguing for your point. Or think that it's not important enough to be worth the effort. Or you may have many other reasons for giving them the impression that you agree with their idea, with their decision or with their argument. But sooner or later they may realise that you hadn't agreed at all. For example, during another conversation at a later point, you revert to what you actually think. Or even worse, if they turn out to be wrong, you begin blaming them for having made the wrong decision, even though at the time you had given the impression that you were on board with it. You had not tried hard enough to argue for a different decision by helping them understand your point of view.

    The solution? We mentioned that honesty is important in communication. Dishonesty will make the other person begin to lose trust in the boat. So don't give them the false impression that you agree, if you don't. But if you are happy to let go of your position despite your disagreement, communicate that as well. Perhaps you can say that you still don't agree but are happy to try it their way. Or you could say that you still don't agree but are tired of continuing the discussion. Or the issue isn't important enough to you to continue debating it. Basically, say it like it is.

When it comes to decision making, teamwork means that you and your partner may not agree about the best course of action and may need to communicate as long as it takes to reach a decision that you're both happy with. This may take time and energy as you both put forth your arguments and together explore all the details. You may each be looking at the issue from a slightly different angle and the best decision becomes clear to you through talking more. But if you don't wish to put in that effort, that's completely okay. As long as you remember that if you choose to hand over the decision making to the other person, then you should not complain about the outcome if it doesn't turn out well. You made the decision to leave them in charge.

Communication and Emotions

Thoughts and emotions impact many areas of our lives, and that includes communication. Communication is not only about what you say externally. An important part of communication is what is going on inside of your mind. For example, if you are overcome by rage or frustration, it may be difficult to communicate effectively, because these emotions can shift your focus away from wanting to understand and be understood, and instead place it on unhelpful strategies like hurting back, blaming or blocking. An emotion like shame might focus your attention on trying to defend yourself so that you don't feel that you are in the wrong. Again, this shifts your attention away from wanting to create true understanding.

Since our emotions can have such a big impact on communication, we need to remember that our ongoing practice of the skills that we have learned in this book, can, over time, improve our relationships.

When our self-image is hurt during communication, the emotions that come up can be particularly explosive. When we feel that our sense of self-worth is questioned, for example, when we are criticised or blamed, or when we think that we're in the wrong, we may feel a range of emotions. These include:

- Shame
- Embarrassment
- Broken pride
- Feeling not good enough
- Feeling belittled
- Feeling humiliated
- Anger or resentment

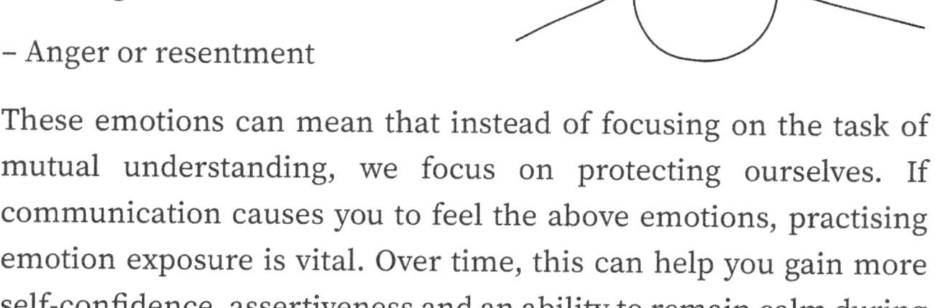

These emotions can mean that instead of focusing on the task of mutual understanding, we focus on protecting ourselves. If communication causes you to feel the above emotions, practising emotion exposure is vital. Over time, this can help you gain more self-confidence, assertiveness and an ability to remain calm during disagreements.

At what points during communication would it be a good idea to practise emotion exposure?

Before communication: At times your emotions are active even before you start communicating. For example, you may be feeling hurt because of something that your friend has done. So, as you approach him to speak about it, you are already feeling emotions all over your body. At other times, the simple act of communication would bring up emotions (e.g. fear of confrontation). It is particularly important to practise emotion exposure when:

- You sense that your emotions may make it hard for you to follow the rules of healthy communication (e.g. you are tempted to yell at your friend with blaming, vengeful or hurtful words. Or all you want to do is to prove to everyone that you are in the right and the other party is in the wrong).
- You notice yourself wanting to avoid communication because it's too uncomfortable or because you are afraid of losing control of your emotions.

At times you may find that your emotions are so intense that you're not interested in practising emotion exposure. You would rather act on your emotions, hoping to find quick relief from them. For example, instead of communicating with the person who has upset you, you may decide to vent to other friends. Or you may vent on social media. What you are after is quick emotional relief as others tell you that they think you are right and the other person is in the wrong. But this quick emotional relief comes at a price. It is unhelpful in the overall aim of bringing islands closer to each other. Before you know it, there will be different parties taking sides and creating more anger, hurt and misunderstanding in your relationship. So as uncomfortable as your emotions may be at the time, resist the urge to act on them. Instead, close your eyes and simply place your attention on your body. If your thoughts are active, allow them to go on. If it helps you, use your imagination to act out your emotions while you practice emotion exposure. Even if it feels like an intense explosion of thoughts and emotions, just remain aware and be patient.

Once the emotions are calmer, find a way to communicate with the person who has upset you.

During communication: As you communicate, try to keep an eye on the movement of emotions within your body, while you are simultaneously paying attention to the conversation with your partner. If the emotions escalate or you notice that they are clouding your judgement or affecting your ability to communicate effectively, ask for time-out.

Make an agreement with your partner, that if emotions make it difficult to communicate effectively, a brief time-out will be given. It's best to discuss this with your partner at a time when emotions are not at an intense level. Perhaps at the beginning of your discussion. Agree with your partner that the aim of timeout is not to avoid communication. As soon as you're both feeling calmer, come back together and resume. During time-out:

- **Find a quiet corner to practise emotion exposure** - Don't try to rush this. Take as much time as necessary to feel your emotions. Your emotions will move on when they are ready to move on.

- **Remind yourself to hold the remote control** - Remember that whatever your partner thinks of you, it is only their opinion. It is not the truth of you.

- **Practise self-compassion** - Remind yourself that even

if your partner is angry or critical of you, you are still good. And you are still deserving of love.

- **Notice old emotions that come into your current relationships** - For example, you might realise that when your partner asks you to do certain things, you feel rebellious just like you did when, as a teenager, your parents told you that you weren't allowed to do something. Speak about these to your partner, or work through the emotions within yourself.
- **If you are feeling particularly hungry or tired, rest and eat** - Remember, our body and mind are connected. By making your body comfortable, you may cope better with stress.

After communication: If you notice that there are left over emotions from your communication, take some time to practise emotion exposure. At times you may notice that you're still feeling uncomfortable emotions even after you've completely resolved the disagreements between you and your partner, and even if there are no logical reasons for these emotions. Remember, emotions don't always follow logical reasoning. So, it's a good idea to give yourself time to process them. Unfortunately, even after an argument is resolved at a rational level, the ongoing emotions in you or your partner can mean that bickering continues. It is important to notice when your conversation is no longer rational, and acknowledge that what is happening is because of leftover emotions and not because of a rational issue. This would be a good time to ask for time-out and focus on these emotions within the body.

Your Partner's Emotions

Just as emotions impact you during the process of communication, your partner can be impacted by their own emotions. As we know, emotions do not always follow reason and logic. If your rational arguments don't result in your partner's emotional reactions disappearing, don't be surprised. Let us repeat that: if your rational arguments do not result in your partner's emotional reactions disappearing, don't be surprised. Your partner may or may not know how to practise emotion exposure to work through their emotional experiences. However, there are a few things that you might be able to do to help:

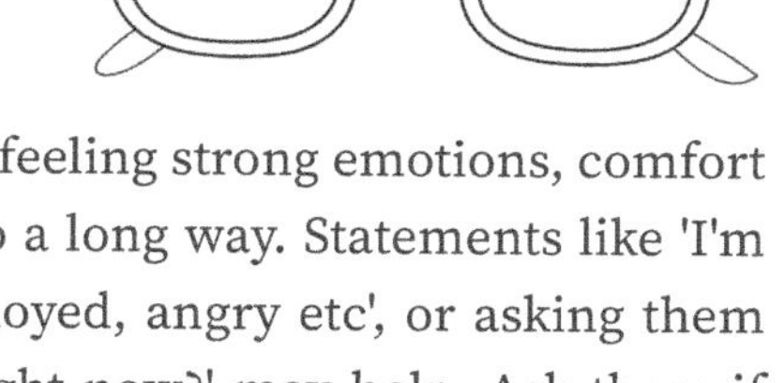

Comfort them - If your partner is feeling strong emotions, comfort them. A bit of comforting may go a long way. Statements like 'I'm sorry, I can see you're upset, annoyed, angry etc', or asking them 'what would you like me to do right now?' may help. Ask them if they would like space, or if they want you to keep talking. Identify the main issues causing pain for your partner and acknowledge that you've heard them.

Do not see it as a personal attack on you - see it for what it is - an emotion that's hurting your partner. If your partner is irritable, explosive or emotionally toxic, it is likely that they are feeling very unhappy within. Acknowledge that to yourself. We often punish hurt people in arguments because we see their hurt as an attack on us. To put it simply, we expect to be blamed or punished. Remind yourself that even if your partner's anger is targeted towards you, it's nothing but an emotion. It is not the reality of your partner, but an angry emotion that they are experiencing at the time.

Emotions are not the truth of a person. They are unstable and ever changing. It is true that while we experience them, emotions seem to be the absolute truth. This is because emotions are like a fog that covers the eyes making it difficult to see beyond them. But once the fog clears, we realise that there is a whole world around us that we missed. You may have experienced this at first hand during your practices of emotion exposure.

"Emotions are not the truth of a person. They are unstable and ever changing.

Unfortunately, people often believe that emotions are the truth of a person. You may have heard statements like 'never forget what an angry person says, because that is when the truth comes out'. That is not the case. Instead remember that anger is an emotion whose aim is often to hurt back, not to communicate the truth! Yes, it is true that, on occasions, anger will create impulsive behaviour and so your partner may let out opinions and thoughts that they had previously held back and not expressed, but the majority of what an angry person says is intended to hurt. So, these statements should not be taken as truth. The statements of an angry person should be regarded as remarks made by a temporary emotional state that will do what satisfies its need to hurt back.

Give them time - if your partner needs time to allow their emotions to de-escalate and to feel calmer, give them that time. If your partner doesn't have effective skills to communicate or to manage their emotions, they may not have the ability to ask you for time out. So, make sure they understand that they can have one if they would like it. Also be clear that the purpose of time out is not to escape communication; it's just a temporary break.

Manage intense outbursts - If your partner's emotional outbursts are very intense, and particularly if they are putting you or anyone else at risk, be assertive in putting boundaries in place. Manage risk behaviours using whatever safety measures are needed. Never encourage risk behaviours or allow them to continue. Assertive boundary setting could also involve discussing outbursts once your partner has calmed down, so that the two of you can agree on rules and safety behaviours. It's important to be assertive in sticking to the rules that you have agreed on. In this way you may gradually motivate your partner to take control of their own emotional outbursts.

Practice

Think of a person with whom you need to communicate. Practise emotion exposure around the emotions that you feel as you think about the emotions that they may display during heated discussions.

Mindful listening

Finally, we would like to teach you a little trick that can take your communication game to another level. Mindful listening is the art of being completely present as you listen to your partner. Present means that you actively place your attention on everything that's happening within you, like your thoughts and emotions, as well as on the other person. Here's how it works:

Close your eyes and start with a mindfulness of sound practice.

Remember: all you need to do is to listen to all the sounds around you.

Now, allow your thoughts in and practise mindfulness of your thoughts. Listen to them, watch them, or feel them in your body.

Now imagine speaking to a person from your list. Just as you are mindful of your thoughts, remain mindful of what they say. Listen to it with all of your attention and awareness. If any emotions rise up in your body, place part of your attention on the emotion or on that part of the body. Keep your attention there until the emotion passes.

When the emotion has passed, once again imagine yourself listening to that person with full awareness.

Post-Conflict Debrief

Even after you and your partner have diligently studied and internalised every detail from the last two chapters on communication, there will be moments during the storm of conflict where you might find yourself questioning if these techniques will truly work for you, or your partner, in the heat of emotions. Can these techniques truly withstand the intensity of emotional conflicts? These doubts are natural and valid, as intense emotions pose the biggest challenge to communication, often interfering with our ability to effectively apply learned techniques.

In these moments, it's important to remember not to blame

yourself or your partner. Slipping up and allowing emotions to take control of the communication does not suggest that you have failed in improving your relationship. This may happen many times, and it's part of the learning process. This is where an important step in communication comes into play: post-conflict debriefing.

Make sure that you and your partner have an agreement, that after each conflict you will commit to a debriefing session. Make it a normal part of your routine. After emotions have settled and you are both feeling more like yourselves again, talk about the parts of your conflict that didn't go so well or could have gone better. This is a teamwork activity, and not a space to blame each other for not doing better. The purpose is to work together to find useful information that will help next time around. The idea is to figure out how, as a team, you could make your next conflict less painful and quicker to resolve. Volunteer to suggest where you could do something differently (e.g. 'Okay, maybe next time I will ask you if you're really blaming me before I assume that you are'). But also suggest to your partner where they could support you through your emotions as well (do this part carefully so it doesn't turn into a blame-game; e.g. 'any chance in the future you could first reassure me that you do see the good things I do for our relationship, before you criticise any shortcomings? Otherwise I'll feel like all you see is my shortcomings. Do you think you could remember to do that next time?').

During this debrief, you and your partner can:

1. **Learn about each other's triggers and the emotions that they activate** - For example, maybe certain triggers remind you of your old traumas. Maybe you start seeing your partner as the

'enemy' and lose trust in them. Maybe you start feeling like you're inadequate and can't do anything right. Whatever it is, if your partner is offering you this information, it's absolute gold. It can help you understand 'where they are' when they're under the influence of emotions. During the next round of conflict, if you understand 'where they are,' you will be far less likely to be triggered yourself. Not getting triggered allows you to be far more helpful in assisting your partner to navigate whatever emotion is active for them, and help them gradually heal the wounds. Be generous with sharing this information about yourself with your partner so that the next time you find yourself triggered, they can offer you the same service.

2. **Learn about how your triggers impact you when they're active** - For example, maybe when you're triggered you find it hard to feel any form of love directed at you, or maybe you feel the need to become physically active (e.g. clean or exercise). Maybe you need practical and solution-focused advice to 'fix' whatever problem is stressing you. Or maybe you're the exact opposite and prefer emotional support without the practical suggestions - what ever it is, let your partner know in as much detail as you can.

3. **Explore ways you and your partner can still operate as a team during the storm of emotions** - If your partner explains to you that when they're triggered they look at you as the 'enemy', spend some time exploring this, and you'll likely find

ways you can act, or things you can say that will help them come back to awareness and find trust in you more quickly.

At times, it's understandable if you're hesitant to do the post-conflict debriefing session as it may feel like opening up a healed wound if you try to discuss a conflict right after it has settled. Although it may feel counter-intuitive, view it as forward-thinking and preparing for the future. It's best to put to good use the conflict you just had by making sure your relationship grows from it. So seize this perfect opportunity for reducing future conflict.

Also remember, these debriefing sessions don't need to be dragged-out or long. A simple 'what can we do better next time?' exercise could do!

Finally, remember that if your partner suggests things that you are not comfortable or in agreement with, this is your opportunity to discuss your reasons and hesitations. If you fail to reach an agreement on this occasion, it is okay to leave certain discussions as an open-book and continue discussing them over time until you eventually reach solutions that you are both happy with. So don't seek perfection. Each time just try to deepen your understanding of yourself and of your partner a little more. In time this will translate to conflict having less power over your life.

This process is a long term commitment. Do it as regularly as you can, and you may gradually find that during conflict your triggers stick around for shorter and shorter periods. You'll start to naturally be able to active think, active listen and stay present with emotional experiences within the body, even during emotional storms.

I've now completed 84% of the book! □

Chapter 12: Kindness

Revision

Close your eyes and remember what you learned in the previous chapter, as well as how you've gone with practising it since. Don't pressure yourself to remember everything. Just allow the remembering to naturally happen at its own pace.

A Fresh Look

Kindness... We're told from a young age 'be kind'... 'be nice to your brother', 'share with your friend', 'help others', and so on. But not many of us are told why we should be kind. Or, in fact, what kindness is and where it comes from. We'll try to answer these questions and take a fresh look at this concept in this chapter.

Let's start with a few definitions. What is kindness? Kindness is a positive, general stance towards yourself and others. In kindness you see everyone as equal and extend warm, caring feelings towards all.

Compassion is kindness, mixed with an awareness that you and others are capable of suffering. So when a compassionate person becomes aware of the suffering in others, they have a wish to relieve it. And a compassionate person feels joy when they see other people's happiness, or a relief to their suffering.

But are kindness and compassion really good things? What's their worth and value? Do they serve a purpose?

Reasons to be Kind

Here are 3 reasons why kindness and compassion can be helpful, positive and important to you and everyone around you. But before we start talking about this topic, put aside any shame that society has taught you to have around unkind thoughts and feelings. Try not to avoid any aspects of your thoughts or emotions, even if you think they would be labelled as 'wrong' or 'unkind'. As we look at the first part of this chapter, set aside any thoughts or questions around how we should act or behave as a result of compassion, and instead just focus on the basics first. The basic questions are: what is compassion? And is it a good thing in the first place? The question of how to act and behave from a place of compassion will be covered later in the chapter.

Reason Number 1

Suffering exists, whether we acknowledge it or not. There is no denying the fact that we are each closest to our own suffering. If you cut your finger, only you can feel the physical pain. If your friend cuts his finger, you can't physically feel it. Similarly, if you are abandoned by your loved ones, you can experience the loneliness and sadness at first hand. But if your colleague is abandoned by their loved ones, it's no longer you who is lonely or sad. This simple reality has resulted in many of us deciding that the pain and suffering of others is not our business.

But here's the thing - someone's reality doesn't disappear just because we're not aware of it. Whether or not you can feel the pain resulting from your friend's wounded finger, that pain is still being felt somewhere, by someone - in this case by your friend. The pain is still taking place. And just as you would find the pain uncomfortable, your friend also finds it uncomfortable. It's this simple acknowledgement that underlies the basis for compassion. Just because I am unaware of the suffering, it doesn't mean that it doesn't exist. And pain is pain, no matter who is experiencing it.

Reason Number 2

Kindness and compassion are essential to the easing of suffering. When we are unkind and non-compassionate towards ourselves or others, we are contributing to suffering. Let's take a moment to examine this.

Lack of compassion and kindness towards yourself – we've already learned about this in previous chapters. Lack of compassion towards ourselves can result in so many emotional issues. When we're not compassionate towards ourselves, we lose sight of the struggles that we have had to face in life. So we focus only on our shortcomings. We focus on self-blame, self-punishment, shame and anger towards ourselves. We forget the simple fact that life can be hard, and we are only doing our best. We turn into harsh, uncaring and aggressive critics of ourselves. The only outcome is increased suffering.

Lack of compassion and kindness towards others – similarly, when we're not compassionate or kind towards others, we lose sight of their suffering and struggles. We start to treat them the same way that we would treat ourselves when we are not compassionate. We lose sight of acceptance and expect them to be something other than what they are at this moment. And, well, that's not going to happen. Change takes time and work and learning. Compassion helps us understand that this person, at this moment, is the only way that they can be. The future can and often does change and shape people. But right now, they can't suddenly go *bam!* and morph into a different person.

But our lack of kindness towards them will impact them in so many ways. By being unkind to them, we are deep down, teaching them to be unkind to themselves. We are teaching them that they are not worthy or deserving of love. But when we are compassionate towards others, we might cultivate in them more compassion towards themselves! And we know that so much good change starts with self-compassion. Let's look at an example. Imagine two different parents. Both of their children came home from school one day, with a note from their teacher saying that they had skipped class and been aggressive to other students. This is how they each reacted:

> **Parent number 1** - This parent asked their child 'what happened? What is your version of the story?' Through active listening, they found out that their child had been teased and ridiculed by his classmates. He had been feeling down, self-doubting and angry. As a result, he started skipping class and getting into verbal and physical conflict.
>
> The parent then acknowledged that this must have been uncomfortable for their child and that they understood. When their child felt heard and understood, he felt calmer and agreed to work with the parent to improve the situation. So,

they collaboratively made a plan to improve things. They agreed to try their plan and if it didn't work, they would talk about it again soon.

Parent number 2 - This parent immediately got angry. They started yelling at the child, telling him that he 'should be doing better' and that 'this was not good enough.' They then went on to talk about how hard they worked to make sure the child had a good education, that the child was ungrateful, unruly, and irresponsible. When the child tried to explain what had been happening for him, the parent said that this was no excuse and that they were not interested in hearing these stories. The child was then grounded. He felt lonely and unfairly treated. Out of fear, he did temporarily stop skipping class, but he felt increasingly unhappy inside.

Put yourself in the shoes of each of the children in our stories. Which child is more likely to experience self-compassion as an adult? Which one is more likely to experience self-blame, self-punishment and anger as an adult? Although both of these parents may have had good intentions for their child, can you see that having compassion in their approach was key to raising happier children?

Reason Number 3

Kindness and compassion are foundations to deep social bonds and a key to their long-term stability - It's easy to see the reasons for this. People yearn to be connected with those who understand them, validate their feelings and are kind towards them. Being treated with lack of compassion, with resentment, harsh criticism and intolerance contributes to relationship challenges and the breaking of bonds between people. To have an enjoyable society to live in, with pleasant emotions and a good atmosphere, kindness and compassion are the number one ingredients. See your kindness and compassion as investments that result in a pleasant society you yourself would enjoy living in.

Similarities and Differences

It's easier to feel compassion towards the people we know well, the people we tend to speak to most, people who have similar backgrounds, age group, experiences and lifestyles to us. The reason for this is obvious. We understand the people who are similar to us. We have similar emotional experiences, because we have shared similar life experiences. When you are similar to someone, you can really appreciate the pain and suffering that they might experience. So, you want to help them and attend to their needs.

The opposite is also true. We often find it hardest to feel compassion towards those who are different to us. We struggle to understand the reasons for their behaviour and emotions. We might find that their emotions are foreign to us, or the way that they express those emotions is foreign to us. We also tend to simplify their problems. What do we mean by that? Well, each of us has spent a lifetime journeying through every single moment of our own struggles and as a result we have been moulded into the person we are today. We didn't just wake up one morning and decide to be who we are. It took years of life experiences to create our unique thoughts and emotional patterns. A person who has never had similar life experiences to us may struggle to appreciate why we are the way we are. They might simplify the situation and think that we should just snap out of those emotions. Or that we should just behave differently, just do what is rational. But when you connect with someone who has had similar life experiences to you, you don't tend to simplify their problems. You understand the types of emotional or physical experiences that push them to act in the ways that they do.

This simple fact results in a world where people team up with like-minded or similar people and conflict starts to grow as a result of our lack of compassion towards those who are different. So how can we extend compassion to those people who are different to us? There is a simple principle that might help. Despite their differences, people share the following 3 characteristics:

1. They dislike suffering, fear, and pain

2. They want to be loved and cared for

3. They want to feel a sense of self-worth

Spend some time reflecting on the individuals or groups of people you feel very different to. Now reflect on the fact that, just like you, they have these 3 characteristics, whether they show it or not. Given that they don't like to suffer, just as you don't, can you imagine yourself feeling compassion towards them?

Can you be critical of someone, but maintain a sense of compassion and kindness? The principle of compassion is not so much about agreeing with a person's opinions, beliefs or behaviours. Rather it is about the fact that underneath those opinions, beliefs and behaviours, they are still a person who experiences pain, fear and discomfort. And closing your eyes to their suffering does not make it go away. Even if, in your opinion, they deserve the suffering, they are still experiencing pain in this moment and they wish to be free from it. Compassion is about not closing your eyes to their pain, but rather acknowledging what they are going through. Suffering is unpleasant, no matter who experiences it.

Think of a person with whom you have disagreements or don't see eye to eye. Write down their perspectives, as you have heard them expressed in the past.

.... Ⓟ

....

....

....

....

Now, try to imagine what they may be feeling underneath their thoughts or beliefs. Without feeling a need to agree with their opinions, or changing your own, imagine extending compassion towards them. This means that you acknowledge the pain they may be experiencing and wish for them to feel better.

Homework

In the days and weeks to come, try to spend some time with people you don't normally spend time with, with the sole purpose of getting to know them and understanding them. This includes people of older or younger generations. Or people from different social or ethnic groups. Practise emotion exposure if strong emotions come up as you interact with them.

Compassionate Disagreement

By now, some of you may be wondering: well does compassion mean that I have to constantly enable, agree, support, and tolerate? What about in the face of bullying, injustice or other harmful behaviour from those around me? What if I have tried to communicate and have been met with no willingness to reconcile? Do I just keep giving and sacrificing?

As we mentioned previously, compassion doesn't necessarily dictate your behaviour. It dictates the state of mind underneath your behaviour. At every moment in your interactions, you make decisions and choices and it may be your logic and rationality that help you choose the best course of action. But underneath those choices, you can always display and feel a sense of kindness and compassion towards the other person. There are times when you need to show that you don't agree or approve of a behaviour, for example if you see your friend making fun of another person. The most compassionate act here could be to display your disapproval of the behaviour. You can use your creativity to find a strategy that works best for each situation. For example, you could simply not laugh at the joke. Or you may express to your friend why you didn't like their behaviour. You could also make a supportive gesture towards the person who is being made fun of. You could do these things while at the same time feeling compassion towards both of the people in this equation.

Unlike regular punishment that seeks to cause pain, the goal of compassionate disagreement is not to hurt ourselves or other people. Instead, its goal is to create opportunities to contemplate and learn. Compassionate disagreement has the following characteristics:

It does not shame or belittle the person - we now know the importance of our self-image to our mental health. Any disagreement that tries to belittle, ridicule, shame or embarrass the person essentially causes harm to their self-image. That only creates more pain, more anger and more resistance. You should also never portray yourself as superior to the other person in any way. That is contrary to kindness. You should simply show your disagreement from the humble position of an equal human.

It is not aggressive - aggression and anger breed more aggression and anger. Violence creates more violence. It's important to learn to communicate our emotions, rather than to punish with them.

It does not seek to control the other person's will power - humans have individual will power. We make our own choices around what to think, what to believe and how to behave. To break a person's will power (whether they are a child or an adult) means taking away their ability to trust themselves, be true to themselves and be able to make decisions for themselves. If forceful approaches are used to break or control the other person's will power, it results in negative consequences. In special circumstances exceptions to this rule may exist (for example, restraining someone who poses a threat to their own safety or the safety of others), but this type of solution should be reserved for when it's absolutely necessary. In day to day life, disagreements should always be respectful of other people's choices. They should be focused on creating real change, not coercing others to act as we would like them to.

It does not replace education and communication with punishment - If the other person does not know how to do any differently, what purpose does punishment serve? We should help others understand why we disagree with their behaviour. We should also try to understand why they behave in the ways that they do. If they don't know how to act any differently, we should help them. For example, if your child can't do any better in their maths class, what purpose does punishment serve? All it does is to create a scared and stressed-out child who still doesn't know how to do maths.

Compassionate disagreement should result from active thinking so that we can make sure it's helpful rather than harmful. It shouldn't be a passive projection of anger or punishment towards the other person.

What Impedes Compassion?

Why are we surrounded by so much lack of compassion? What causes such a scarcity of compassion in our societies? There are three major factors that impede compassion. Let's take a look at them now.

The first one is our old friend, **experiential avoidance!** We know that we avoid things because they are uncomfortable. Becoming aware of the suffering of others can be uncomfortable. We are often tempted to push this awareness aside, ignore it and forget all about it. We use a variety of mental strategies to convince ourselves that 'it is not so bad', that 'it is not my business' or 'it is not worth my time'. Or we simply blame the victim for their suffering as a way to feel better about it. This means that on a large global level, suffering continues, and we don't allow the power of our compassion to create positive change. But now we know that before we can have positive change, we first need to accept what is here right now. Whether we like it or not. Acceptance helps us to stop avoiding. Close your eyes for a minute. Take some time to remind yourself of the principle of acceptance: that reality is as it is in this moment. So, we might as well stop internally fighting it. Instead, practise emotion exposure around those uncomfortable emotions that you tend to feel when exposed to the suffering of others. Take a minute now to do that.

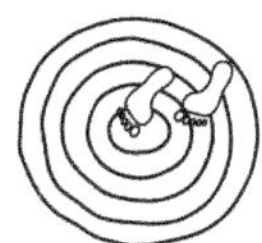

There are also individuals who have relied on experiential avoidance so often and in so many areas of their lives that they have become strangers to their own emotions. They may feel a sort of emotional 'numbness.' In these cases, the individual not only struggles to feel or understand their own emotions, but also struggles to understand other people's emotions or appreciate their suffering. Naturally, this results in reduced compassion overall.

The second reason is **lack of self-compassion.** How can you truly love others if you don't love yourself? People who are blaming or harsh towards others are often just as blaming and harsh towards themselves. If this still applies to you after what we have learned in this book, continue working on it using everything that you have learned. You will find that your ability to be kind and compassionate towards others may grow as you become kinder towards yourself. Along with this, emotions to do with jealousy or inferiority can often make us most unkind. The reason again is that when you compare yourself to others and see yourself as less worthy, you often develop feelings of anger and a wish to punish yourself and others. The answer is to continue working on your ability to reach true self-compassion by pulling yourself out of the world of comparisons and the coin.

And thirdly, **anger and frustration** can block our ability to feel compassion. At times anger can make us uncaring or cause us to want to hurt others or take joy in their misfortune. Just like any emotion, the answer is to recognise it, find it in the body and feel it. Even if you strongly believe that your life circumstances justify your anger and frustration, we suggest that you still process these emotions as you would with any emotion. Any non-compassionate stance will result in more collective pain and more collective mental health problems. So be the change that starts to create a kinder world - even if no one else around you is on board yet.

If you believe that you have bigger issues than the others around you, and hence they should be compassionate towards you but not the other way around, consider this: imagine two people with headaches. One of them has a headache that's twice as bad as the other one. But the person with a less severe headache is still hurting. And you can't expect them to ignore their own pain because it's less severe in comparison with the other person's. A headache is a headache. You don't sit there and compare them to determine which person needs more compassion. Both of these people need compassion, and to the degree that their focus on their own headache allows, they can both acknowledge the pain of the other person and show them compassion.

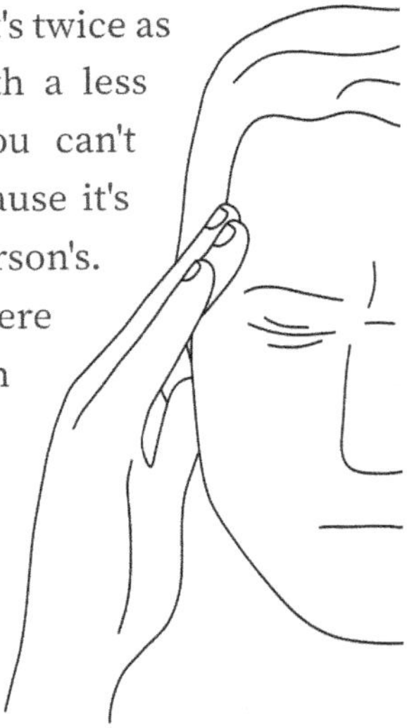

Close your eyes and see if you can remember any emotions that may at times cause you not to feel compassionate. Remember, the purpose is not to fight the emotion or to make it go away. Emotions are normal and okay. The purpose is to feel the emotion with all of your awareness. If you keep your attention on your body, you may notice that the emotion feels better after some time. If the emotion has many layers, treat it like the onion we discussed in chapter 5 and focus on whatever layer you notice next.

Compassion Impersonators

We have spoken about what compassion is. Now, let us take a look at some common experiences that we may have mistaken for compassion. These experiences look a lot like compassion, but they are, in fact, unhelpful thought errors or emotions that are best dealt with so that they don't stifle our happiness.

Personal emotions: At times, seeing others in suffering activates your own emotions. It may trigger personal worries and fears for your own future, if the same thing was to happen to you. It may bring back painful emotions attached to a similar past experience of yours. It may act as a reminder for some of your personal struggles. This is no longer about compassion towards the other person. It's an activation of your own personal emotions. The emotional pain can be intense or, at times, it could go on for hours or days. If seeing others in pain envelops you in strong emotional pain, remember to take time to practise active thinking and emotion exposure around what you are feeling.

Feeling sorry: The basis of compassion is kindness and a sense of equality with the other person. But for some people, the idea of feeling 'sorry' for others can have an underlying tone of 'looking down' on them. This form of 'feeling sorry' involves negative emotions towards those who are less fortunate. For example, the person may feel a fear of turning out like the person that they feel sorry for. They may believe that if they are not doing well in life, they are somehow 'inferior'. It goes back to the coin and our sense of superiority and inferiority.

To put it simply, this type of attitude is missing the important element of kindness. If you tend to feel this way for those suffering, remind yourself that doing well in life or being free of pain is not a sign of superiority. It is a sign that certain elements of life have lined up for you, which have made it easier for you to do well. Practice emotion exposure and become familiar with these emotional experiences in your body.

Self-image: What if we want to make others happy and help them because we expect ourselves to be a model citizen and fear not being a kind, compassionate and overall 'good' person? We may not want the other person to judge us negatively or dislike us. Or we may fear being disappointed in ourselves for not being a caring helper. As you can see, in these scenarios it is no longer the compassion that is the driving factor. Rather it is fear of not being good enough. In other words, your driving factor is about you and not purely about the other person. Fear of going to the negative side of the coin and being an unworthy person. Fear of our self-image being turned negative and unpleasant. If this applies to you from time to time, make sure you use the skills that you have learned in this book to work through your fears and recognise the unhelpful thought errors.

Self-sacrifice tendency: If you habitually neglect your own needs or wants, because you have developed an automatic tendency to always put others first, especially people you consider needy or dependent on you, this may apply to you. The self-sacrifice tendency can turn into an automatic feeling of guilt or anxiety every time you attend to your own needs or want to do something nice for yourself. There is always someone else who needs you. There is always a reason why you can't stop and enjoy things in life. You may even feel that you shouldn't complain or take your own needs or difficulties seriously, because there is always someone who has it worse. However, the self-sacrifice tendency results from anxiety, guilt or other unhelpful thoughts or emotions that in the long run don't serve anyone in the equation.

More Information for Self Sacrificers

Here are some problems with the self-sacrifice tendency:

1. **Sometimes you come first** - sometimes you need something more. Sometimes you are tired. Sometimes you are hurting. Sometimes you have to heal yourself just as much. You are not any less important than anyone else. You are here to live life, as well as to help others. Remember, the purpose of helping others is for humans to have a better experience in life. For them to suffer lessand enjoy more. Well, you suffer too! You should have a better experience too. If the purpose of compassion is to want happiness for anyone who is capable of suffering, how can you forget yourself in this equation? Your experience matters just as much as

anyone else's experience. Because you are one of those humans who deserve to be happy and enjoy life.

2. **You need to be healthy to help others** - sometimes you have to heal yourself first, before you can heal anyone else. If you are burnt out, tired or unhealthy, how can you be of benefit to anyone else? So have the courage to look after yourself when you need looking after.

3. **Your behaviour is training others** - a big problem with the self-sacrifice tendency is that those who are affected by it forget that by continually protecting and shielding the other person or people, they are also taking away from them the opportunity to learn, to grow and to develop the resilience to cope with their own problems. Yes, it's not nice to see others suffer. But at times, teaching them to overcome their own problems is far more valuable than rescuing them over and over again. Unfortunately, self-sacrificers have a tendency to make the people around them dependent on them. Like a mother who has always done everything for their child to make sure that the child doesn't have to deal with life's hardships. But at some point, this mother may realise that since their child has not learned how to deal with those small or large obstacles, they now anxiously run to others for help every time they are in need. Self-sacrificers also often train other people to take for granted that they are the person who will look after things. When there is work to be done, others sit back and everyone sees it as the self-sacrificer's job. So, they feel

run down and exhausted. They don't make a system where people learn to collaborate and chip in. They take on all the burden and it becomes the new norm for everyone.

4. **Self-sacrificers often end up being too tired, too burnt out and too angry because of everything that they have had to shoulder** - many reach a point where they start harbouring anger and resentment towards the people they have been looking after. They may go to the other extreme where they don't want to do anything for anyone anymore. This is when the self-sacrificer might start acting in unkind and non-compassionate ways, which is exactly the opposite of what they had intended at first.

So, if you are a self sacrificer, see if you can make an internal decision to turn things around and gradually relinquish responsibility where you can. If emotions like guilt or worry are preventing you from doing this, work through them using the skills that you have learned so far in this book.

Joining the Unhappy Pool: compassion doesn't mean being unhappy and down in a world full of suffering. Imagine if the whole population of the world was 100 people. There were 99 unhappy people there, and you were the 100th person. Does compassion mean joining the pool of unhappy people, and as a result causing happiness to go extinct in the world? Where would be the sense in that?

The answer is simple; you have the choice to be happy. And

> “The best place to extend kindness from is a place of emotional peace and joy. Not from a place of pain and anxiety. So even if you see everyone around you being unhappy, give yourself the permission to be happy.

perhaps, through your happiness, you can make more people around you happy. It doesn't help anybody if you join the pool of suffering. Compassion means caring, wishing happiness for those who are unhappy and extending kindness. And the best place to extend kindness from is a place of emotional peace and joy. Not from a place of pain and anxiety.

So even if you see everyone around you being unhappy, give yourself the permission to be happy. Yes, as a result of compassion you could experience painful emotions like sadness or grief, but these emotions shouldn't become your constant state. Give yourself the right to pull yourself up, instead of going down into the unhappy pool.

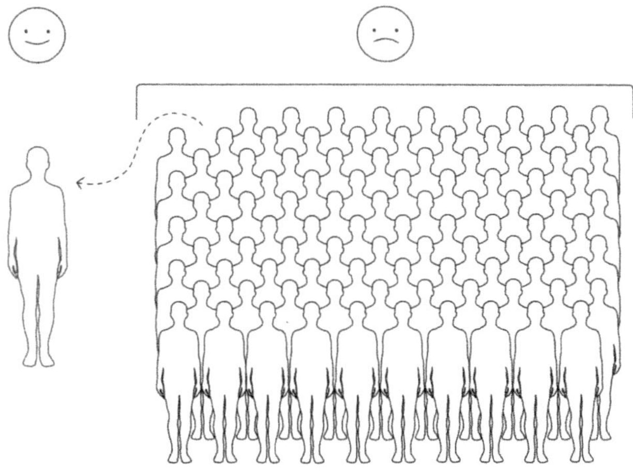

Remember: like most people, you are given your own fair share of happy and unhappy moments in life. And the same applies to everyone around you. Grabbing on to the unhappiness of others will increase the load of your unhappiness but will not reduce theirs. You're only increasing overall suffering for humans. But true compassion and kindness can help to reduce the suffering of others.

Acts of Altruism

Altruism means acting on your compassion. This is where your skills in active thinking and compassion can come together to create something great. Compassion means that your focus can be placed on efforts to make the world a better place for yourself and for others, to multiply happiness and to increase mental health. At times, it's not easy to see how achieving this goal is possible, when so much is out of our control. But active thinking can bring about creativity. It can bring about seeing things with a fresh new look and finding solutions that didn't exist before. We may be able to stop saying 'it's not possible' and start wondering 'how can I achieve it?' This means that where you see problems and suffering, you begin using active thinking to find helpful solutions. Remember to use tricks like writing or speaking to someone who understands to help you along in your active thinking process.

Remember: at times helping others may mean teaching them to help themselves, or trusting their strength to fight their own battles. You may need to encourage them to stop avoiding their fears and face them instead. Try to consider what actions might help the person most in the long run.

Coping with Compassion

Compassion can cause us emotional pain, especially at times when it is not within our capacity to help someone, or to help everyone. As we have previously learned, emotions are not bad. Uncomfortable emotions are not a sign of mental illness. It's how we process those emotions that results in mental health or illness. So, it's important that when compassion causes us emotional pain, we don't resort to experiential avoidance. Instead we must make a habit of practising emotion exposure: meaning that you remain with the emotion, place your full focus on the experience of the emotion and practise emotion exposure.

We should also remember the principle of acceptance. Acceptance comes from the place of knowing that things are as they are, whether we like them or not.

And finally, stay in the present moment. That means that after the emotions have passed, there is no need to hold on to the unhappy thoughts. Permit yourself to experience happiness again, while trusting in the other person's ability to handle challenges. Remember that each person will have their share of happy and unhappy experiences in life. And there is no sense in you joining 'the unhappy pool'.

Faces Ⓕ

Grab a photo album, a magazine or a newspaper or try running an online search for pictures of people's faces. Take a look at each face and see if, within you, you can tell what they might be feeling. This exercise is about helping you to internally connect with the person experiencing the emotion. You don't necessarily need to know what their emotion is called.

Now have a think about this question: if you were feeling these emotions, how would you like to be treated by those around you? How would you like them to interact with you?

Think about a person you've interacted with recently. Can you remember their facial expression and body language? How do you believe they were feeling? Close your eyes and imagine what that would feel like. If you were feeling that way, how would you have liked to be treated?

In the days to come, make a practice of noticing the facial expressions and body language of those around you, imagining what they might be feeling inside and extending compassion and kindness towards them.

Exercise Ⓖ

Let's finish this chapter with a few exercises around practical real life scenarios of compassion.

Everyone is capable of experiencing suffering, regardless of:

How intelligent they are

True ☐

False ☐

Where they are from

True ☐

False ☐

How much money they have

True ☐

False ☐

How educated they are

True ☐

False ☐

What they look like

True ☐

False ☐

Their ability to logically understand the world around them

True ☐

False ☐

What gender they are

True ☐

False ☐

What age they are

True ☐

False ☐

How nice or helpful they are

True ☐

False ☐

We should be compassionate to people because we like them, agree with them, they are related to us, or they are similar to us.

True ☐

False ☐

We should be compassionate to people because they can suffer.

True ☐

False ☐

People suffer, even if their suffering doesn't directly impact us.

True ☐

False ☐

To be kind you need to see the other person as your equal, and feel care and warmth towards them.

True ☐

False ☐

Read the following scenarios and decide which ones are compassionate:

Continuing a joke, even though your friend finds it hurtful. You don't think the joke should hurt them, so you tell them to stop being 'oversensitive'.

Compassionate ☐

Not compassionate ☐

Criticising people a lot as soon as you don't like something about them.

Compassionate ☐

Not compassionate ☐

Calling a friend soon after you have had an argument with them, because you don't want them to feel bad for too long, or to go to bed with negative emotions.

Compassionate ☐

Not compassionate ☐

Refusing to do your friend's assignment, but instead offering to help them figure out how to do it on their own.

Compassionate ☐

Not compassionate ☐

Commenting on your friends' weight, appearance, fashion sense or other characteristics, without considering how your comments might make them feel about themselves.

Compassionate ☐

Not compassionate ☐

Feeling relieved about the fact that a person you owe money to does not know their legal rights, because that way you can get away with not paying them.

Compassionate ☐

Not compassionate ☐

Cutting communication with a friend, with no explanation of what they have done to upset you. In your mind you feel justified because they shouldn't have done what they did to hurt you. Meanwhile the other person doesn't know why they are being punished and begins guessing and second guessing everything they did, and their worth to you as a friend.

Compassionate ☐

Not compassionate ☐

Blaming a person for the wrongs done by other people, simply because they happen to have shared characteristics like cultural background, skin colour, gender, facial features etc. If they are similar enough to the people responsible for the wrongs committed, then it's safe to assume that they would act in similar ways.

Compassionate ☐

Not compassionate ☐

Woah,
I've completed
92% of the
book! ☐

Chapter 13: Health, Rest and Leisure

The Body

We often tend to consider the body as completely unrelated to our minds or mental health. But that could not be further from the truth. By now, you can no doubt see that it is in the body that we feel our emotions. In fact, we often confuse purely physical sensations, like hunger, or tiredness, or hormonal changes with emotions. You may have noticed this yourself: one day you wake up with a sore throat, an achy body and a heavy head. Great! You are coming down with a cold. But it looks like today every emotional thing gets to you a bit more as well. The same could happen when you are hungry or tired and suddenly everything feels more negative. This is, at least in part, because we often confuse uncomfortable sensations within the body with emotions. On days when your body feels great, it is much easier to also feel great emotionally.

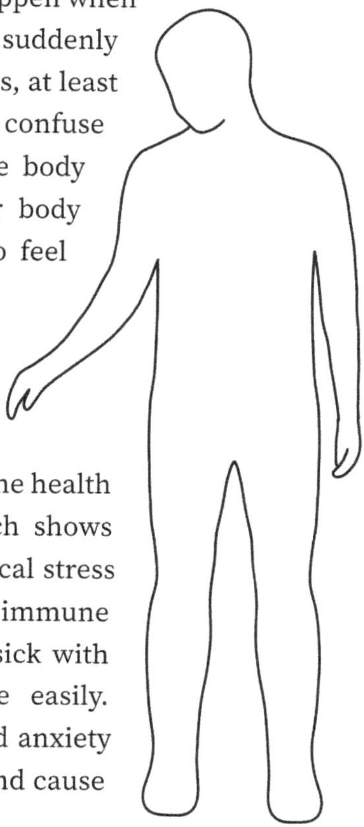

The connection between the mind and the body goes even further than that. Firstly, the health of our emotions can, in many ways, impact the health of our bodies. For example, research shows that people going through psychological stress may experience a weakness in their immune system, meaning that they may get sick with things like the cold and flu more easily. Emotional factors like depression and anxiety can make us more sensitive to pain and cause us to experience pain more intensely. Emotional factors can even create pain in the body where there are no underlying physical reasons for it. On the other hand, for people experiencing physical pain or illness, exercises like mindfulness and relaxation can reduce the experience of pain and discomfort.

What does all of this mean for you? Well, for starters, it means that when you feel pain or discomfort in your body, you now have some tricks up your sleeve to help you cope better. Practising mindfulness techniques, or emotion exposure around any emotions or sensations in the body could help you along. So next time you're at home in bed because you've had to take sick leave from work or studies, use the opportunity. In these kinds of situations, it might sometimes be hard to distinguish emotions from physical discomfort. Don't worry too much about trying to tell them apart. Just close your eyes and focus on whatever the body is feeling. Take your time. You may gradually notice that you're feeling a bit better. Pain and discomfort may still be there, but feelings like anxiety or restlessness can turn into a calm, peaceful state and that might make the whole illness easier to tolerate. Once your mind is calm, start practising mindfulness. You could practise mindfulness of the sounds around you, mindfulness of the body, you could watch your thoughts or focus all of your attention on the flavour of that soup or medicine that you have to have! These are all opportunities for mindfulness.

The strong connection between the body and mind also means that to improve our mental health, we should try to look after our bodies. How do we do that? That's a very big question, and it's outside the scope of this course to fully answer it. We suggest that you make it a personal goal to learn about the many factors that can help make your body healthier. You can research by speaking to health professionals, reading reputable books, journal articles and so on. In this section, we will touch on a few things that we can do to help our bodies along, things that research has shown to have particularly strong benefits for our mental health.

Exercise: exercise helps increase those chemicals in the brain that are responsible for making us feel happy. Exercise is a funny thing. Those who are fit and exercise regularly, talk about it as if it were a miracle drug. They enjoy it and say that it improves their mood. But those of us who haven't exercised for a long time, or who are very unfit might initially struggle with it. The key with exercise is to continue it, even if at first it doesn't make you feel good. Change will be gradual. As your body gets fit, you'll start to experience so many benefits to your body and mind. If it helps, start with really small, easy exercises and shorter amounts of time. Pick activities that you enjoy. Different people might find different types of activity enjoyable - some prefer solo exercises, some team exercises, some like to learn new skills and for some it's just about having fun using physical games or dance. As long as you're pushing your body a little bit each time, you're helping create more fitness. Gradually your gentle walk could turn into a jog. Or you could lift heavier weights at the gym.

Diet: what we eat and the vitamins and minerals that are available to our bodies, have an important role in the happy chemicals in our brain. For example vitamin D (which you can get from certain foods, as well as from sunlight), vitamin Bs (which you need to get from a variety of sources), vitamin C (which you get from many fresh fruits and vegetables), and good oils (such as olive oil or those found in walnuts, chia seeds, flaxseeds, fish etc) are only a few factors that can positively influence depression or anxiety. Reducing inflammation also helps, so anti-inflammatory food such as turmeric could be helpful. Amino acids can be converted to happy chemicals in the brain, so they can help with mental health problems.

On the other hand, research shows that those things that are generally bad for your body, such as fast food, food full of bad sugars or fats, and food that's so processed that it doesn't have many nutrients left in it, are linked with increases in issues like depression and anxiety. So it helps to eat plenty of unprocessed, nutritious foods, like fresh fruits and vegetables. But at times, for various reasons, even eating plenty of good food won't be enough to give your body all the vitamins and minerals that it needs. It may help to see your doctor from time to time to check if your body is deficient in something. For example, if your doctor has let you know that you are iron deficient, it's important to correct that, as it can have a significant impact on your mental health. You can also introduce into your diet a good multivitamin/mineral supplement. Please check with your doctor or pharmacist to make sure that the supplements you plan to take won't interact negatively with any health issues that you may have or medications that you are taking.

Sleep: the relationship between sleep and mental health is an interesting one. Having enough good quality sleep helps improve our mental health, but also a healthy mind helps improve our sleep. Having enough sleep is associated with improved ability to cope with stress and trauma, and a reduction of depression and anxiety symptoms. Good sleep can also improve our concentration and learning. If you struggle with sleep issues, here are a few things that you can try:

1. Practise emotion exposure and mindfulness before bed, or while lying in bed, to help you relax and slow down thinking.

2. Try to sleep at a similar time every night and wake up at a similar time every morning. Our bodies have an internal clock and feel best when we don't meddle with that clock too much. You may have experienced how travelling and being jet lagged affects your mood. So it might be a good idea to help your body clock to not get too confused by constantly changing sleeping or waking times by large amounts.

3. If you tend to stay up really late and wake up quite late in the day, it might be a good idea to make some changes. Research shows that night people have a higher chance of suffering from mental health problems. Even if it feels like right now your mind is most alert and your energy at its peak later in the night, and even if being awake in the morning seems to be a complete waste of time, change is possible. Shifting your body clock slowly by sleeping only a little bit earlier each night and waking up a little bit earlier each morning might be a good approach that is not too difficult.

4. Stay away from caffeine and cigarettes close to bedtime. Too much alcohol close to bedtime isn't a good idea either! Many people use alcohol to help them fall asleep more quickly. The problem is that even though you may fall asleep more easily,

the quality of your sleep may be affected. You may have lighter or more broken sleep.

5. You may like to try keeping your bedroom quiet, dark and free of electronic screens. Turn off the TV or computer. Put your mobile phone on flight-mode or turn it off completely.

6. Expose yourself to sunlight during the day (use sun- protection if needed), especially first thing in the morning.

7. Don't try to force yourself to fall asleep – people who suffer from insomnia often get very fixated on the need to fall asleep, worry about staying awake, or try to use their will power to fall asleep. These thought patterns simply result in anxiety and agitation and won't help with sleeping. Our biology has shaped us in a way that when we are anxious, we become more alert and ready to fight any threats. So instead of getting anxious about not falling asleep, it's best to focus on practising relaxation and mindfulness exercises. If needed, practise emotion exposure around your fear of not falling asleep.

Drugs and Alcohol

The link between our body and mind is also clear when we look at the way in which drugs and alcohol impact us. Of course, we all know that using drugs and alcohol has an immediate impact on the way our minds work. They can relax us, stimulate us, or trigger various pleasant or unpleasant psychological experiences. But many people are not aware of the long-term impact of drugs on our mental health.

Research shows a strong relationship between drugs and mental health issues. People with mental disorders are a lot more likely to be addicted to drugs than the general public. The reverse is also true: those who are addicted to drugs are much more likely to suffer from a mental disorder. Why is that? Well, there are several reasons:

1. People suffering from mental health problems are more likely to use drugs as they try to find a way to avoid and escape their negative emotions.
2. Using drugs or alcohol increases the likelihood of mental disorders being started or getting worse. We will learn more about this shortly.
3. Drugs can cause problems to our relationships, work and financial wellbeing. They further impact our mental health in this way. For example, one night of abusing alcohol may lead to serious conflict with a loved one, breaking the law or other actions that may result in long term consequences. Overtime, this can reduce the quality of our lives.

First, let's take a look at why drugs and alcohol make us feel good. Meet the two happy chemicals in our brain: dopamine and serotonin.

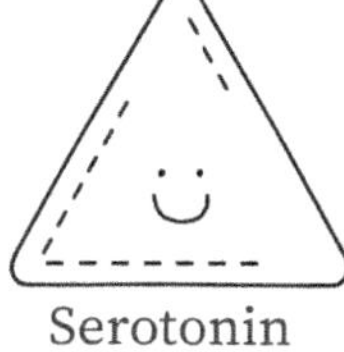
Serotonin

Dopamine

They are 'feel-good chemicals' in the brain that are meant to reward you when you do things that are good for you, like eating good food, getting sleep or doing exercise. But many drugs hijack the dopamine and serotonin systems. This includes alcohol, cannabis and harder drugs like opium, heroin, methamphetamine, cocaine and ecstasy. Each drug uses a different method, but what they all have in common is that they bombard your brain with higher than normal amounts of dopamine or serotonin.

How much of the extra chemical is poured into your brain depends on the type of drug and how much you have used. But regardless of the type, all drugs create a higher than normal amount of dopamine or serotonin inside the brain.

So far it all sounds great, doesn't it? The thing is, your brain is a clever machine. It responds to things and tries to protect itself. For your brain, this is a state of emergency, it's way too much dopamine or serotonin! So, to combat this emergency, it reduces its natural release of these happy chemicals, or closes off the gates for them to be received.

What that means is that once the impact of the drug wears off, you end up with even less happy chemicals than you started with. The reduced dopamine or serotonin in your brain is there to stay for a while, and in the case of some stronger drugs, for a long, long time.

Suddenly normal, daily things that used to make you happy, won't lead to as much of the happy chemicals in your brain anymore. So you don't enjoy things as much. To experience the same level of enjoyment or happiness, you may then be drawn to using drugs again and again, and need to use more of the drug each time.

Addiction

Experimenting with drugs may seem harmless to many people. Some people believe that they are strong enough to keep their drug use in check, not abuse drugs or develop an addiction. Unfortunately, for many, this plan doesn't quite work. Here are two reasons for this:

1. If you used a magic potion that took away a headache once, what's stopping you from using it again when you have another headache a few months down the track? The first time you used it, it seemed harmless enough, and right now all you want is for your headache to go away! Now what happens if your headache starts happening daily? Then you start to use that magic potion every single day. And what if, unbeknown to you, the potion was gradually increasing the frequency or severity of your

headaches - meaning that you had to use it even more often or in higher doses?

Let's say that instead of that headache, it was emotional pain that you were suffering with. And instead of the magic potion, it was one of the drugs we just looked at that took the emotional pain away. What happens when you go through another patch of emotional pain in life? And another patch? And another patch? Can you see that there might be opportunities for that drug use to become more and more frequent? Avoiding painful thoughts and emotions, such as traumatic memories, anxieties, lack of satisfaction and boredom are common reasons that cause many people to develop an addiction.

2. Often addiction happens when we least expect it. With some drugs it creeps in as we deny the fact that we are, more and more, depending on the drug to stay happy and fulfilled. With highly addictive drugs such as heroin, cocaine and methamphetamine, it's often the people who rely heavily on their will power who are trapped into addiction. Many people report that before using the drug, they believed themselves to have strong will power and never thought they would give in to an addiction. However, the strong pull with some of these drugs was not what they had imagined. So, trying these sorts of drugs even once can become a life sentence. And it's commonly those people who believe they will not get addicted who decide to 'just try it once'. Before they know it, they may feel pulled back to using the drug 'just one more time' and 'one more time'. This is how addiction develops.

Educating your children about these issues may be a good idea, as it could protect them against any misleading information that they may be surrounded with in the society or media.

Beating the Dependence

When you are ready to give up, remember the rules of classical conditioning. Do you remember the story from chapter 1 about the street that became conditioned to remind our character of eating lollies? In the same way, for drug users, anything can become conditioned and cause cravings. This includes people, places, times of the day and even emotions. So the first step might be to identify your conditioned triggers. The next step is to work on reconditioning those by not giving into the cravings, or by replacing them with other, healthier things. Something that could really help is noticing the bodily sensations of your cravings and practising emotion exposure around them, instead of acting on them. You may need to repeat emotion exposure around those sensations over and over again, as you train your brain to respond differently. A few other things that you could try are:

- To gradually reduce the amount of the drugs or alcohol that you use, as well as how often you use them. You could even use tricks like drinking really slowly or diluting your drink with non-alcoholic drinks
- Find new friends who don't drink or use drugs, or ask your friends and family to support you
- Don't keep drugs or alcohol in the house
- While trying to give up or reduce your use, do not lose hope if you

have a bad day - it's important to just get back on the horse and not beat yourself up if you don't do well one day. Just keep going and don't look back. Every time you resist the addiction, you are progressing and moving forward.

Home Practice

Make some plans to improve your physical health. These could include improvements around your exercise, diet, sleep or giving up harmful habits. Set small achievable goals and try to work towards them in the week ahead.

.... Ⓟ

....

....

....

Relaxation and Breathing

Let's repeat the relaxation exercise from chapter 1. Remember: This exercise involves tensing and relaxing different muscles in your body. If you have injuries in any part of your body, please skip that part and don't put extra tension on those muscles.

Sit down in a comfortable position. Start with the muscles in your feet and lower legs. First tense and then relax your muscles. Now move up to the muscles in your upper legs and thighs. Again, tense and then relax those muscles. Now repeat the same process for the muscles in your abdomen and lower back: tense, and then relax. Now your chest and upper back. Now move on to your shoulders, arms and hands. We will repeat the shoulders again. This time tense and relax the muscles in your shoulders and neck. Now tense up the muscles in your face. Don't be shy, go ahead and make a face! And relax. And finally, tense the muscles in your jaw, around your ears and all over your head. And relax.

Take a few moments, close your eyes and enjoy the relaxation in your body. If any parts of your body refuse to relax, tense and relax those muscles one more time and keep your attention on that part for a little while.

Now, let's take a minute to learn about breathing. Unhealthy breathing is shallow and quick. Like this:

Healthy breathing is deep and slow, like this:

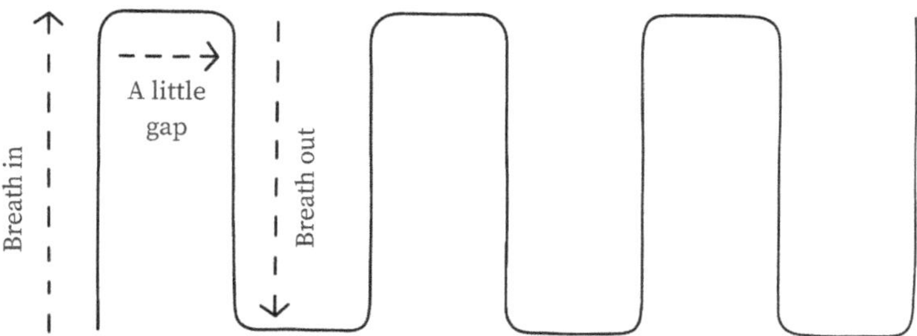

Between a breath in and a breath out, there's a little bit of a gap. No need to rush to the next breath. In that little gap, you can relax the muscles in your chest. Try it. Close your eyes, breathe more slowly, and deeply. And before you rush to the next breath, enjoy the feeling of relaxation in your chest. Take your time. Let this process be effortless and natural.

How did you find this exercise? If you enjoyed it, feel free to use it before bedtime, or whenever you need to de-stress.

Undervaluing Leisure

Do you work to live? Or do you live to work? Many of us have forgotten that we are here to live and there is more to life than work. We undervalue all the sweet things in life. Like leisure, rest, laughter, spending time with our loved ones, arts, music, creativity and so on. We see life as a series of obstacles that we need to get through just to survive. Things that need to be done. Obligations. We forget who we are and turn into robots programmed just to push through one goal after another. Is that how you want to live?

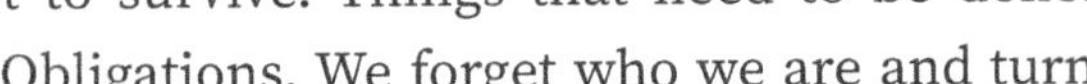

Of course, often the realities of life mean that we don't have a lot of time for rest, leisure or creative activities. We need to work, to earn a living and look after our families. So not all that we do is in line with our personal interests. And that's alright. We need to find ways to make work enjoyable and work through any negative emotions that we may have attached to it. But the point that we're trying to make is that while doing the things we have to do, we must take care not to lose sight of the things we want to do.

When many of us were young children, we may have learned from our parents or other important adults, that creativity and play were less important than studies or chores. So, we may have grown up into adults who continue to undervalue pleasurable activities. We might feel guilty or anxious if we're not doing something that's considered productive. We might feel a fear of 'wasting time'. But rest and enjoyable activities increase positive emotions and are important to our mental health. Living without them can result in exhaustion and a general loss of joy. And not only that, being overworked can result in a drop in our productivity and reduce our ability to cope with pressure. So our work also suffers.

Perhaps most importantly, this will result in losing touch with our own reality. As children, we freely express ourselves using play and art activities. We follow our genuine interests and go about our day with an attitude of ease and freedom. As adults, we often rely on things like deadlines, necessities and a feeling of 'I have to' to motivate us. We often lose touch with what we really want to do.

The time you spend in leisure and creative pursuits is your chance to be that child again! To be you again. It is the segment of time during your day or week, that you allocate to being who you are, expressing yourself freely and enjoying the activities that you are naturally drawn to.

Tip 1

Length of time doesn't matter. If you find that you're too busy to allocate generous amounts of time for rest, leisure and creativity, then allocate small blocks of time to them.

Try to keep these blocks of time regular. Practise discipline to make sure your blocks of leisure take place regularly, even if they are brief. Don't give in to the thoughts that tell you that these blocks are a waste of time or are less important than work.

Tip 2

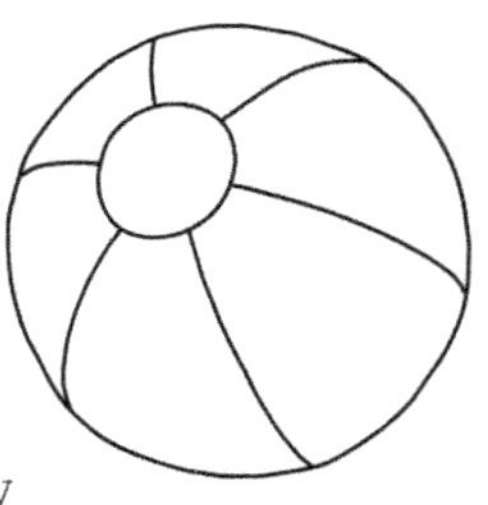

Don't allow competitiveness and perfectionism into your periods of creativity and play. Remember, the point of these activities is freedom of expression and restful joy. Competitiveness and perfectionism can create more stress for you. Before you know it, you may find yourself grappling with fear of failure or a need to preserve a positive self-image. If you enjoy pushing yourself, mastering a new skill or creating helpful or beautiful things, focus on the challenge and not on whether or not you're good enough in comparison to others. If you enjoy creativity and self-expression, forget about trying to create an impressive image that everyone will like. Focus on expressing yourself. Focus on enjoying the process of creating, not worrying about the outcome.

Exercise Ⓕ

Make a list of all of your old and new hobbies. Your hobbies can be anything that you enjoy doing. Anything at all. Even if, to other people, it's not considered a hobby. If you can't think of any hobbies, maybe write down a list of a few things that you wouldn't mind trying. You don't have to be good at it. You just need to be interested in trying it or curious to see if you may enjoy it.

....

....

....

....

....

Now close your eyes and imagine letting go and enjoying one of your hobbies. Do you feel any guilt or anxiety around resting or not doing productive work? Where do you feel these emotions in the body? Close your eyes and focus on these emotions, until they pass.

Fear of Time

For some of us, the idea of truly relaxing and being able to enjoy leisure, needs a bit of extra work. This is especially the case for those who have developed a fear of time passing. Fear of time takes so many shapes and forms. Here are 4 common types:

1. **Time is passing by** - we often receive messages from the society around us that time is running out, it's passing by, it needs to be seized! We keep looking at calendar days, or

remembering how old we are, and then feel anxious about the passing of the time. This is a bit of a mental trick. It's okay for time to pass by. The problem is that those of us who have developed anxiety around this will not be able to relax and make the most of each of these passing moments. It's like eating an ice cream, and with every bite feeling sad or anxious that the ice cream is running out. It would be a bit difficult to enjoy your ice cream that way, wouldn't it? Living in the present moment means that you focus on what is happening right now, instead of getting anxious about what is in the past or the future. Worrying that your time is running out or that you've wasted time is not living in the present moment. Living in the present moment means relaxing and thinking of nothing, other than enjoying what is here right now.

As a result, many of us get a bit anxious if we want to take a break and rest. This is worth working through. Yes, the activity of your choice might not be what we're used to seeing as productive. But that doesn't make it any less valuable. So as tempting as it is to put that soccer ball down and go do something more 'productive', resist the urge for a minute. Instead, work through the emotions in the body that are making you feel anxious about having a bit of fun. Let's try that for a minute. Close your eyes and think about time passing by, resting or doing things that you consider unproductive. Practise emotion exposure around any emotions that come up.

2. **Regret** - thinking that a large portion of your time has been

wasted in the past, regret over things that you should have done, or could have achieved.

Now of course there are times in life when regret has a place. A short-lived regret may help us reconsider unhelpful aspects of our lives and look for more helpful alternatives. But this thinking style means that you may blame yourself or blame others for the wasted time, continue feeling regret for long periods of time, or feel overwhelmed with negative emotions.

Often, those affected by this thinking style are unable to make the most of their present moment, as they are so focused on their past. Feeling disappointed in yourself or in your life makes it hard to set new goals, to work hard towards those goals or tolerate possible challenges as you work towards your goals. It's easy for feelings of self-blame and failure to surface as soon as we face challenges. They can cause us to give up more easily. This then means that you may feel you are 'wasting' more and more time.

Tips for shifting this thinking style:

- Practise acceptance around the time that you feel you have wasted. Just as you would accept any other unwanted but true circumstances in your life (e.g. grieving the death of a loved one). Give yourself time to grieve if you need to, until you are able to accept the reality that this time that has passed will not return, no matter how much you internally fight it. Accept that what is done, is done, whether we like it or not. We must stress the importance of allowing plenty of time for this step and not trying to rush or bypass it.

- Consider the fact that time is relative. We're all given different amounts of time in this life. Imagine that your time starts now.
- Practise emotion exposure around any remaining emotions of regret, guilt, anxiety, sadness etc.

3. **Life Deadlines** - thinking that you're falling behind in life. Setting up mental deadlines for yourself and feeling unfulfilled if you fall behind. Some examples are: 'I need to be married and have children by the time I'm 30', or 'I need to have achieved my career goals by the time I'm 40' and so on.

   In previous chapters, we learned that goals can be useful. But goals need to be flexible, and we need to be brave enough to entertain plan Bs, in case we don't achieve our original goals. Because, as people, we can rarely control all the various factors that lead to future outcomes in life. So being fixated on these types of mental deadlines can lead to feeling dissatisfied or anxious. It's important to practise acceptance if certain factors are outside your control and do not go according to plan. Remember, when present realities are outside our control, refusing to accept them won't change those realities. It will only make us less happy. So, see if you can come up with a plan B and spend time coming to terms with it, and finding your happiness within that alternative plan.

   ....(P)

   ....

....

....

Close your eyes and see if you can practise acceptance around those areas of your life that are not going to plan. If you need to, place your attention on the body. Practise emotion exposure around any emotions that come up.

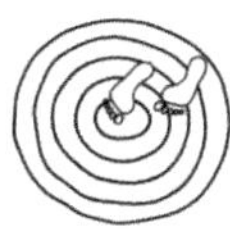

The 'Happiness Judge'

At times, our worry and anxieties attach themselves to the most pleasant things in our lives, telling us that we owe it to ourselves to have fun, be happy, experience life, make the most of our money, make the most of our opportunities etc. The happiness judge says 'why aren't you happy enough?', 'you should be doing more with your life', 'you shouldn't miss out'. So we may feel regretful, unsatisfied, angry or down. Mundane, normal and ordinary life circumstances disappoint the happiness judge. You may spend so much time glorifying a holiday, a new car, a new house, getting married, reaching a career goal, and so on. You may feel like these events will finally bring you lasting happiness and excitement. Alas the holiday might be ruined by bad accommodation, the new car or house will eventually become old, getting married will not free you from your painful thoughts and emotions and reaching the career goal might have a period of excitement followed by new challenges and hard work. At the end of the day, all exciting experiences are temporary and they are followed by the mundane - the ordinary.

At times the happiness judge causes you to feel conflicted when making decisions, because you fear not picking the best option. No matter how thoroughly you consider your options, you realise that even the best choices could have flaws, or that something better might be around the corner. This then turns the harsh, internal judge against you, saying 'I made a mistake and now I'm going to miss out'.

Comparison is a large part of the happiness judge. A slice of pizza bought from an ordinary, humble pizza shop might be very delicious. But if you compare it to that slice of pizza you had at a high end restaurant with an award winning Italian chef, you would most likely be disappointed. Taking comparisons out of the ordinary moments of life can help us enjoy each moment free of any expectations.

The thing to remember is that if we stop thinking and comparing, this present moment and our ordinary life are the very sources of happiness we have been seeking. Research shows that we are happiest when we are concentrated on the present moment, as opposed to thinking of the past or future. Focusing on the present moment means placing your complete attention on the taste of that cup of tea you are drinking, laughing with a friend, lying down in bed on a summer night while listening to the singing of the crickets, or taking a warm shower after a long day at work. Enjoying these ordinary moments with your complete attention and free of any other thoughts is cheap and available to everyone!

A Break from Thinking

It's not only our bodies that need rest and relaxation. The mind also needs a break. We have already learned that thinking is like work. So, when the mind rests, it needs a break from thinking. A common question at this point is: 'but if I'm not thinking, what will I do? What will my mind do instead of thinking?'

This question comes up for people because they are so used to thinking all the time, like a person who has worked hard for years, without ever taking a break. If you encourage them to take some time off, they will not know what to do with themselves! They are so used to working, and that is all they know.

The simple answer is that the thing you do when you are not thinking is simply being aware of what is happening at this moment. In other words, mindfulness. When you think, you create mental images, you create ideas, you control or shape or logically analyse things. You could say that your thoughts are your creations. And creating is work.

But when you are mindful, you're not creating anything. You're not changing or controlling or analysing. You are just paying attention to what is already here. You let go of mind-based creation and just become one with what is already here. And in giving up that creation and control, you give yourself permission to rest. It's true that at times what is here may not be very pleasant. But if we relax and stop avoiding what is here, we know that uncomfortable emotions can give way to peace. So you can feel calm and rested within the reality that's surrounding you. Let's take a few minutes to practise a mindfulness exercise.

Sit comfortably and begin by practising mindfulness of sound.

Now shift your attention to your thoughts, allow the thoughts in and listen to, watch or feel your thoughts.

Then shift your attention to the feelings in your body and practise mindfulness of your body sensations. Begin by wiggling your toes and noticing how they feel. Then rest them and continue feeling them. Now work your way upwards and notice each part of your body, all the way to your head.

Now shift your attention to your breath. Relax the muscles in your chest, allow your breathing to become slower and deeper. No fast or shallow breathing. Take small breaks between each breath where you relax your chest muscles. Don't force this process, let it be natural.

Now shift your attention back to your thoughts, allow the thoughts in and listen to, watch or feel your thoughts. Notice how you are in charge of where you place your attention. Your attention may occasionally wander off, but you can always bring it back.

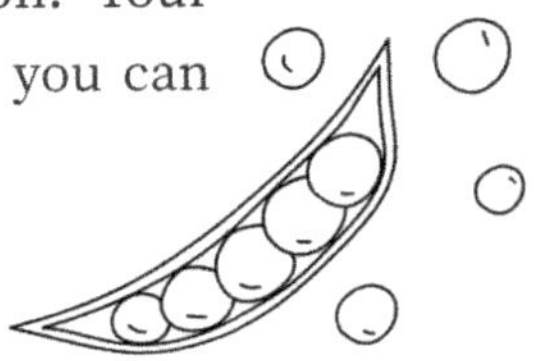

Once again shift your attention away from thoughts and back to sounds. If your attention initially wanders off, gently bring it back to the sounds. Notice the movement of your attention. And notice that you are in charge of your attention.

Can you see the peace and relaxation of your mind as you take a break from thinking?

Now you are about to be asked to once again allow in your thoughts. Except that, this time, be mindful of how your body feels. Does it shift from rest to tension? Notice the emotions in your body. Take a moment to practise emotion exposure around whatever your body is feeling. Stay with the emotions in your body without fighting them or trying to get rid of them. Feel them until they feel relieved. Take your time.

Remembering This Book

Now let's try remembering what we've learned in this booked. Close your eyes and go through what we have covered, from the beginning of this book, till now. Don't pressure yourself to remember everything. Just allow the remembering to naturally happen at its own pace. What moments, thoughts or realisations come to your mind? Can you remember your own thought processes and emotions as you were journeying through each chapter? What have you already begun practising and what do you still need to practise? How and when do you plan to practise these?

If you like, create a contract with yourself. You can start with 'I promise to myself...', and then write down those things that you have learned in this book that you would like to keep working on. For example, you could make plans to continue your mindfulness practices, active thinking and emotion exposure.

Tip: Experience shows that revisiting this book from time to time can help you get more and more out of it. So, you may like to work this into your plan.

....Ⓕ

....

....

....

Again, remember to revisit this book from time to time. This brings us to the end of this Book. Well done and enjoy the rest of this journey. Don't forget: mental health is a task for all of us!

A Little Note to Readers:

Pass It On!

This book marks a major change in how we teach and spread mental health knowledge. The Fount™ framework offers a fresh new approach that does away with the need for available mental health experts, opening up exciting new possibilities for reaching people all over the world more easily and swiftly.

There's only one catch: the success of this framework relies on everyone's help. This includes you! The Fount™ framework focuses on growth through a community-driven approach, relying on readers of *Mind Wellbeing* to pass on the knowledge and create a ripple effect!

How, you may ask? It's simple: the idea is for readers to form their own *Mind Wellbeing* study groups with their social circles in order to spread the benefits to others. Without relying on available mental health experts or trained facilitators, every reader of *Mind Wellbeing* has the power to help spread this knowledge to their communities, families, coworkers, and friends.

When you form a *Mind Wellbeing* study group, you're getting more out of the book by re-reading it, which, especially in a group setting, can help you find new insights and deepen your understanding. But also, you become part of something bigger—a movement to tackle the global mental health crisis!

Are you keen to give us a hand in achieving this goal? Then keep reading... It's easier than you might think!

As people read a book or complete a course that can improve their life, they often think about others who would also benefit from what they're learning. Was this your experience as you read *Mind Wellbeing*? If so, who did you wish you could share *Mind Wellbeing* with? Feel free to write down their names below:

Would you consider reaching out to one or several of these people and inviting them to join you in forming a group or book club to study Mind Wellbeing together? Take a moment to active think about the practical steps or communication strategies you need to organise for this to become a reality. You may like to refer to the section 'Studying This Book With a Group' on page XIX for a reminder on how to form a group.

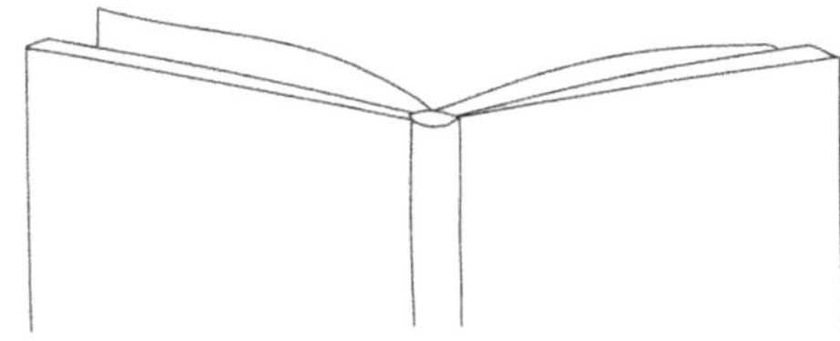

Use the space below to brainstorm your ideas and plans, and write down any potential challenges you might face along with possible solutions. You can even role-play (by yourself or in your group) how you could overcome any challenges.

 368

Planning Space Ⓕ

Human groups need leadership to work together and achieve their common goals. Without a leader, groups can struggle to organise themselves, lose focus, and struggle to make decisions or manage time. A leader is simply someone who helps guide the group and keeps things on track. In your group, you might like to assume the role of the group leader or facilitator, or pass on this role to another group member. The group members could even take turns to have this role. The leader or facilitator would organise the group, make sure plans go ahead, help the group stay focused and on task, manage time effectively, and create a supportive and inclusive environment.

How do you feel about assuming the role of the group leader or facilitator? Ⓕ

1. I'm comfortable to take on this role. ☐
2. I'm not feeling very confident, but keen to take on the challenge. ☐
3. I'm not comfortable to take on this role and not keen to take on this challenge. I would prefer to pass on the role of leadership to another group member ☐

Take a moment to reflect on ways to increase your own confidence or invite another group member to take on the role of the group leader/facilitator:

....

....

....

....

Challenging Member Dynamics

Creating a supportive and effective group dynamic is essential for the success of Mind Wellbeing groups. Below are a few points to consider on how to facilitate group interactions, encourage meaningful participation, and handle challenging member dynamics.

The good news is that most challenging group dynamics can be resolved with two ingredients that you learn about in the book:

1. Good Communication Skills

2. Compassion and Acceptance

Below we explore a few common scenarios where these two ingredients can help you navigate challenging group dynamics.

Refocusing Conversations - During group discussions, members could at times overly dominate discussions, or digress and go on a tangent. What are some things you could do in these situations to bring your group back to focus? Here's how compassion and communication strategies can help you manage this situation. As you try to refocus the group, take every measure to make sure you're not shaming the person who is speaking. A good way to achieve this is to thank them for the interesting points they are raising, or acknowledge any other value that you can find in their comments before attempting to refocus the group. You could also suggest a later point to continue that discussion.

Handling Questions and Clarifications - Participants may have questions or need clarifications as they go through the book. Remind them that Mind Wellbeing is comprehensive and often answers many common questions as they progress. If you think a participant's question is addressed in a particular section of the book, refer them to that section. At other times, encourage patience by explaining that the answers to most questions will fall into place as they learn various pieces of the puzzle and practice exercises from multiple sessions. Group leaders and facilitators should avoid using their own interpretations of the book's contents in a way that suggests they know the definitive answer. Instead, feel free to share your reflections while making it clear that this is your personal understanding of the content, not an authoritative answer.

Catering for People with More Severe Mental Health Issues - In the section 'When to Seek Further Help' on page XVIII, we touched on the idea that individuals with more significant mental health challenges may require additional help beyond what is offered in a self-help program like this. These individuals may struggle with concentration, motivation, and energy levels, making it hard for them to consistently attend or fully benefit from the program. At times, these individuals may benefit from participating in Mind Wellbeing alongside intensive, personalised support from mental health professionals. In other cases, it might be best to wait until they are more stabilised and less overwhelmed before they engage with the program.

Programs like Mind Wellbeing are designed to promote overall mental wellness but are not equipped to handle situations like acute crises or severe distress. If you ever encounter a group member who seems too unwell to benefit from the program or if they are disturbing other participants and preventing them from benefiting, have a gentle and supportive chat with them to explore if they feel ready to participate at this stage. Aim to reach a mutual decision with the participant about whether it might be best for them to wait until they are more ready. Asking them questions about how they are feeling and whether they are benefiting from the program could be a good strategy to help them reflect on their current experience and readiness. Encourage them to seek professional treatment if they haven't already and provide reassurance that the program will be there for them when they are ready.

Other Dynamics that Benefit from Compassion and Communication - These two ingredients can be used to resolve a variety of challenges that your group may face. For instance, if members are having conflicts or not getting along, encourage open communication between them, while using empathy to understand each person's perspective and provide them with support. If members are late to sessions or missing sessions, take every care to avoid shaming them as they could be facing a variety of challenges. Instead, have a supportive chat to encourage them to catch up on the reading they missed. Specifically, encourage participants who have missed Chapter 5 to catch up on it, or ideally try their best not to miss it, as it is a foundational chapter that all future chapters depend on.

Considering Cultural Factors - As a reader of Mind Wellbeing, you are an expert in your own culture. Think about what factors might enhance learning or participation within your cultural context. For example, in some cultures, it might be necessary to slowly and gradually introduce art activities or games, as they might be seen as childish. In other cultures, there might be a need for more art or other activities to foster engagement. Use your initiative to tailor the program to fit cultural sensitivities and preferences. We value your feedback and cultural insights to improve the program. Please share your feedback with us via info@fount.com.au

So now, how do you feel about creating and nurturing a group that can foster an environment for learning and healing? Feel free to write down any other reflections you have, or active think about any hesitations you have below:

.... Ⓕ

....

....

....

By forming and nurturing your own *Mind Wellbeing* study groups, you're contributing to a global movement aimed at improving mental health on a larger scale. You are helping to create a ripple effect that extends far beyond your immediate circle, reaching more people and making a significant impact on global mental health. Now that you have worked out most of the details, all you need to do is let it happen and enjoy seeing everyone in your group flourish and achieve inner wellbeing, one session at a time!

Certificate of Completion

Fount™ - Mind Wellbeing Program

Presented to ....

(Print Name)

for successfully completing 100% of the Mind Wellbeing manual.

Signature: ....

Name of the Person Signing: .... Date: ....

☐ I am signing my own certificate of completion *

☐ I am the Mind Wellbeing group facilitator/leader/organiser

☐ We studied Mind Wellbeing together or as part of the same group

☐ Other (please specify your relationship to the participant):

....

* *This certificate is based on an integrity-based honour system, allowing participants to sign their own certificate of completion to affirm that they have completed the program.*

Essential Terms Cheat Sheet

Acceptance

Acceptance is a realisation that reality can't be any different in this moment, so by releasing our resistence against the reality of this moment, we can free ourselves from unnecessary emotional struggle. Acceptance isn't about giving up or stopping efforts to improve our circumstances. It is an internal quality that can lead to inner calm while still working toward improving external circumstances.

Active and Passive Thinking

Passive Thinking is when your mind is running on autopilot. Thoughts are churning in the background without you paying much attention. Automatic thoughts repeat the same ideas or concerns without being questioned or leading to any solutions.

Active Thinking is when you're aware of your thoughts and actively pay attention to them. You engage with what's going on in your mind, assess your thoughts, and question them. By becoming an active participant in your thinking, you can manage your thoughts better, break free from unhelpful patterns, and find solutions to problems.

Blame

Blame is focusing on finding someone to hold responsible and punish when things go wrong—whether it's ourselves or others. It's the opposite of compassion and a form of non-acceptance, where we resist the reality of our own and other people's challenges and ignore that someone might not have known better or couldn't help it. Instead of helping us find solutions blame focuses on the problem - channelling frustration or rage.

Compassion

Compassion is the ability to recognise and empathise with the suffering or difficulties of others, coupled with a desire to help alleviate it. It can also result in joy when we see other people's happiness, or a relief to their suffering. Compassion encompasses empathy - being able to put yourself in someone else's shoes - and the ability to be present with suffering, without judgement or efforts to avoid or suppress it.

Conditioning and Exposure Therapy

Conditioning is the process where our brain links two unrelated things, often through repeated experiences. For example, we might learn to associate a harmless situation with fear because of a past negative experience.

Exposure Therapy is a method to unlearn those unwanted connections by intentionally facing the things we fear or dislike in a safe and controlled way. By repeatedly facing the feared situation without any negative consequences, our brain automatically adjusts, and our anxiety decreases.

Emotion Exposure

Emotion exposure is the process of fully experiencing an emotion by giving it your full attention without trying to change, suppress, or control it. Instead of using logic or reasoning to manage emotions, you focus on the physical sensations of the emotion in your body—like heaviness, restlessness, or pressure—and allow them to exist as they are. By staying present with the emotion you allow the emotion to be felt, processed, and eventually relieved. Mastering this skill and practicing it regularly can become a powerful tool for improving your mental health and wellbeing.

Experiential Avoidance

Experiential avoidance is any internal effort to avoid, escape, or control psychological experiences like thoughts, emotions, beliefs, sensations, memories, or impulses. This might involve distracting ourselves, suppressing certain thoughts, or pretending uncomfortable realities don't exist. While it might feel helpful in the moment, avoiding these experiences often leads to more challenges in the long run.

Mindfulness

Mindfulness means being fully present in the moment without judging it—paying attention to your thoughts, emotions, and surroundings as they are without trying to change or control them. Mindfulness is not about thinking about the past or future, nor is it about coming up with new ideas or other thought-based activities. It's simply paying attention to what's already here.

Self-Compassion

Self-compassion means showing yourself kindness and understanding, especially during times of weakness, imperfection, or struggle. Just as you might comfort an injured animal or a crying child, self-compassion involves offering that same care to yourself. Instead of harsh self-criticism or blame, it involves approaching your struggles with curiosity and care, seeking to understand challenges and find constructive solutions. This mindset fosters emotional healing while also helping you address and improve the areas of you're not satisfied with.

Self-Image

Your self-image is how you see yourself—the mental pictures, opinions, and emotions you associate with who you are. It shapes your sense of identity and how you feel about yourself as a person. There are two main components to self-image:

Thoughts: These are your beliefs and opinions about who you are, how others see you, your worth, and your value. This is often referred to as your sense of identity.

Emotions: These are the feelings tied to being you or the emotions that feel closest to your sense of self—your 'you-ness'. They are often experienced in the body, just like any other emotion.

The Coin

'The coin' is a metaphor for how we measure self-worth in a world of comparisons. One side represents superiority, believing 'I am better', while the other represents inferiority, believing 'I am not good enough.'

In this cycle, we chase the 'good' side and fear the 'bad,' but both are inseparable. The higher we base our worth on being 'better,' the harder the fall when we feel we have failed. 'The coin' creates unnecessary emotional pain, tying our worth to how we rank against others. True freedom lies in stepping away from this coin and finding self-worth beyond comparison.

Sifters and Moulders

Sifters and moulders are people with two different approaches to relationships:

Sifters focus on searching for people who won't hurt or disappoint them. They often test relationships, disconnecting from others when trust is broken or when their expectations aren't met. This can leave sifters feeling lonely or struggling to trust others, as misunderstandings and emotional mistakes are common in all relationships. Sadly, sifters can eventually give up on relationships altogether, feeling that no one truly meets their standards.

Moulders accept that people can make mistakes as a result of emotions, errors in judgement or misunderstandings. So they attempt to gradually shape their relationships into healthy, happy connections through open communication. Moulders seek to understand others, find common ground, and don't give up on relationships easily. While they know not every relationship can be saved—since both people need to be willing to work on it—they have a better chance of building deep, meaningful connections.

The World of Comparisons and Absolutes

The world of comparisons is where worth is measured by comparing one thing to another. In this world, we label things as 'better' or 'worse,' 'superior' or 'inferior,' based on how they stack up. We judge and measure people, expecting them to meet certain standards or be like someone else. This leads to unnecessary emotional pain, as we might feel inadequate if we don't measure up or fail to appreciate others for who they truly are.

The world of absolutes is where things are viewed as they are, without comparison. In this world, people's unique qualities are appreciated without being measured against others, fostering acceptance and reducing emotional stress.

Your Own Definitions

Use the space below to jot down any other definitions or key terms you'd like to add for quick reference later on. This is your personal glossary—customise it to your liking!

....

....

....

....

....

....

....

....

....

....

....

....

....

....

....

References

American Psychiatric Association. (2000). Diagnostic and statistical manual of mental disorders (4th ed., text rev.). Author.

Antypa, N., Vogelzangs, N., Meesters, Y., Schoevers, R., & Penninx, B. W. (2016). Chronotype associations with depression and anxiety disorders in a large cohort study. Depression and Anxiety, 33(1), 75-83.

Arntz, A. (2002). Cognitive therapy versus interoceptive exposure as treatment of panic disorder without agoraphobia. Behaviour Research and Therapy, 40(3), 325-341.

Batson, C. D., Turk, C. L., Shaw, L. L., & Klein, T. R. (1995). Information function of empathic emotion: Learning that we value the other's welfare. Journal of Personality and Social Psychology, 68, 300–313.

Batson, C. D. (1998). Altruism and prosocial behavior. In D. T. Gilbert, S. T. Fiske, & G. Lindzey (Eds.), The Handbook of Social Psychology (Vol. 2, pp. 282–316). McGraw-Hill.

Bell, I. R., Edman, J. S., Morrow, F. D., Marby, D. W., Mirages, S., Perrone, G., et al. (1991). B complex vitamin patterns in geriatric and young adult inpatients with major depression. Journal of the American Geriatrics Society, 39(3), 252–257.

Bloom, D. E., Cafiero, E. T., Jané-Llopis, E., Abrahams-Gessel, S., Bloom, L. R., & Fathima, S., et al. (2011). The global economic burden of noncommunicable diseases. World Economic Forum.

Bloomfield, M. A., Ashok, A. H., Volkow, N. D., & Howes, O. D. (2016). The effects of Δ9-tetrahydrocannabinol on the dopamine system. Nature, 539(7629), 369–377. https://doi.org/10.1038/nature20153

Boettcher, H., Brake, C. A., & Barlow, D. H. (2016). Origins and outlook of interoceptive exposure. Journal of Behavior Therapy and Experimental Psychiatry, 53, 41-51.

Boulanger, J. L., Hayes, S. C., & Pistorello, J. (2010). Experiential avoidance as a functional contextual concept. In A. M. Kring & D. M. Sloan (Eds.), Emotion regulation and psychopathology: A transdiagnostic approach to etiology and treatment (pp. 123-153). Guilford Press.

Bourre, J. M. (2005). Dietary omega-3 fatty acids and psychiatry: Mood, behavior, stress, depression, dementia and aging. The Journal of Nutrition, Health & Aging, 9, 31–38.

Bourre, J. M. (2006). Effect of nutrients (in food) on the structure and function of the nervous system: Update on dietary requirements for brain, Part 1: Micronutrients. The Journal of Nutrition, Health & Aging, 10(5), 377–385.

Brake, C. A., et al. (2016). Mindfulness-based exposure strategies as a transdiagnostic mechanism of change: An exploratory alternating treatment design. Behavior Therapy, 47(2), 225-238.

Chawla, N., & Ostafin, B. (2007). Experiential avoidance as a functional dimensional approach to psychopathology: An empirical review. Journal of Clinical Psychology, 63(9), 871-890.

Dohrenwend, B. S., & Dohrenwend, B. P. (Eds.). (1974). Stressful life events: Their nature and effects. Wiley.

Doherty, A. M., & Gaughran, F. (2014). The interface of physical and mental health. Social Psychiatry and Psychiatric Epidemiology, 49(5), 673-682.

Eckert, M., Ebert, D. D., Lehr, D., Sieland, B., & Berking, M. (2016). Overcome procrastination: Enhancing emotion regulation skills reduces procrastination. Learning and Individual Differences, 52, 10-18.

Eifert, G. H., & Heffner, M. (2003). The effects of acceptance versus control contexts on avoidance of panic-related symptoms. Journal of Behavior Therapy and Experimental Psychiatry, 34(3-4), 293-312.

Eisenberg, N. (2000). Emotion, regulation, and moral development. Annual Review of Psychology, 51, 665–697.

Facer-Childs, E. R., Middleton, B., Skene, D. J., & Bagshaw, A. P. (2019). Resetting the late timing of 'night owls' has a positive impact on mental health and performance. Sleep Medicine, 60, 236-247.

Flett, G. L., Besser, A., Hewitt, P. L., & Davis, R. A. (2007). Perfectionism, silencing the self, and depression. Personality and Individual Differences, 43(6), 1211-1222.

Foster, R. G., Peirson, S. N., Wulff, K., Winnebeck, E., Vetter, C., & Roenneberg, T. (2013). Sleep and circadian rhythm disruption in social jetlag and mental illness. Progress in Molecular Biology and Translational Science, 119, 325-346.

Ginat-Frolich, R., Kara-Ivanov, A., Strauss, A. Y., Myers, A., & Huppert, J. D. (2022). Mechanisms underlying interoceptive exposure: Belief disconfirmation or extinction? A preliminary study. Cognitive Behaviour Therapy, 51(3), 224-237. https://doi.org/10.1080/16506073.2021.2009781

Garland, E. L., & Howard, M. O. (2018). Mindfulness-based treatment of addiction: Current state of the field and envisioning the next wave of research. Addiction Science & Clinical Practice, 13(1), 1-14.

Gordon, R. (1983). An operational classification of disease prevention. Public Health Reports, 98(2), 107–109.

Gross, J. J. (1998). Antecedent- and response-focused emotion regulation: Divergent consequences for experience, expression, and physiology. Journal of Personality and Social Psychology, 74(1), 224-237.

Gross, J. J., & Muñoz, R. F. (1995). Emotion regulation and mental health. Clinical Psychology: Science and Practice, 2(2), 151-164.

Gross, J. J., & Thompson, R. A. (2007). Emotion regulation: Conceptual foundations. In J. J. Gross (Ed.), Handbook of emotion regulation (pp. 3-24). Guilford Press.

Guzek, D., Kołota, A., Lachowicz, K., Skolmowska, D., Stachoń, M., & Głąbska, D. (2021). Association between vitamin D supplementation and mental health in healthy adults: A systematic review. Journal of Clinical Medicine, 10(21), 5156. https://doi.org/10.3390/jcm10215156

Han, Q. Q., Shen, T. T., Wang, F., Wu, P. F., & Chen, J. G. (2018). Preventive and therapeutic potential of vitamin C in mental disorders. Current Medical Science, 38(1), 1-10. https://doi.org/10.1007/s11596-018-1840-2

Hayes, S. C., Luoma, J. B., Bond, F. W., Masuda, A., & Lillis, J. (2006). Acceptance and commitment therapy: Model, process and outcomes. Behaviour Research and Therapy, 44(1), 1-25.

Hayes, S. C., Strosahl, K., & Wilson, K. G. (1999). Acceptance and commitment therapy: An experiential approach to behavior change. Guilford Press.

Hayes, S. C., Wilson, K. G., Gifford, E. V., Follette, V. M., & Strosahl, K. (1996). Experiential avoidance and behavioral disorders: A functional dimensional approach to diagnosis and treatment. Journal of Consulting and Clinical Psychology, 64(6), 1152-1168.

Holmgren, R. A., Eisenberg, N., & Fabes, R. A. (1998). The relations of children's situational empathy-related emotions to dispositional prosocial behavior. International Journal of Behavioral Development, 22(1), 169–193.

Horney, K. (1951). Neurosis and human growth: The struggle toward self-realization. Routledge.

Ingram, R. E. (1990). Self-focused attention in clinical disorders: Review and a conceptual model. Psychological Bulletin, 107(2), 156–176.

Izard, C. E. (2002). Translating emotion theory and research into preventive interventions. Psychological Bulletin, 128(5), 796-824.

Janicak, P. G., Lipinski, J. F., Davis, J. M., Comaty, J. E., Waternaux, C., & Cohen, B., et al. (1988). S-adenosylmethionine in depression: A literature review and preliminary report. Alabama Journal of Medical Sciences, 25, 306–313.

Johnson, J. H., & Sarason, I. G. (1979). Recent developments in research on life events. In V. Hamilton & D. M. Warburton (Eds.), Human stress and cognition (pp. 3-23). Wiley.

Johnson, S. L., Carver, C. S., & Fulford, D. (2010). Goal dysregulation in the affective disorders. In A. M. Kring & D. M. Sloan (Eds.), Emotion regulation and psychopathology: A transdiagnostic approach to etiology and treatment (pp. 221-245). Guilford Press.

Karekla, M., Forsyth, J. P., & Kelly, M. M. (2004). Emotional avoidance and panicogenic responding to a biological challenge procedure. Behavior Therapy, 35(4), 725-746.

Kashdan, T. B., Barrios, V., Forsyth, J. P., & Steger, M. F. (2006). Experiential avoidance as a generalised psychological vulnerability: Comparisons with coping and emotion regulation strategies. Behaviour Research and Therapy, 44(9), 1301-1320.

Kessler, R. C., Aguilar-Gaxiola, S., Alonso, J., Chatterji, S., Lee, S., & Ormel, J. (2009). The global burden of mental disorders: An update from the WHO World Mental Health (WMH) Surveys. Epidemiologia e Psichiatria Sociale, 18(1), 23–33.

Khalsa, S. S., et al. (2018). Interoception and mental health: A roadmap. Biological Psychiatry: Cognitive Neuroscience and Neuroimaging, 3(6), 501–513. https://doi.org/10.1016/j.bpsc.2017.12.004

Khoury, N. M., Lutz, J., & Schuman-Olivier, Z. (2018). Interoception in psychiatric disorders: A review of randomized controlled trials with interoception-based interventions. Harvard Review of Psychiatry, 26(5), 250-263.

Kumari, V., et al. (2017). The mindful eye: Smooth pursuit and saccadic eye movements in meditators and non-meditators. Consciousness and Cognition, 48, 66-75.

MacBeth, A., & Gumley, A. (2012). Exploring compassion: A meta-analysis of the association between self-compassion and psychopathology. Clinical Psychology Review, 32(6), 545-552.

Matiz, A., Crescentini, C., Fabbro, A., Budai, R., Bergamasco, M., & Fabbro, F. (2019). Spontaneous eye movements during focused-attention mindfulness meditation. PLOS ONE, 14(1), e0210862.

Mikkelsen, K., Stojanovska, L., Polenakovic, M., Bosevski, M., & Apostolopoulos, V. (2017). Exercise and mental health. Maturitas, 106, 48-56.

Mrazek, P. J., & Haggerty, R. J. (Eds.). (1994). Reducing risks for mental disorders: Frontiers for preventive intervention research. National Academy Press.

Neff, K. D. (2003). Self-compassion: An alternative conceptualization of a healthy attitude toward oneself. Self and Identity, 2(2), 85-101.

Neff, K. D. (2004). Self-compassion and psychological well-being. Constructivism in the Human Sciences, 9(2), 27-37.

Neff, K. D., Kirkpatrick, K. L., & Rude, S. S. (2007). Self-compassion and adaptive psychological functioning. Journal of Research in Personality, 41(1), 139-154.

National Institute on Drug Abuse. (2022, March 22). Drugs and the brain. https://nida.nih.gov/publications/drugs-brains-behavior-science-addiction/drugs-brain

Ochsner, K. N., Knierim, K., Ludlow, D. H., Hanelin, J., Ramachandran, T., & Glover, G., et al. (2004). Reflecting upon feelings: An fMRI study of neural systems supporting the attribution of emotion to self and other. Journal of Cognitive Neuroscience, 16(8), 1746-1772.

Ohrnberger, J., Fichera, E., & Sutton, M. (2017). The relationship between physical and mental health: A mediation analysis. Social Science & Medicine, 195, 42-49.

O'Grady, D., & Metz, J. R. (1987). Resilience in children at high risk for psychological disorder. Journal of Pediatric Psychology, 12(1), 3-23.

Rao, T. S., Asha, M. R., Ramesh, B. N., & Rao, K. S. (2008). Understanding nutrition, depression and mental illnesses. Indian Journal of Psychiatry, 50(2), 77–82. https://doi.org/10.4103/0019-5545.42391

Scott, A. J., Webb, T. L., & Rowse, G. (2017). Does improving sleep lead to better mental health? A protocol for a meta-analytic review of randomised controlled trials. BMJ Open, 7(9), e016873. https://doi.org/10.1136/bmjopen-2017-016873

Scott, A. J., Webb, T. L., Martyn-St James, M., Rowse, G., & Weich, S. (2021). Improving sleep quality leads to better mental health: A meta-analysis of randomised controlled trials. Sleep Medicine Reviews, 60, 101556. https://doi.org/10.1016/j.smrv.2021.101556

Segal, Z. V., Williams, J. M. G., & Teasdale, J. D. (2002). Mindfulness-based cognitive therapy for depression: A new approach to preventing relapse. Guilford Press.

Segerstrom, S. C., & Miller, G. E. (2004). Psychological stress and the human immune system: A meta-analytic study of 30 years of inquiry. Psychological Bulletin, 130(4), 601–630. https://doi.org/10.1037/0033-2909.130.4.601

Seligman, M. E. P. (1995). The optimistic child. Houghton Mifflin.

Shaheen Lakhan, S. E., & Vieira, K. F. (2008). Nutritional therapies for mental disorders. Nutrition Journal, 7, 2. https://doi.org/10.1186/1475-2891-7-2

Sharma, A., Madaan, V., & Petty, F. D. (2006). Exercise for mental health. Primary Care Companion to the Journal of Clinical Psychiatry, 8(2), 106. https://doi.org/10.4088/pcc.v08n0208a

Spira, A. P., Beaudreau, S., Jimenez, D., Kierod, K., Cusing, M., & Gray, H., et al. (2007). Experiential avoidance, acceptance and depression in dementia family caregivers. Clinical Gerontologist, 30(4), 55-64.

Steven, J. L., & William, S. S. (2011). Impact of psychological factors in the experience of pain. Physical Therapy, 91(5), 700–711. https://doi.org/10.2522/ptj.20100330

Stewart, S. H., & Watt, M. C. (2008). Introduction to the special issue on interoceptive exposure in the treatment of anxiety and related disorders: Novel applications and mechanisms of action. Journal of Cognitive Psychotherapy, 22(4), 291-302.

Swann, W. B. (1996). Self-traps: The elusive quest for higher self-esteem. Freeman.

Vadivelu, N., Kai, A. M., Kodumudi, G., Babayan, K., Fontes, M., & Burg, M. M. (2017). Pain and psychology-A reciprocal relationship. The Ochsner Journal, 17(2), 173–180.

van der Kolk, B. A. (1994). The body keeps the score: Memory and the evolving psychobiology of posttraumatic stress. Harvard Review of Psychiatry, 1(5), 253–265. https://doi.org/10.3109/10673229409017088

Volkow, N. D., Fowler, J. S., & Wang, G.-J. (2002). Role of dopamine in drug reinforcement and addiction in humans: Results from imaging studies. Behavioural Pharmacology, 13(5-6), 355-366.

Volkow, N. D., Michaelides, M., & Baler, R. (2019). The neuroscience of drug reward and addiction. Physiological Reviews, 99(4), 2115-2140.

Werner, E. E., & Smith, R. S. (1992). Overcoming the odds: High risk children from birth to adulthood. Cornell University Press.

Werner, K., & Gross, J. J. (2010). Emotion regulation and psychopathology: A conceptual framework. In A. M. Kring & D. M. Sloan (Eds.), Emotion regulation and psychopathology: A transdiagnostic approach to etiology and treatment (pp. 29-54). Guilford Press.

Wolf, A. W., Schubert, D. S. P., Patterson, M. B., Grande, T. P., Brocco, K. J., & Pendleton, L. (1988). Associations among major psychiatric diagnoses. Journal of Consulting and Clinical Psychology, 56(2), 292–294.

World Health Organization. (1998). Primary prevention of mental, neurological and psychosocial disorders. Author.

World Health Organization. (2000). International Consortium in Psychiatric Epidemiology. Cross-national comparisons of the prevalences and correlates of mental disorders. Bulletin of the World Health Organization, 78(4), 413-426.

World Health Organization. (2001). Mental health: New understanding, new hope. Author.

Young, S. N. (2007). Folate and depression: A neglected problem. Journal of Psychiatry and Neuroscience, 32(2), 80–82.

Zahn-Waxler, C., Cole, P. M., Welsh, J. D., & Fox, N. A. (1995). Psychophysiological correlates of empathy and prosocial behaviors in preschool children with problem behaviors. Development and Psychopathology, 7(1), 27–48.

About Fount™

The dictionary meaning of the word fount is a fountain, spring, source, or origin. Why was this name chosen for our institute? Because a plant, at its source or origin, already contains what it takes to grow and flourish. All it needs is for unhelpful parasites to be removed and for helpful nutrients and water to be supplied. It will then grow and reveal its unique and brilliant qualities!

Our educational materials are developed based on the idea that, similar to a plant, human beings have at their source and origin what it takes to grow and flourish their wonderful inner qualities. They just need a bit of help to:

- Reverse the harmful effects of unhealthy past environments
- Develop healthier ways of coping with stress
- Improve how they manage relationships and relate to the world

Fount™ educational materials aim to enhance common knowledge about the human mind and promote happier, more fulfilled lives. The following are a few principles of our programs:

- Prevention is better than cure.
- Mental health is not merely the absence of mental illness; it is about optimising your sense of wellbeing, peace, and life satisfaction.
- Your mental wellbeing will impact the mental wellbeing of those around you.

About the Author

Sahba Saberi is passionate about mental health, cats, and food. She first realised the importance of mental health when she was a teenager. 'Why isn't everyone getting excited about this?' she thought, 'The world would be a different place if we all did!'

So it's not surprising that she went on to become a psychologist, developing courses aimed at educating everyone, absolutely everyone, about mental health! Her career spans almost two decades of work as a psychotherapist, alongside years of dedicated study into the latest developments in the fields of therapy and prevention.

Not only has she authored works aimed at improving mental health on a global scale, she is also trying to figure out how to stop summer holidays from ever running out.

www.ingramcontent.com/pod-product-compliance
Lightning Source LLC
LaVergne TN
LVHW010557100826
845148LV00014B/2748

* 9 7 8 1 7 6 4 7 1 2 4 9 1 *